The World Of
Risk Management

Serving the Profession and Academia

The World Of Risk Management

editor

H. Gifford Fong

World Scientific

NEW JERSEY • LONDON • SINGAPORE • BEIJING • SHANGHAI • HONG KONG • TAIPEI • CHENNAI

Published by

World Scientific Publishing Co. Pte. Ltd.
5 Toh Tuck Link, Singapore 596224
USA office: 27 Warren Street, Suite 401-402, Hackensack, NJ 07601
UK office: 57 Shelton Street, Covent Garden, London WC2H 9HE

British Library Cataloguing-in-Publication Data
A catalogue record for this book is available from the British Library.

THE WORLD OF RISK MANAGEMENT

ISBN 981-256-517-5

Typeset by Stallion Press
E-mail: enquiries@stallionpress.com

Printed in Singapore by Mainland Press

CONTENTS

INTRODUCTION

The World Of Risk Management is a collection of extremely high quality papers previously published in the *Journal Of Investment Management* (JOIM). JOIM is a fully refereed publication, which serves the practitioner, academic and student by bridging the theory and practice of investment management.

This book brings together authors who are the thought leaders from both academia and the practice of investment management to provide a rigorous and insightful analysis of various topics in risk management. For those interested in the broad landscape of risk management as well as specific details of implementation, this book will serve as a useful resource.

The first paper "Design of Financial Systems: Towards a Synthesis of Function and Structure", by Merton and Bodie describes a unifying framework for financial systems and products. Ho then puts in context the use of asset/liability management for an insurance company in "Asset/Liability Management and Enterprise Risk Management of an Insurer". A pathbreaking paper, "It's 11pm—Do You Know Where Your Liquidity Is? The Mean–Variance–Liquidity Frontier" by Lo, Petrov and Wierzbicki addresses one of the most challenging and not well researched areas of risk management. A legend in his own time, Treynor provides important insights in his "Time Diversification" paper on the topic of risk management by diversification. Michaud in "A Practical Framework for Portfolio Choice" covers a number of points with regard to portfolio optimization. An improved methodology for both pricing and risk analysis using Monte Carlo techniques is covered in "A Markov Chain Monte Carlo Method for Derivative Pricing and Risk Assessment" by Das and Sinclair. Measuring the nature of active risk is discussed by Qian and Hua in "Active Risk and Information Ratio". Griffiths and Winters test a year end effect for risk and liquidity in "The Year-End Price of Risk in a Market for Liquidity." Markowitz and Usmen in their "Resampled Frontiers vs. Diffuse Bayes: An Experiment" test two alternatives in the use of mean-variance optimization. Last but not least, Stutzer in "Fund Managers May Cause Their Benchmarks to be Priced 'Risks'" asserts a problem in using a benchmark for risk analysis.

Let me also take this opportunity to thank the staff of Gifford Fong Associates for their support of this activity. In addition, let me extend gratitude to World Scientific Publishing Co. (WSPC) for their sponsorship of this book.

Cordially,
H. Gifford Fong
Editor

Journal Of Investment Management
3658 Mt. Diablo Blvd., Suite 200
Lafayette, CA 94549
Telephone: 925-299-7800
Facsimile: 925-299-7815
Email: editor@joim.com

PRACTITIONER'S DIGEST

The "Practitioner's Digest" emphasizes the practical significance of manuscripts featured in this book. Readers who are interested in extracting the practical value of an article, or who are simply looking for a summary, may look to this section.

DESIGN OF FINANCIAL SYSTEMS: TOWARDS A SYNTHESIS OF FUNCTION AND STRUCTURE — PAGE 1

Robert C. Merton and Zvi Bodie

This paper explores a functional approach to financial system design in which financial functions instead of institutions are the "anchors" of such systems and the institutional structure of each system and its changes are determined within the theory. It offers a rudimentary synthesis of the neoclassical, neoinstitutional, and behavioral perspectives on finance to describe a process for driving changes in the institutional structures of financial systems over time and to explain their differences across geopolitical borders.

The theory holds that within an existing institutional structure, when transaction costs or dysfunctional financial behavioral patterns cause equilibrium asset prices and risk allocations to depart significantly from those in the "frictionless," rational-behavior neoclassical model, new financial institutions, financial markets, and supporting infrastructure such as regulatory and accounting rules evolve that tend to offset the resulting inefficiencies. Thus, market frictions and behavioral finance predictions, along with technological progress, are central in explaining financial system design and predicting its future evolution. However, in the longer-run equilibrium, after offsetting institutional structures have had time to develop, the predictions of the neoclassical model, albeit as a reduced form, will be approximately valid for asset prices and resource allocations.

The paper lays out the principles behind the theory and illustrates its application using many examples, several drawn from the field of investment management. The analysis offers insights on the development of the asset management industry in the past as well as direct implications for its future evolution. Whether or not it holds as a descriptive theory, the analytical framework offers a useful prescriptive approach to the design of new investment products.

ASSET/LIABILITY MANAGEMENT AND ENTERPRISE RISK MANAGEMENT OF AN INSURER — PAGE 29

Thomas S. Y. Ho

The purpose of this paper is to provide an overview of some of the risk management techniques used currently. And the paper then proposes the corporate model approach to manage enterprise risks of the firm. Section 1 reviews the current practices, which are considered most effective in risk management for the life insurers. In a similar fashion, Section 2 describes the practices for the property/casualty insurance. Section 3 discusses the challenges that these current practices face in our current environment and describes the corporate model approach to deal with these challenges. Finally, Section 4 contains the conclusions.

IT'S 11 PM—DO YOU KNOW WHERE YOUR LIQUIDITY IS? THE MEAN–VARIANCE–LIQUIDITY FRONTIER PAGE 47

Andrew W. Lo, Constantin Peirov and Martin Wierzbicki

Although liquidity has long been recognized as one of the most significant drivers of financial innovation, the collapse of several high-profile hedge funds such as Askin Capital Management in 1994 and Long Term Capital Management in 1998 has refocused the financial industry on the importance of liquidity in the investment management progress. Many studies—both in academic journals and more applied forums—have made considerable process in defining liquidity, measuring the cost of immediacy and price impact, deriving optimal portfolio rules in the presence of transactions costs, investigating the relationship between liquidity and arbitrage, and estimating liquidity risk premia in the context of various partial general equilibrium asset-pricing models. However, relatively little attention has been paid to the more practical problem of integrating liquidity directly into the portfolio construction process.

In this paper, we attempt to remedy this state of affairs by modeling liquidity using simple measures such as trading volume and percentage bid/offer spreads, and then introducing these measures into the standard mean–variance portfolio optimization process to yield optimal mean–variance–liquidity portfolios. We begin by proposing several measures of the liquidity of an individual security, from which we define the liquidity of a portfolio as the weighted average of the individual securities' liquidities. Using these liquidity metrics, we can construct three types of "liquidity-optimized" portfolios: (1) a mean–variance efficient portfolio subject to a liquidity filter that each security in the portfolio have a minimum level of liquidity; (2) a mean–variance efficient portfoilio subject to a constraint that the portfolio have a minimum level of liquidity; and (3) a mean–variance–liquidity efficient portfolio, where the optimization problem has three terms in its objective function: mean, variance, and liquidity.

Using three different definitions of liquidity–turnover, percentage bid/offer spread, and a nonlinear function of market capitalization and trade size—we show empirically that liquidity-optimized portfolios have some very attractive properties, and that even simple forms of liquidity optimization can yield significant benefits in terms of reducing a portfolio's liquidity-risk exposure without sacrificing a great deal of expected return per unity risk. Our framework adds an important new dimension—literally as well as figuratively—to the toolkit of quantitative portfolio managers. In particular, with three dimensions to consider, portfolio management can no longer operate within a purely numerical paradigm, and three- and four-dimensional visualization techniques will become increasingly central to industrial applications of portfolio optimization.

TIME DIVERSIFICATION PAGE 93

Jack L. Treynor

The risk surrounding the market's rate of return—change in dollar value, divided by initial dollar value—is roughly stationary across time. To maintain constant dollar risk, investors concerned with their terminal wealth must sell when the stock market rises and buy when it falls. The frequent trading is probably the reason why few investors have tried to time diversify.

Consider an asset whose *dollar* gains and losses are in one-to-one correspondence with the stock market's *rate of return*: if the risk surrounding the latter is indeed stationary across time, then the risk surrounding the former will also be stationary. Using this principle and elementary calculus, we derive the asset.

Although an asset with constant dollar risk does not exist in nature, it can be approximated with actual investment positions. The key to the approximation is the fact that a diversified asset's beta expresses a power relation between its value and the market level.

A PRACTICAL FRAMEWORK FOR PORTFOLIO CHOICE PAGE 111

Richard O. Michaud

Optimal portfolio choice is the central problem of equity portfolio management, asset allocation, and financial planning. Common optimality criteria such as the long-term geometric mean, utility function estimation, and return probability objectives have important theoretical or practical limitations. A portfolio choice framework consisting of resampled efficient portfolios and geometric mean analysis is a practical alternative for many situations of investment interest. Mean–variance optimization, the typical framework for defining an efficient portfolio set in practice, is estimation error sensitive and exhibits poor out-of-sample performance characteristics. Resampled efficiency, a generalization of mean–variance efficiency, improves out-of-sample performance on average and has important additional practical benefits. Geometric mean analysis gives the distribution of the multiperiod financial consequences of single-period efficient investments to clearly visualize the tradeoffs between risk and return and for assessing an appropriate level of risk. While Monte Carlo financial planning is a more flexible framework, geometric mean analysis may be less error prone, theoretically justifiable and convenient. Controversies that have limited geometric mean analysis applications are resolvable by improved understanding of distributional properties and rational decision-making issues. The special case of asset allocation for defined benefit pension plans is addressed. Geometric mean analysis is also useful in rationalizing a number of interesting investment paradoxes.

A MARKOV CHAIN MONTE CARLO METHOD FOR DERIVATIVE PRICING AND RISK ASSESSMENT PAGE 131

Sanjiv R. Das and Alistair Sinclair

This paper explores a novel algorithm for the pricing of derivative securities. There are now hundreds of different types of derivative securities, each with their own peculiar characteristics. Yet, no single approach works for every type of contract and, indeed, the literature in finance is replete with a vast number of different pricing models.

The goal in this paper is to propose a novel pricing model that is tailored to some derivatives of more recent interest, for which dominant models do not as yet exist. The algorithm is based on a Markov chain Monte Carlo approach, developed in a different context by Sinclair and Jerrum (1989). While the use of Monte Carlo methods is well established for pricing derivatives, our approach differs in several respects: it uses backtracking to prevent the accumulation of errors in importance sampling; it has rigorously provable error bounds; and it is, in principle, applicable to derivative pricing on any nonrecombining lattice. In addition to describing the algorithm, we also present some initial experimental results that illustrate its application to a simple barrier option pricing problem.

ACTIVE RISK AND INFORMATION RATIO PAGE 151

Edward Qian and Ronald Hua

Many practitioners are bewildered by the fact that ex post active risks of their portfolios are often significantly higher than ex ante tracking errors estimated by risk models. Why do risk models tend to underestimate active risk? The answer to this question has important implications to active management, in the areas of risk management, information ratio estimation, and manager selections.

We present an answer to this puzzle. We show there is an additional source of active risk that is unique to each strategy. It is unique because its contribution to active risk depends on the variability of the strategy's information coefficient through time. We name this risk the strategy risk. Consequently, the true active risk must consist of both the strategy risk and the risk-model tracking error; and, the active risk is often different from, and in many cases, significantly higher than the risk-model tracking error. Based on this result, we further show that a consistent estimation of information ratio is the ratio of average information coefficient to the standard deviation of information coefficient. We provide corroborating empirical evidence in support of our analysis and demonstrate the practicality of our findings. Specifically, we show how the understanding of strategy risk leads to more accurate ex ante forecasts of active risk and information ratio.

THE YEAR-END PRICE OF RISK IN A MARKET FOR LIQUIDITY PAGE 169

Mark D. Griffiths and Drew B. Winters

Money markets (Kidwell, Peterson and Blackwell, 1997) are generally described as short-term markets for liquidity where the lenders that provide the liquidity demand debt securities with low default risk and high marketability. Recent evidence shows both repo rates (Griffiths and Winters, 1997) and commercial paper rates (Musto, 1997) increase dramatically prior to the year-end and that the identified changes are consistent with a preferred habitat for liquidity at the year-end. Musto (1997) suggests that the price of risk in commercial paper may increase at the year-end.

Using daily rates on 7-day, 15-day, and 30-day nonfinancial commercial paper from two different risk classes (AA and A2/P2), we find, across all terms and for both risk classes, that rates increase when a security begins to mature in the new-year and that rates decline across the year-end with the decline beginning a few days before the end of the year. These changes are consistent with the hypothesis of a year-end preferred habitat for liquidity. In addition, we find that the spread between the two risk classes, across all terms, increases at the same time indicating that the price of risk also increases at the year-end. In other words, when the lenders in the commercial paper market need their cash at the year-end they increase the rate charged for commercial paper across all borrowers, but they increase the rate more for higher risk borrowers.

Our results provide additional support for the Chicago Mercantile Exchange's introduction of an interest rate futures contract designed to address the turn effect in interest rates which has been attributed (Burghardt and Kirshner, 1994) to the pressures applied to year-end financing rates caused by the demand for cash.

RESAMPLED FRONTIERS VERSUS DIFFUSE BAYES: AN EXPERIMENT PAGE 183

Harry M. Markowitz and Nilufer Usmen

This paper reports an experiment that tests two proposals for handling the fact that historical means, variances, and covariances, sometimes used as inputs to MPT portfolio analyses, are themselves noisy. One method is that of Michaud (1998). The other is an implementation of the diffuse Bayes approach widely discussed in texts and tracts on Bayesian inference.

The experiment contains a simulated referee and two simulated players, namely a Michaud player and a Bayes player. The referee selects a "true" probability distribution of returns on eight asset classes. Given this probability distribution, the referee generates 217 monthly observations for the eight asset classes. These observations are handed to each player who then proceeds in its prescribed manner. The object of each player is to pick a portfolio which maximizes a specified function of portfolio mean and variance. This process is repeated for three different objective functions, for 100 historical samples drawn from a given truth, and for 10 truths. One of the investor objectives is long run growth. The others are two other "utility functions."

The two players, and therefore their methodologies, are evaluated in terms of their ability to provide portfolios which give greatest value to the objective function, and their ability to estimate how well they have done. The results of the experiment have implications for the relative merits of the two methodologies, and for probable weaknesses in other methods of estimating the inputs to an MPT portfolio analysis.

FUND MANAGERS MAY CAUSE THEIR BENCHMARKS TO BE PRICED "RISKS" PAGE 203

Michael Stutzer

Fund managers now commonly try to beat specific benchmarks (e.g., the S&P 500), and the widespread dissemination of return statistics on both index and actively managed funds makes it plausible that some individual investors may also be trying to do so. Academics now commonly evaluate fund performance by the size of the "alpha" from a multifactor generalization of the familiar Capital Asset Pricing Model, i.e. the size of the intercept in a linear regression of the fund's returns on the returns of a broad based market index and other "factor" portfolios (e.g., those proposed in the influential work of Eugene Fama and Kenneth French).

This paper theoretically and empirically argues that these two seemingly disparate facts may be closely connected. Specifically, the attempt of fund managers and/or individual investors to beat benchmark portfolios may *cause* those benchmarks (or proxies for them) to appear in the multifactor performance evaluation models advocated by academics. This casts additional doubt on the currently problematic academic presumption that the non-market factors proxy for predictors of fundamental risks that can affect future investment opportunities. Instead, the non-market factors in the Fama and French equity fund performance evaluation model may proxy for growth-oriented index portfolios, which some try to beat, and value-oriented index portfolios, which others try to beat.

Journal Of Investment Management
Vol. 3, No. 1 (2005), pp. 6–28

DESIGN OF FINANCIAL SYSTEMS: TOWARDS A SYNTHESIS OF FUNCTION AND STRUCTURE*

Robert C. Merton[a] *and Zvi Bodie*[b]

This paper proposes a functional approach to designing and managing the financial systems of countries, regions, firms, households, and other entities. It is a synthesis of the neoclassical, neo-institutional, and behavioral perspectives. Neoclassical theory is an ideal driver to link science and global practice in finance because its prescriptions are robust across time and geopolitical borders. By itself, however, neoclassical theory provides little prescription or prediction of the institutional structure of financial systems—that is, the specific kinds of financial intermediaries, markets, and regulatory bodies that will or should evolve in response to underlying changes in technology, politics, demographics, and cultural norms. The neoclassical model therefore offers important, but incomplete, guidance to decision makers seeking to understand and manage the process of institutional change. In accomplishing this task, the neo-institutional and behavioral perspectives can be very useful. In this proposed synthesis of the three approaches, functional and structural finance (FSF), institutional structure is endogenous. When particular transaction costs or behavioral patterns produce large departures from the predictions of the ideal frictionless neoclassical equilibrium for a given institutional structure, new institutions tend to develop that partially offset the resulting inefficiencies. In the longer run, after institutional structures have had time to fully develop, the predictions of the neoclassical model will be approximately valid for asset prices and resource allocations. Through a series of examples, the paper sets out the reasoning behind the FSF synthesis and illustrates its application.

1 Introduction

This paper explores a functional approach to the design of a financial system in which financial functions are the "anchors" or "givens" of such systems and the institutional structure of each system and its changes are determined within the theory.[1] The term "institutional structure," as used here, includes financial institutions, financial markets, products, services, organization of operations, and supporting infrastructure such as regulatory rules and the accounting system. The financial functions may be provided by private-sector, governmental, and family institutions. The proposed framework can be

[a]Harvard Business School, Soldiers Field, Boston, MA 02163, USA.

[b]Boston University School of Management, 595 Commonwealth Avenue, Boston, MA 02215, USA.

*First presented orally by the first author as a keynote lecture at the European Finance Association Annual Meeting, Barcelona, Spain, August 2001. The first written version with the same title circulated as Harvard Business School Working Paper #02-074, May 2002.

applied both as a *descriptive* theory to predict the design structure of existing financial systems and as a *prescriptive* one to explore how such systems should be designed.

For nearly three decades, the science of finance, largely based on neoclassical finance with its assumptions of frictionless markets and rational behavior, has had a significant impact on the global practice of finance, as highlighted in Section 2. Prospectively, we see that influence continuing and indeed expanding into a broader domain of applications. However, as outlined in Section 3, the neoclassical paradigm, as an effective abstraction from complex reality, is being challenged by two alternative paradigms, the new institutional (or neo-institutional) finance and behavioral finance.

Instead of examining each as competing alternatives, our central methodological thesis for implementing a functional theory of financial institutions is a synthesis of the neoclassical, the new institutional, and the behavioral perspectives on finance. We call this attempt to synthesize these three perspectives, *Functional and Structural Finance* (FSF). Section 4 frames that functional synthesis by offering a number of examples to illustrate the basic approach. Section 5 offers an overview of the key elements of FSF. The concluding section of the paper discusses the significant influence of a well-functioning financial system on long-term economic growth as further motivation for the systematic examination of financial system design.

Although the manifest purpose of the paper is to explore the design of the financial system and the synthesis of behavioral and transaction cost finance with traditional neoclassic finance, the analysis has direct implications for the process of investment management and for prospective evolution of the asset management industry. Indeed, several of the finance examples used to illustrate this approach to a functional synthesis are drawn from investment management.

The attempt at synthesis offered here is surely far from a complete and axiomatic development of FSF. Nonetheless, we harbor the hope that this first pass will stimulate further thought along these lines.

2 On the Impact of Finance Science on Finance Practice

New financial product and market designs, improved computer and telecommunications technology, and advances in the theory of finance over the last generation have led to dramatic and rapid changes in the structure of global financial markets and institutions. The scientific breakthroughs in finance theory in this period both shaped and were shaped by the extraordinary innovations in finance practice that coincided with these revolutionary changes in the structure of world financial markets and institutions. The cumulative impact has significantly affected all of us—as users, producers, or overseers of the financial system.

Finance science has informed practice across a wide spectrum of finance applications, with powerful prescriptions for valuation, asset allocation, performance measurement, risk management, and corporate financial decision-making. Surely the prime exemplifying case is the development, refinement, and broad-based adoption of derivative securities such as futures, options, swaps, and other contractual agreements.

Practitioner innovations in financial-contracting technology have improved efficiency by expanding opportunities for risk sharing, lowering transaction costs, and reducing information and agency costs. Those innovations would not have been possible without the Black–Scholes option-pricing methodology, which was developed entirely within the academic research community.[2]

Indeed, in providing the means for pricing and risk measurement of derivative securities, finance science has contributed fundamentally to the remarkable rate of globalization of the financial system. Inspection of the diverse financial systems of individual nation-states would lead one to question how much effective integration across geopolitical borders could have taken place, since those systems are rarely compatible in institutional forms, regulations, laws, tax structures, and business practices. Still, significant integration did take place.

Derivative securities designed to function as adapters among otherwise incompatible domestic systems were important contributors to effective integration. In general, the flexibility created by the widespread use of derivatives as well as specialized institutional designs provided an effective offset to dysfunctional country-specific institutional rigidities. Furthermore, derivative-security technologies provide efficient means for creating cross-border interfaces without imposing invasive, widespread changes within each system.

An analogy may prove helpful here. Imagine two countries that want to integrate their pipelines for transporting oil, gas, water, or anything else. Country A has a pipeline that is square, while country B's pipeline is triangular. Country A's plan for integrating the pipelines is to suggest to B that it replace its triangular pipeline with a square one. This, of course, will require a very large and disruptive investment by B. Decision makers in country B, not surprisingly, have an alternative—country A should tear up its square pipeline and replace it with a triangular one.

But rarely would either of those two plans make sense. Almost always, the better solution is to design an efficient *adapter* that connects the two existing pipelines with minimum impediments to the flow across borders.

This pipeline analogy captures much of what has been happening during the past twenty years in the international financial system. Financial engineers have been designing and implementing derivative contracts to function as efficient adapters that allow the flow of funds and the sharing of risks among diverse national systems with different institutional shapes and sizes.

More generally, financial innovation has been a central force driving the financial system toward greater economic efficiency. Both scholarly research and practitioner experience over that period have led to vast improvements in our understanding of how to use the new financial technologies to manage risk.

As we all know, there have been financial "incidents," and even crises, that cause some to raise questions about innovations and the scientific soundness of the financial theories used to engineer them. There have surely been individual cases of faulty engineering designs and faulty implementations of those designs in finance just as there have been in building bridges, airplanes, and silicon chips. Indeed, learning from (sometimes even tragic) mistakes is an integral part of the process of technical progress.[3]

However, on addressing the overall soundness of applying the tools of financial engineering, it is enough to note here the judgment of financial institutions around the world as measured by their practice. Today no major financial institution in the world, including central banks, can function without the computer-based mathematical models of modern financial science. Furthermore, the specific models that these institutions depend on to conduct their global derivative pricing and risk-management activities are based typically on the Black–Scholes option pricing methodology.

So much for the past: What about the impending future?

With its agnosticism regarding institutional structure, neoclassical finance theory is an ideal driver to link science and global practice because its prescriptions are robust across time and geopolitical borders. Future development of derivative-security technologies and markets within smaller and emerging-market countries could help form important gateways of access to world capital markets and global risk sharing. Financial engineering is likely to contribute significantly in the developed countries as well; as for instance in the major transitions required for restructuring financial institutions both in Europe and in Japan.[4]

But will the same intense interaction between the science and practice of finance continue with respect to the new directions of scientific inquiry?

3 The Challenge to Neoclassical Finance

With its foundation based on frictionless and efficient markets populated with atomistic and rational agents, the practical applicability of the neoclassical modeling approach is now challenged by at least two alternative theoretical paradigms. One, *New Institutional Economics*, focuses explicitly on transaction costs, taxes, computational limitations, and other frictions.[5] The other, *Behavioral Economics*, introduces non-rational and systematically uninformed behavior by agents.[6] In contrast to the robustness of the neoclassical model, the prescriptions and predictions of these alternatives are manifestly sensitive to the specific market frictions and posited behavioral deviations of agents.[7] Perhaps more latent is the strong sensitivity of these predictions to the institutional structure in which they are embedded.

There is a considerable ongoing debate, sometimes expressed in polar form, between the proponents of these competing paradigms. Those who attack the traditional neoclassical approach assert that the overwhelming accumulation of evidence of anomalies flatly rejects it.[8] They see a major paradigm shift to one of the new alternatives as essential for progress. Defenders of the neoclassical paradigm respond that the alleged empirical anomalies are either not there, or that they can be explained within the neoclassical framework, and that in either case, the proposed alternatives do not offer a better resolution.[9] That debate so framed is best left to proceed anomaly by anomaly and we say no more about it here.

Instead, we take a different approach. Rather than choose among the three competing theoretical perspectives, we believe that each, although not yet of the same historical significance, can make distinctive contributions to our understanding and each has its distinctive limitations.

In neoclassical theory, institutions "do not matter" in the sense that equilibrium prices and the allocation of resources are unaffected by specific institutional structures. As long as markets are efficient and frictionless, one can use almost any convenient financial system in a model for analyzing asset demands and the derived equilibrium asset prices and risk allocations will be the same as in models with more realistic and more complex financial systems.

In criticizing neoclassical theory, proponents of both neo-institutional and behavioral finance often posit the same simple financial institutional structure in their models, and then proceed to show how the introduction of market frictions and deviations from rationality can cause significant changes in equilibrium allocations and asset price behavior. But this is not a valid argument. Unlike the frictionless and rational neoclassical case, there is no longer the invariance of optimal asset demands to institutional specifications. Hence, proper assessments, theoretical and empirical, of market allocational and informational efficiency and interpretations of apparent distortions on capital asset pricing from behavioral and transactional dysfunctions cannot be undertaken without explicit reference to a realistic modeling of the institutional environment. Thus, as major changes take place in the institutional structure for trading financial assets and allocating risks, one would expect that the impact of such frictions on asset prices would change. Indeed, from the FSF perspective, the particular institutions and organizational forms that arise within the financial system are an endogenous response to minimize the costs of transaction frictions and behavioral distortions in executing the financial functions common to every economy.[10] As a consequence, in well-functioning financial systems, high transaction costs and dysfunctional cognitive dissonance among individuals may not have a material influence on equilibrium asset prices and risk allocations. Therefore, from this perspective, market-friction and behavioral predictions may not provide reliable insights about observed asset prices and resource allocations, but they will be centrally important—along with technological progress—in explaining the actual institutional structure of the financial system and the dynamics of its change.

4 The Functional Synthesis

The central conclusion of FSF is that in well-developed financial systems, predictions of the neoclassical theory of finance will be approximately correct for asset prices and resource allocations, after the endogenous changes in institutional structure have taken place.[11] Furthermore, FSF can be used to predict likely changes in institutional structure and to identify targeted changes in that structure that might lead to more efficient allocations.

Many of the issues facing decision makers around the world today are about institutional change. In China, for example, decentralization and privatization of large parts of the economy during the past decade have produced remarkable improvements in standards of living. Public officials and business leaders now see an urgent need to create a financial infrastructure to support continued economic development. In Japan, officials are considering fundamental changes in the structure of their banking system to overcome economic stagnation. And in Europe and the United States, pension and Social Security reform has become a top priority. A critical issue everywhere is controlling the risk of default by financial institutions.

Neoclassical theory generally serves as a good starting point in addressing such policy issues. It can identify properties of an efficient equilibrium resulting from the assumptions of rational optimizing behavior and perfect competition. In the posited frictionless environment of neoclassical models, however, multiple alternative institutional structures are possible to support the same equilibrium asset prices and risk allocations.[12]

For example, the celebrated Coase theorem shows that in the absence of transaction costs, a variety of organizational structures can result in optimal resource allocation.[13] In such an environment there would be no reason for firms to exist, since the simpler neoclassical structure of atomistic agents interacting directly in competitive markets would work just as well. As Coase shows, however, when transaction costs are brought into the analysis, then organizational structure matters. Some economic activities are best undertaken in large hierarchical firms, while other activities are best organized through atomistic markets.

Another well-known example of neoclassical assumptions leading to indeterminacy in structural form is the celebrated M&M Propositions regarding the capital structure of firms.[14] Modigliani and Miller prove that in the absence of transaction costs, agency costs, and taxes, firms would be indifferent with respect to their financing mix between debt and equity. When these frictions are taken into account, however, a firm's capital structure can matter a great deal.[15]

In both examples—the Coase Theorem and the M&M Propositions—the neoclassical model serves as a starting point for analysis of institutional structure. However, the neoclassical model alone cannot in general identify the most efficient structure. The new institutional and behavioral theories can be used to help identify features of the environment that may make one structure superior to another in a particular setting at a particular time.

Thus, the neoclassical model by itself offers some limited guidance to decision makers seeking to understand and manage the process of institutional change. In FSF, neoclassical, institutional, and behavioral theories are *complementary* rather than *competing* approaches to analyzing and managing the evolution of financial systems. By employing all three modes of analysis, FSF can perhaps help policy analysts to choose among competing structural solutions to real-world problems.

Instead of attempting a highly formal development of FSF, which is still quite tentative, we frame its synthesis of the different schools of thought using a series of illustrative examples.

The two fundamental tenets of FSF are:

- Neoclassical theory is approximately valid for determining asset prices and resource allocations (albeit as a reduced-form model), but offers little to explain which organizational structures for production and performing various financial functions and which particular market instruments and financial intermediaries will evolve.

- Neo-institutional and behavioral theories are centrally important in analyzing the evolution of institutions including market instruments and financial intermediaries, but are unlikely to provide significant and stable explanations of asset prices and resource allocations.[16]

4.1 Example 1. Transaction Costs and Option Pricing

A quarter century ago, Hakansson (1979) wrote about the "Catch 22" of the option pricing model. His point was that *if* the conditions for Black–Scholes pricing are satisfied, then the option is a *redundant* security with no social purpose; and if the conditions are *not* satisfied, then the pricing model is *wrong*.[17] The seeming paradox can be resolved, however, by considering transaction costs.

In reality most investors face substantial transactions costs and cannot trade even approximately continuously. But in a modern, well-developed financial system, the lowest-cost transactors may have marginal trading costs close to zero, and can trade almost continuously. Thus, the lowest-cost producers of options can approximate reasonably well the dynamic trading strategy, and their cost of replicating the payoffs to the option is approximately the Black–Scholes price.[18]

As in any competitive-equilibrium environment, price equals marginal cost. As is typical in analyses of other industries, the equilibrium prices of financial products and services are more closely linked to the costs of *efficient* actual producers than to *inefficient* potential ones. The result in this context is that high-trading-cost individuals can become customers of low-trading-cost financial intermediaries and buy options at nearly the same price *as if* those individuals could trade continuously without cost.

The underlying force driving the development of efficient institutional structures is Adam Smith's "invisible hand"—firms seeking to maximize their profits in competitive product markets. Potential customers have a demand for the contingent payoffs associated with options, and profit-seeking financial firms compete to supply the options using the lowest-cost technology available to them. As marginal trading costs for the financial firms approach zero, equilibrium option prices approach the Black–Scholes dynamic-replication cost. Thus, we should find that with an efficient, well-developed financial system, over time, the neoclassical model gives the "correct" pricing as a reduced form, but options and other derivative financial instruments and the institutions that produce them are certainly not redundant.[19]

4.2 Example 2. Continuous-Time Portfolio Theory

Our second example is closely related to the first one, but carries it a step further. Consider the Intertemporal CAPM and the assumptions of frictionless markets and continuous trading used in deriving it.[20] It is well known that by introducing transaction costs into a model with an institutional structure in which individuals all trade for themselves directly in the markets, one can get very different portfolio demand functions and thus very different equilibrium prices.[21] But in the presence of substantial information and transaction costs it is not realistic to posit that the *only* process for individuals to establish their optimal portfolios is to trade each separate security for themselves directly in the markets. Instead, individuals are likely to turn to financial organizations such as mutual and pension funds that can provide pooled portfolio management services at a much lower cost than individuals can provide for themselves. Equilibrium asset prices will, therefore, reflect the lower marginal transaction costs of those financial-service firms and not the higher transaction costs of the individuals.

Neoclassical portfolio theory also offers some guidance in identifying the likely nature of the services to be provided by financial intermediaries. The theory of portfolio selection tells us that in the absence of transaction costs and with homogeneous expectations, individuals would be *indifferent* between choosing individually among all assets and choosing among a small number of optimized portfolios. This is the classic "separation" theorem of portfolio theory.[22] But in the presence of significant information and transaction costs, the separation theorem turns into an elementary theory of financial intermediation through mutual funds.

Mutual funds are the investment intermediaries that specialize in producing optimized portfolios by gathering the information needed (expected returns, standard deviations, and correlations among the full set of risky assets) and combining them in the right proportions (the efficient portfolio frontier). Because of economies of scale in gathering information, processing it, and trading securities, the transaction costs for mutual funds will be significantly lower than for individuals, so individuals will tend to hold mutual funds rather than trade in the individual securities themselves.

This view also addresses the issue of heterogeneous expectations in the Capital Asset Pricing Model by offering a justifying interpretation for its standard assumption of homogeneous beliefs: namely, investors in mutual funds in effect "agree to agree" with the return-distribution estimates of the professionals who manage those funds. Furthermore, since professional investors tend to use similar data sets and methods of statistical analysis, their estimates may be more homogeneous than would otherwise be the case if individuals were gathering data and making forecasts directly for themselves.[23]

In more realistically complete models of lifetime portfolio selection, individuals may have complex optimal dynamic strategies. Here too, neoclassical theory offers a useful starting point for a theory of financial structure. As shown in Merton (1989), *for every dynamic trading strategy there exists an equivalent contingent contract or derivative security.* Black, Merton, and Scholes derived the option pricing model by showing that there is a dynamic trading strategy that replicates the payoffs from a call option. That same approach applies to any derivative security.[24] The contingent-claim-equivalence to dynamic portfolio strategies can be derived by running the option-pricing derivation "in reverse."[25]

From contingent-claim-equivalence it follows that a low-transaction-cost financial intermediary can sell to high-transaction-cost customers fully hedged ("immunized") contracts that have the contingent payoffs associated with an optimized portfolio strategy. The intermediary pursues the dynamic trading strategy at its lower transaction costs and provides the specified contractual payoffs to its customers.[26]

Note that under this view of the process of financial intermediation, the products traditionally provided by investment management firms tend to merge with the long-term contracts traditionally produced by the life insurance industry. This convergence transformation has been going on for many years in the market for variable annuities in the United States, although it has largely been motivated by the tax-deferral advantages of annuities.

If this view is correct, then as transaction costs continue to decline, financial intermediaries will produce more complicated-to-produce products that combine features of investments and insurance. They will be customized to provide easy-to-understand, seamless solutions to complex life-cycle risk management needs of households.

Households today are called upon to make a wide range of important and detailed financial decisions that they did not have to in the past. For example, in the United States, there is a strong trend away from defined-benefit corporate pension plans that require no management decisions by the employee toward defined-contribution plans that do. There are more than 9000 mutual funds and a vast array of other investment products. Along with insurance products and liquidity assets, the household faces a daunting task to assemble these various components into a coherent effective lifetime financial plan.

Some see this trend continuing with existing products such as mutual funds being transported into technologically less-developed financial systems. Perhaps this is so, especially in the more immediate future, with the widespread growth of relatively inexpensive Internet access to financial "advice engines." However, the creation of all these alternatives combined with the deregulation that made them possible has consequences: deep and wide-ranging disaggregation has left households with the responsibility for making important and technically complex micro-financial decisions involving risk—such as detailed asset allocation and estimates of the optimal level of life-cycle saving for retirement—decisions that they had *not* had to make *in the past*, are *not* trained to make *in the present*, and are *unlikely* to execute efficiently *in the future*, even with attempts at education.

The availability of financial advice over the Internet at low cost may help to address some of the information-asymmetry problems for households with respect to commodity-like products for which the quality of performance promised is easily verified. However, the Internet does not solve the "principal–agent" problem with respect to more fundamental financial advice dispensed by an agent. That is why we believe that the future trend will shift toward more integrated financial products and services, which are easier to understand, more tailored toward individual profiles, and permit much more effective risk selection and control.[27]

Production of the new brand of integrated, customized financial instruments will be made economically feasible by applying already existing financial pricing and hedging technologies that permit the construction of custom products at "assembly-line" levels of cost. Paradoxically, making the products more user-friendly and simpler to understand for customers will create considerably more complexity for their producers. The good news for the producers is that this greater complexity will also make reverse engineering and "product knockoffs" by second-movers more difficult and thereby, protect margins and create franchise values for innovating firms. Hence, financial-engineering creativity and the technological and transactional bases to implement that creativity, reliably and cost-effectively, are likely to become a central competitive element in the industry.

These developments will significantly change the role of the mutual fund from a direct retail product to an intermediate or "building block" product embedded in the more integrated products used to implement the consumer's financial plan. The "fund of funds" is an early, crude example. The position and function of the fund in the future will be much like that of individual traded firms today, with portfolio managers, like today's CEOs, selling their stories of superior performance to professional fund analysts, who then make recommendations to "assemblers" of integrated retail financial products.

4.3 Example 3. Irrational Pessimism/Optimism

Having given two examples of how transaction costs can endogenously determine financial structure and the production process while neoclassical models remain valid as reduced-form predictors of equilibrium asset prices and allocations, we now offer an example of how behavioral factors can have similar effects. As we know from the empirical studies done by Kahneman, Tversky, and other behavioral scientists, people's financial behavior can differ systematically from the neoclassical assumptions of rationality. In particular, it has been shown that when individual choices depend on probabilities, subjective estimates of these probabilities are often subject to large biases. It does not necessarily follow, however, that the market prices of products whose demand depends on probability estimates—products such as insurance—will reflect those biases. To see why, consider the market for life insurance.

Suppose that people systematically underestimate their life expectancies. Then, if they are risk-averse (or even risk-neutral) the price they will be willing to pay for life insurance will be "too high" relative to the actuarially fair price. For example, suppose that the actuarially fair annual price is \$20 per \$10,000 of insurance, but people would be willing to pay \$40 as their "reservation" price. What would be the likely institutional dynamics of price formation in this market?

Life insurance firms that enter this market early might earn large profits because they can charge the reservation price of \$40 while their underwriting cost will be the \$20 expected loss. But others will examine the mortality data, calculate the spread between price charged and the objective costs of supplying life insurance, and soon discover the profit opportunity available. If there are no effective barriers to the entry of new firms, price competition will drive the price to the zero excess-profit point.[28]

Thus, in the long-run, competitive equilibrium, life insurance prices will reflect the rational unbiased probabilities of mortality, even though every buyer of life insurance has biased estimates of these probabilities. The institutional structure of providers of this risk-intermediating function and its dynamics of evolution may be greatly affected by this behavioral aberration even though asymptotically it has no effect on equilibrium price and once again neoclassical pricing obtains, as a reduced form.[29]

4.4 Example 4. Home Bias

Now consider the well-documented "home-bias" effect in portfolio selection.[30] Several rational explanations for this effect have been proposed in the economics and finance literature—for example, higher information costs for foreign vs. domestic shares.[31] But suppose that the reason is indeed an *irrational* bias against investing abroad. Thus, US residents prefer to invest in the shares of US corporations just because they are domiciled in the United States. They, therefore, invest far *less* abroad than is optimal according to the neoclassical model of optimal diversification.

Does the posited behavioral "aberration" result in an equilibrium allocation different from the neoclassical prediction?

Not necessarily. If US corporations were to invest only in US capital projects, then with investor home bias the equilibrium cost of capital and expected return on shares for US companies would be lower than in the neoclassical equilibrium, and higher for non-US projects and firms. However, with value-maximizing managers and absent legislative restrictions on investment, this equilibrium is not sustainable. With the lower cost of capital for the shares of US corporations, US firms will find that direct investments abroad will have higher net present value than domestic ones.[32] Asymptotically in the limiting case of no other imperfections except investor home bias, US corporations would end up issuing shares in the United States and investing overseas until they reach an asset allocation and cost of capital that is the same as predicted in a neoclassical no-home-bias equilibrium.

Thus, the final equilibrium asset prices and allocations will be as predicted by neoclassical finance theory. However, the *institutional structure* in which specific financial functions are executed may be materially determined by investor home bias. Of all possible institutional structures that are consistent with the neoclassical equilibrium, FSF looks for the one that most effectively mitigates the distortionary effects of home bias. Thus, instead of mutual funds and other investment intermediaries exclusively serving the function of international diversification on behalf of US residents, home bias may cause domestically based manufacturing and service companies to perform this diversification function through direct investment.

Much the same story would be true at a more micro-level for regional biases within a country's borders. For example, Huberman (1999) reports that people invest disproportionately in the shares of their *local* Bell Operating Systems. Again, we argue that this behavior does not necessarily lead to a distortion in equilibrium prices of shares relative to the neoclassical prediction. However, this behavior would lead one to predict that Bell operating companies located in more investor-rich regions might branch out and invest directly in operating companies in other less wealthy regions. Cross-regional diversification would thus be performed by the operating telephone companies themselves rather than by mutual funds and other "pure" financial intermediaries.

Note the operation here of the "invisible hand." Each individual investor retains his/her home-biased behavior, and firm actions are driven by the motive of maximizing net present value, without requiring any explicit awareness of that behavior.

Recognition that endogenous institutional changes may affect the influence of home bias on asset prices, if that bias is behaviorally driven, suggests some interesting time series tests which compare the amounts of stock of companies held directly by "locals" who are not managers of the firms in the 1950s, 1970s, and 1990s. One might expect that the much larger institutional holdings of stocks in the latter periods would mitigate the home bias effect.[33] Much the same tests could be applied to investments in local mutual fund groups that over time have moved into investing in shares of foreign companies.

4.5 Example 5. Regret Aversions[34]

Now consider another example from investing to illustrate how institutions might respond to an irrational behavior pattern by creating new financial instruments. Suppose that people do indeed have an aversion to feeling sorry after-the-fact for earlier investment decisions they made. If this behavioral trait is widespread, then we might expect to find a demand in the market for "look-back" options. A look-back call option gives its owner the right to buy an underlying security at the lowest price at which it traded during the term of the option. Similarly, a look-back put option gives its owner the right to sell the underlying security at the highest price at which it traded during the term of the option.[35] Thus, by paying a fixed insurance-like premium, the investor is assured of no regret from his investment decisions during the subsequent period covered by the option, because he will buy the stock at the lowest price (or sell it at the highest price) possible. There is of course a prospect for regret from paying for the option itself, if the *ex post* gain from the option does not exceed its cost. However, such regret, if any, may well be minimal because the premium is fixed in advance (bounding the amount of regret) and the "base" price for comparison (if the investor had sold or bought at some point instead of purchasing the option) is likely to be "fuzzy." Furthermore, if the marketing of the option frames it psychologically as "regret insurance," then investors may be no more at risk of realizing regret from paying the premium than from the purchase of other standard forms of insurance, such as fire and theft protection on a house or car.

Those regret-averse investors who would otherwise hold sub-optimal portfolio strategies because of strong regret aversion may well be willing to pay a premium price for such an option. The theory laying out the production technology and production cost for an intermediary to create look-back options first appeared in the scientific literature more than two decades ago.[36] Today, look-back options are available widely over-the-counter from investment and commercial banks.

The point of this example is to suggest that if regret aversion is indeed a significant behavioral phenomenon, then FSF theory predicts an institutional response in the form of creating products like look-back options. If regret is so widespread that it affects equilibrium prices, then at a given point in time, one investor's regret concern about selling a security is likely to mirror another investor's regret concern about buying that security. If so, a properly designed institution or market may be able to "pair off" these offsetting demands and neutralize the regret effect on asset demands. Thus, the theoretically predicted incremental effect that this behavioral phenomenon might have had on equilibrium asset prices and allocations in an institutional environment without look-back options or another functionally equivalent institution can be mitigated or eliminated entirely with their inclusion by institutionally rational intermediaries.[37]

4.6 *Example 6. Organizational Design*

In this example, we move from financial products to consider how organizational design itself might offset dysfunctional individual behavior and produce an end result that is in line with neoclassical predictions. For example, suppose that when making investment decisions individually, analysts tend to be optimistic and overconfident in their forecasts for the securities they study.[38] Let us suppose further that when individual analysts, each of whom has studied a different security, are brought together in a group and asked to form a group consensus regarding all of the securities, the bias is mitigated or altogether eliminated.[39]

FSF theory would predict a strong tendency for asset-management and other financial-service firms to organize investment selections as a group process including creating investment committees to evaluate the recommendations of individual security analysts and portfolio managers. The committees would have the effect of mitigating the bias of the individual analysts. Consequently, there would be little or no impact of this individual bias on actual investment choices and equilibrium asset market prices.

4.7 *Example 7. Don't Change Behavior; Solve with Institutions*

Now suppose it were possible to change the behavior of individuals to make them less optimistic and overconfident when analyzing individual securities. Although such a change in behavior would eliminate the bias, it might be better not to tinker with the behavior of individuals. The reason is that although optimism and overconfidence are dysfunctional in the domain of security analysis, they may be functional in other domains vital to individual success. That is, there can be unintended and unanticipated consequences of this action. By eliminating a person's optimism and overconfidence in general, we may therefore do more harm than good. Thus, it may be considerably better to rely on investment committees as a means of offsetting the individual bias caused by overconfidence than to attempt to alter the behavior of the individual analyst.

4.8 *Example 8. Sociological Elements of Behavioral Finance*[40]

The preceding examples of behavioral distortions of efficient risk allocation and asset pricing all involve cognitive dissonance of individual agents. However, there is another dimension of potential behavioral effects that is sociological in nature in that it derives from the social structure of the financial system. Sociological behavior is neither under the control of individuals within that social structure nor a direct consequence of simple aggregation of individual cognitive dysfunctions. A classic instance within finance is the Self-Fulfilling Prophecy (SFP),[41] applied for instance to bank runs: a bank would remain solvent provided that a majority of its depositors do not try to take their money out at the same time. However, as a consequence of a *public* prophesy that the bank is going to fail, each depositor attempts to withdraw his funds and in the process of the resulting liquidity crisis, the bank does indeed fail. Each individual can be fully rational and understand that if a "run on the bank" does not occur, it will indeed be solvent. Nevertheless, as a consequence of the public prophesy, each depositor decides rationally to attempt to withdraw his savings and the prophecy of bank failure is fulfilled. As we know, one institutional design used to offset this dysfunctional collective behavior is deposit insurance. There are of course others.

"Performativity" or Performing Theory has been employed as a mode of analysis with respect to the accuracy of the Black–Scholes option pricing model in predicting market prices of options, exploring whether the model's widespread public dissemination and use by option traders may have actually caused market pricing to change so as to make the model's predictions become more accurate.[42] Other recent work applying sociological analysis to finance issues includes studies of the sociology of arbitrage and understanding the development of derivative and other financial markets.[43]

5 Elements of Functional and Structural Finance

In this section we review the main analytical elements of FSF as exemplified by the cases of the preceding section.

5.1 Functions are the "Anchors"

When studying the dynamics of financial systems, it is best to adopt an analytical framework that treats *functions* rather than *institutions* as the conceptual anchors.[44] In this analytical framework the functions are exogenous, and the institutional forms are endogenously determined.

5.2 The Point of Departure is the Neoclassical Paradigm

When analyzing changes in parts of the financial system, a useful point of departure is the neoclassical paradigm of rational agents operating opportunistically in an environment of frictionless markets. If existing prices and allocations fail to conform to the neoclassical paradigm, it is helpful to focus on why this is so. The possible causes of such a failure might be:

- Existing institutional rigidities, in which case we might consider applying institutional design techniques to circumvent their unintended and dysfunctional aspects or abolish them directly, if the institutional sources are no longer needed.
- Technological inadequacies, which may disappear over time as a result of innovation.
- Dysfunctional behavioral patterns that cannot be offset by institutional changes.

5.3 Theory as a Predictor of Practice

As technology progresses and transaction costs continue to fall, finance theory is likely to provide increasingly more accurate predictions and prescriptions for future *product* innovations. Combining behavioral theory with neoclassical theory, together with existing theory within New Institutional Economics, should produce better predictions and prescriptions for the kinds of *institutional* changes to expect.[45]

5.4 Institutional Rationality Versus Individual Irrationality

Even when individuals behave in ways that are irrational, institutions may evolve to offset this behavior and produce a net result that is "as if" the individuals were behaving rationally. This is a version of Adam Smith's "invisible hand." Structural models that include transactions costs, irrational behavior, or other "imperfections" may give distorted predictions when framed in a neoclassical "minimalist" institutional setting of atomistic agents interacting directly in markets. It is, therefore, essential to include the endogenous institutional response. Studies of the impact of transactions costs or irrational behavior patterns would be greatly enhanced if as a matter of format, they included a section on institutional designs that have the potential to mitigate the effects of these patterns on prices and allocations. The resulting institutional design, if not already in place, can be seen as providing either a prediction about the dynamics of future institutional change or as a normative prescription for innovation.

5.5 Synthesis of Public and Private Finance

The FSF approach has no ideological bias in selecting the best mix of institutions to use in performing financial functions. It treats all institutions, whether governmental, private-enterprise or family based, as potential solutions. The same techniques of financial engineering apply whether the financial system is dominated by governmental institutions or by private-sector ones or by a balanced mix of the two. FSF seeks to find the best way to perform the financial functions for a given place at a given time.

For example, consider alternative systems for financing retirement. In recent years, there has been great interest around the world on this subject, and big changes are occurring in the institutional means for providing this essential financial function. In some countries where the economy is primarily based on traditional agriculture, retirement income is provided almost entirely by the retiree's family. In other countries it is provided by government, or by a mix of government and private-sector pension plans.

This is not by accident. The best institutional structure for providing income to the retiree population varies from country to country, and within a single country it changes over time. That best structure depends on a country's demographics, its social and family structure, its history and traditions, and its stage of economic development. And it changes with changes in technology.

These changes in retirement systems are sometimes treated as exogenous events or framed as the result of policy mistakes of the past. Instead, we propose that they be viewed systematically as part of a dynamic process of institutional change that can be analyzed and improved using the latest financial technology.[46]

5.6 *The Financial Innovation Spiral*[47]

The evolution of retirement systems, and indeed the financial system as a whole, can be viewed as an innovation spiral, in which organized markets and intermediaries compete with each other in a static sense and complement each other in a dynamic sense. That intermediaries and markets compete to be the providers of financial products is widely recognized. Improving technology and a decline in transactions costs has added to the intensity of that competition. Inspection of Finnerty's (1988, 1992) extensive histories of innovative financial products suggests a pattern in which products offered initially by intermediaries ultimately move to markets. For example:

- The development of liquid markets for money instruments such as commercial paper allowed money-market mutual funds to compete with banks and thrifts for household savings.
- The creation of "high-yield" and medium-term note markets, which made it possible for mutual funds, pension funds, and individual investors to service those corporate issuers who had historically depended on banks as their source of debt financing.
- The creation of a national mortgage market allowed mutual funds and pension funds to become major funding alternatives to thrift institutions for residential mortgages.
- Creation of these funding markets also made it possible for investment banks and mortgage brokers to compete with the thrift institutions for the origination and servicing fees on loans and mortgages.
- Securitization of auto loans, credit-card receivables, and leases on consumer and producer durables, has intensified the competition between banks and finance companies as sources of funds for these purposes.

This pattern may seem to imply that successful new products will inevitably migrate from intermediaries to markets. That is, once a successful product becomes familiar, and perhaps after some incentive problems are resolved, it will become a commodity traded in a market. Some see this process as destroying the value of intermediaries. However, this "systematic" loss of successful products is a consequence of the functional role of intermediaries and is not dysfunctional. Just as venture-capital firms that provide financing for start-up businesses expect to lose their successful creations to capital market sources of funding, so do the intermediaries that create new financial products expect to lose their successful and scalable ones to markets. Intermediaries continue to prosper by finding new successful products and the institutional means to perform financial functions more effectively than the existing ones, all made possible by the commodization of existing products and services.

Thus, exclusive focus on the time path of individual products can be misleading, not only with respect to the seemingly secular decline in the importance of intermediation, but with respect to understanding the functional relations between financial markets and intermediaries. Financial markets tend to be efficient institutional alternatives to intermediaries when the products have standardized terms, can serve a large number of customers, and are well-enough understood for transactors to be comfortable in assessing their prices. Intermediaries are better suited for low-volume customized products. As products such as futures, options, swaps, and securitized loans become standardized and move from intermediaries to markets, the proliferation of new trading markets in those instruments makes feasible the creation of new custom-designed financial products that improve "market completeness," to hedge their exposures on those products, the producers (typically, financial intermediaries) trade in these new markets and volume expands; increased volume reduces marginal transaction costs and thereby makes possible further implementation of more new products and trading strategies by intermediaries, which in turn leads to still more volume. Success of these trading markets and custom products encourages investment in creating additional markets and products, and so on it goes, spiraling toward the theoretically limiting case of zero marginal transactions costs and dynamically complete markets.

Consider, for example, the Eurodollar futures market that provides organized trading in standardized LIBOR (London Interbank Offered Rate) deposits at various dates in the future. The opportunity to trade in this futures market provides financial intermediaries with a way to hedge more efficiently custom-contracted interest-rate swaps based on a floating rate linked to LIBOR. A LIBOR rather than a US Treasury rate-based swap is better suited to the needs of many intermediaries' customers because their cash-market borrowing rate is typically linked to LIBOR and not to Treasury rates.

At the same time, the huge volume generated by intermediaries hedging their swaps has helped make the Eurodollar futures market a great financial success for its organizers. Furthermore, swaps with relatively standardized terms have recently begun to move from being custom contracts to ones traded in markets. The trading of these so-called "pure vanilla" swaps in a market further expands the opportunity structure for intermediaries to hedge and thereby enables them to create more-customized swaps and related financial products more efficiently.

As an example, consider the following issue faced by smaller countries with funded pension plans sponsored by either the government or by private institutions. Currently, these pension funds invest almost entirely in domestic securities—debt and equity issued by local firms, municipalities, and other entities. Although there would appear to be significant potential benefits from international risk-sharing by pension funds, this has not yet happened to any significant extent.

One way for such international risk-sharing to occur is for the small-country pension funds to invest abroad and for foreign financial institutions to offset this flow of funds by investing in the small country. However, there are significant barriers to such international flows of investment funds. Small country governments fear that the outflows will not be matched by inflows of funds, and therefore impose restrictions on the amount that pension funds can invest abroad. At the same time, investors in large countries are reluctant to invest in smaller countries for fear of manipulation and expropriation of their investments.

To circumvent many of these obstacles and obtain better international diversification, pension funds may rely increasingly on international swap contracts.[48] A swap contract consists of two parties exchanging (or "swapping") a series of payments at specified intervals (say, every 6 months) over a specified period of time (say, 10 years). The payments are based upon an agreed principal amount (called the "notional" amount), and there is no immediate payment of money between the parties. Thus, as in forward and futures contracts, the swap contract itself provides no new funds to either party. The size of each swap payment is the difference between the actual value of the item specified in the contract (e.g., an exchange rate or an interest rate) and the value specified in advance in the contract. International pension swaps would enable a small country to diversify internationally without violating restrictions on investing capital abroad.[49]

Swap contracts provide an excellent example to illustrate the importance of institutional details that are routinely ignored in neoclassical analysis. As mentioned earlier in this paper, the neoclassical theory of derivatives focuses on the equivalences among various combinations of derivatives and the underlying assets. Thus, in a frictionless perfect-market environment, leveraged cash market positions, swaps, forward contracts, and futures contracts all perform fundamentally the same economic function of risk-transfer, and their prices are all linked to each other by a pricing relation that rules out arbitrage profits. In this limited sense, given cash or forward or futures contracts, swaps are "redundant."

But in the actual world of contemporary international finance, small differences in the institutional details can have material implications for the speed of implementation. Futures contracts are *multilateral-party* exchange-traded instruments, whereas swap contracts are *bilateral* and are almost never traded on an exchange. To introduce a new type of futures contract requires a formal process of approval by the governing body of the exchange, representing a consensus of the exchange members, which can number in the hundreds. In sharp contrast, to introduce a new type of swap contract requires only consensus between the two counterparts to the contract. This difference makes it possible to innovate and execute new types of swap contracts in a fraction of the time required to introduce a new futures contract.

Today's swap contracts also differ from a series of back-to-back loans or forward contracts. Like swaps, forward contracts are flexible bilateral instruments, but they lack a uniform standard. Modern swap contracts follow a standard format developed during the early 1980s by the International Swap Dealers Association (ISDA). The ISDA's standard contract has been tested in a variety of jurisdictions around the world. Over the years the document has been amended and has evolved to meet legal and regulatory requirements virtually everywhere.

Now that the legal infrastructure has been thoroughly tested and practitioners and regulators have developed confidence in it, the pace of swap innovation is likely to proceed at a much faster rate and with much lower transaction costs.[50] With the infrastructure in place, the cost of implementing new types of swaps involving other underlying securities, commodities, economic indexes, and the like, will be relatively low.

A well-established legal and transactional infrastructure for swaps together with the enormous scale of such contracts outstanding[51] set conditions for the prospective use of swaps and other contractual agreements to manage the economic risks of whole countries in a non-invasive and reversible fashion.[52] Thus, countries can modify their risk exposures separately from physical investment decisions and trade and capital flow policies. This application of financial technology offers the potential for a country to mitigate or even eliminate the traditional economic tradeoff between pursuing its comparative advantages, which by necessity requires it to focus on a relatively few related activities and achieving efficient risk diversification, which requires it to pursue many relatively unrelated activities.

6 Conclusion: Finance and Economic Growth

We have framed and illustrated by examples the FSF approach to the design of financial systems. We conclude here with some observations connecting the design and implementation of a well-functioning financial system with the broader economic issues of promoting long-term economic growth.

Nearly a half century ago, Robert Solow's fundamental work on the long-run determinants of economic growth concluded that it was technological progress, not high rates of saving or population growth, that account for the vast bulk of growth. Subsequent studies have tried to reduce the unexplained residual by adding other measurable inputs. A large body of recent research work suggests that well-functioning financial institutions promote economic growth. These conclusions emerge from cross-country comparisons,[53] firm-level studies,[54] time-series research,[55] and econometric investigations that use panel techniques.[56] And in their historical research, North (1990), Levine (2002), Neal (1990), and Rousseau and Sylla (2003) have all concluded that those regions—be they cities, countries, or states—that developed the relatively more sophisticated and well-functioning financial systems were the ones that were the subsequent leaders in economic development of their times.

An integrated picture of these findings suggests that in the absence of a financial system that can provide the means for transforming technical innovation into broad enough implementation, technological progress will not have a significant/substantial impact on the economic development and growth of the economy. Therefore, countries like China or even Japan, that need to undertake restructuring of their financial systems, should consider not only their short-run monetary and fiscal policies, and not only the impact of these policies on national saving and capital formation, but also how changes in their financial institutions will affect their prospects for long-term economic development.

But substantial changes and adaptations in the institutional implementation will be necessary in different countries. There are at least two reasons: (1) national differences in history, culture, politics, and legal infrastructure, and (2) opportunities for a country that is in the midst of restructuring its financial system to "leap frog" the current best practices of existing systems by incorporating the latest financial technology in ways that can only be done with "a clean sheet."

There is not likely to be "one best way" of providing financial and other economic functions. And even if there were, how does one figure out which one is best without assuming an all-knowing benevolent ruler or international agency? One must take care to avoid placing the implementation of all economic development into one institutionally defined financial channel.

Fortunately, innovations in telecommunications, information technology, and financial engineering offer the practical prospect for multiple channels for the financing of economic growth. Multiple channels for capital raising are a good idea in terms of greater assurance of supply at competitive prices. They also offer the prospective benefits of competition to be the best one in a given environment at a given point in time.

Much of the traditional discussion of economic policy focuses on its monetary, fiscal, currency management aspects and on monitoring capital and trade flows. These are important in the short run, and thus also in the long run, in the sense that one does not get to the long run without surviving the short run. However, if financial innovation is stifled for fear that it will reduce the effectiveness of short-run monetary and fiscal policies (or will drain foreign currency reserves), the consequences could be a much slower pace of technological progress. Furthermore, long-run policies that focus on domestic saving and capital formation as key determinants of economic growth do not appear to be effective. Policies designed to stimulate innovation in the financial system would thus appear to be more important for long-term economic development.

Notes

1 That is, in this theory, financial functions are *exogenous* factors and the institutional structure is *endogenous*.

2 For an overview of the impact of option pricing on finance theory and practice, see Merton (1998) and Scholes (1998).

3 For a detailed exposition of this view see Petrosky (1992). See also Draghi *et al.* (2003, pp. 27–35) for application of financial science and technology to anticipating and managing macro-financial crises.

4 For early applications of the FSF approach to bank reform and pension reform, see Merton and Bodie (1993) and Bodie and Merton (1993), respectively.

5 See International Society for New Institutional Economics, www.isnie.org. Transaction Cost Economics is a central part of the paradigm; see Williamson (1998).

6 Behavioral Economics has its intellectual roots in the work of Kahneman *et al.* (1982). Barbaris and Thaler (2003) provide a recent and comprehensive survey on behavioral finance. A very different approach to behavioral finance is to study the relations between emotions and rational financial decision-making by measuring physiological characteristics. See, for example, Lo and Repin (2002).

7 Intersecting Transactions Cost Finance and Behavioral Finance is Experimental Finance, which takes explicit account of learning by market participants and its effects on financial market price paths and derives and tests behavior in laboratory experiments; cf. Bossaerts (2002) and Bossaerts and Plott (forthcoming) and the Caltech Laboratory for Experimental Finance, www.hss.caltech.edu/~pbs/LabFinance.html.

8 See the papers by Hall (2001), Hirshleifer (2001), Lamont and Thaler (2003), Shiller (1999), Shleifer (2000), and Thaler (1993, 2000).

9 See Fama (1998), Ross (2002, 2004), Rubinstein (2001), Schwert (2003), and Weitzman (2004).

[10] Fama (1980), Fama and Jensen (1983a,b), Jensen and Meckling (1976) and Ross (1973) also provide a theory of endogenous determination of organization design and institutions, driven by minimizing agency costs.

[11] That approximation becomes precise asymptotically as the underlying system approaches a complete market functionally.

[12] Thus, since the actual institutional environment does not matter with respect to its predictions about asset prices and resource allocations, the frictionless neoclassical model should be treated as a reduced-form model, not a structural one. As noted earlier in the text, that same institutional robustness does not apply to predictions of asset price behavior in transaction-cost and behavioral models.

[13] See Coase (1937, 1960).

[14] See Modigliani and Miller (1958).

[15] In offering their proposition, Modigliani and Miller did not assert that capital structure "doesn't matter" in the real world. Instead, by identifying sufficient conditions, they isolate where to look to explain why it does matter.

[16] Gilson and Kraakman (2003) reach a similar conclusion on relative importance with respect to behavioral finance from a different analytical framework.

[17] The formal derivation of the Black–Scholes model assumes that all agents can trade continuously without cost. Under some further restrictions on asset price dynamics, there exists a dynamic trading strategy in the underlying stock and the risk-free asset that would exactly replicate the payoffs to the option. Hence, by ruling out arbitrage, the option price is determined.

[18] The case is further strengthened by taking into account the fact that such intermediaries only need to dynamically hedge their *net* exposures after offsetting them within the firm; see Merton (1989) and footnote #26 here.

[19] For further discussion, see Merton (1989, pp. 251–254, 1992, pp. 466–467) on "quasi-dichotomy."

[20] Merton (1973, 1992).

[21] Constantinides (1986).

[22] Cass and Stiglitz (1970), Markowitz (1952), Tobin (1958), and Merton (1971, 1973, 1992).

[23] As evidence for this convergence in data sources, consider the ubiquitous CRSP data or COMPUSTAT. Sharpe (2004) provides a simulation-based model which computes equilibrium optimal portfolio allocations for investors with heterogeneous beliefs and compares those optimal portfolios to the CAPM-predicted ones.

[24] See Merton (1992, Chapter 13).

[25] This type of procedure is developed in Haugh and Lo (2001) and in Merton (1989, pp. 250–254, 1992, pp. 450–464). See also Merton (1995, pp. 477–479, 2002, pp. 62–63) for its application to central bank open-market operations.

[26] A more accurate assessment of the real-world impact should also take into account other risk-management tools that intermediaries have to reduce transaction costs. For instance, as developed in analytical detail in Merton (1992, pp. 450–457), intermediaries need only use dynamic trading to hedge their *net* derivative-security exposures to various underlying assets. For a real-world intermediary with a large book of various derivative products, netting can vastly reduce the size and even the frequency of the hedging transactions necessary. Beyond this, as part of their optimal risk management, intermediaries can "shade" their bid and offer prices among their various products to encourage more or less customer activity in different products to help manage their exposures. The limiting case when the net positions

of customer exposures leaves the intermediary with no market exposure is called a "matched book."

27 For more detailed discussions, see Aaron (1999), Bodie (2003), Bodie *et al.* (2001) and Merton (2002, 2003).

28 In the realm of investing, see Coval and Thaker (forthcoming) for a prime demonstration with a formal model of the role of institutionally rational intermediaries in bridging the dysfunctional behavior between irrationally optimistic individual entrepreneurs and irrationally pessimistic individual investors. Cohen, Gompers, and Vuolteenaho (2002) provide empirical evidence that institutional investors tend not to make cognitive errors of under-reaction to corporate cash-flow new that individual investors appear to do.

29 Benink and Bossaerts (2001) and Benink *et al.* (2004) present an alternative, "Neo-Austrian" view of the dynamic adjustment process in which asset prices tend to move *toward* an efficient and stable equilibrium but never *reach* that equilibrium and thus, are always inefficient and inconsistent with neoclassical pricing.

30 See, for examples, Coval and Moskowitz (1999), Cronqvist and Thaler (2004), Hong, Kubik, and Stein (2004), Huberman (1999), Lewis (1998) and Portes and Rey (forthcoming).

31 More generally, see Merton (1987) for a portfolio and asset pricing model in which passive indexing investment strategies are permitted but active investors trade only in firms they know about, and the cost of information limits the number of firms an active investor knows about.

32 For some preliminary evidence that can be used to support this view, see Baker, Foley and Wurgler (2004).

33 Although a time series test has not yet been undertaken, the findings of Hong *et al.* (2004) appear to support this view in a cross-sectional analysis of firms.

34 Regret aversion is the tendency to avoid taking any action due to a fear that in retrospect it will turn out to be less than optimal.

35 Look-back options are a particular version of exotic options, a major financial industry line of products.

36 Goldman *et al.* (1979); see more recently, Shepp and Shiryaev (1993).

37 A similar approach could be taken for mitigating other types of psychological factors that may also influence investment decisions dysfunctionally. For a convenient listing of those factors affecting investing, see http://www. altruistfa.com/behavioralinvestingpitfalls.htm. Thaler and Benartzi (2004) provide a real-world example of correcting the economic impact of cognitive errors with a product designed to use pre-commitment to offset the dysfunctional behavior affecting individual retirement saving. Another example is found in Miller (2002) who shows how collective non-cooperative behavior in markets can learn to avoid bubbles.

38 Thaler (2000) writes: "We all tend to be optimistic about the future. On the first day of my MBA class on decision-making at the University of Chicago, every single student expects to get an above-the-median grade, yet half are inevitably disappointed."

39 Scherbina (2004) finds evidence that the presence of institutional investors in equity markets tends to exert corrective pressure on share prices against the distorting information-processing errors of individual investors. Cohen (2003) finds that individuals reduce their equity exposures more than institutions after a market decline and increase their exposures more than institutions after a market rise, which could be the result of greater risk aversion for individuals or price-change-sensitive optimism or pessimism. It would be interesting to

explore whether this difference between institutional and individaul investing behavior is related to greater use of group decision-making by institutions.

40 See Smelser and Swedberg (1994) and Swedberg (2003) for an overview of economic sociology.

41 See R.K. Merton (1948, 1957).

42 See MacKenzie (2004a, b, forthcoming) and Mackenzie and Millo (2003). The distinction between Performativity and a SFP is subtle but significant. Performativity implies that the widespread belief in the model causes pricing in the market to change toward greater conformity with the model than before. The concept of a SFP applies only if the prophesized event—in this case the model-predicted option pricing—would not have occurred in the absence of its public proclamation, usually suggesting that the proclamation (the model) was dysfunctionally "unjustified." Hence, even if widespread public knowledge of the model's adoption leads others to use it, it is not a SFP if the model is economically valid or would be justified, even in the absence of its public proclamation. See Merton (1992, p. 471).

43 See MacKenzie (2000, 2003, 2004a, b, forthcoming).

44 See Merton (1993) on the functional perspective. The functional analytical framework presented here is developed in Crane *et al.* (1995). Financial functions for financial institutions are also used in a different analytic framework that originates from the important work of Diamond and Dybvig (1986).

45 As discussed in Footnote 42 for pricing models, Performativity can apply as well to the evolution of institutional change. If a better theory of institutional dynamics starts to become more widely adopted, its predictions about those dynamics will become more accurate as its adoption spreads and more players use it to make decisions about institutional changes.

46 Bodie (2000).

47 See Merton (1993, pp. 27–33). The description here draws heavily on Merton and Bodie (1995).

48 Bodie and Merton (2002).

49 This swap innovation, including with capital controls, is set forth in Merton (1990).

50 The cost of doing a standard interest-rate swap is today about 1/2 of a basis point—that is only $5000 on a notional amount of $100 million!

51 It has been estimated that the *notional* amount of derivative contracts outstanding globally is $216 trillion. Some large banking institutions have several trillion dollars each on their balance sheets.

52 See Draghi *et al.* (2003, pp. 37–44) and Merton (1999, 2002, pp. 64–67, 2004) for development of this idea.

53 See King and Levine (1993a, b) and Demirguc-Kunt and Levine (2001).

54 See Demirguc-Kunt and Maksimovic (1998, 1999).

55 See Rousseau and Wachtel (1998, 2000).

56 See Levine *et al.* (2000).

References

Aaron, H. (ed.) (1999). *Behavioral Dimensions of Retirement Economics*. Washington, DC: Brookings Institution.

Baker, M., Foley, C.F. and Wurgler, J. (2004). "The Stock Market and Investment: Evidence for FDI Flows." Harvard Business School manuscript (September).

Barberis, N. and Thaler, R.H. (2003). "A Survey of Behavioral Finance." In: G.M. Constantinides, M. Harris and R. Stultz (eds.), *Handbook of the Economics of Finance*. Elsevier Science, B.V.

Beck T., Demirguc-Kunt, A. and Levine, R. (2001). "Law, Politics, and Finance." World Bank Working Paper, #2585 (April).

Beck, T., Levine, R. and Loayza, N. (2000). "Finance and the Sources of Growth." *Journal of Financial Economics* **58**(1–2), 261–300.

Benink, H. and Bossaerts, P. (2001). "An Exploration of Neo-Austrian Theory Applied to Financial Markets." *Journal of Finance* **56**(3), 1011–1028.

Benink, H., Gordillo, J.L., Pardo, J.P. and Stephens, C. (2004). "A Study of Neo-Austrian Economics using an Artificial Stock Market." Rotterdam School of Management, Erasmus University (March).

Bodie, Z. (2000). "Financial Engineering and Social Security Reform." In: J. Campbell and M. Feldstein (eds.), *Risk Aspects of Investment-Based Social Security Reform*. Chicago: University of Chicago Press.

Bodie, Z. (2003). "Thoughts on the Future: Life-Cycle Investing in Theory and Practice." *Financial Analysts Journal* **59**(1), 24–29.

Bodie, Z. and Merton, R.C. (1993). "Pension Benefit Guarantees in the United States: A Functional Approach." In: R. Schmitt (ed.), *The Future of Pensions in the United States*. Philadelphia: University of Pennsylvania Press.

Bodie, Z. and Merton, R.C. (2002). "International Pension Swaps." *Journal of Pension Economics and Finance* **1**(1), 77–83.

Bodie, Z., Hammond, P.B. and Mitchell, O.S. (2001). "New Approaches to Analyzing and Managing Retirement Risks." *Benefits Quarterly* **17**(4), 72–83.

Bossaerts, P. (2002). *The Paradox of Asset Pricing*. Princeton: Princeton University Press.

Bossaerts, P. and Plott, C. (forthcoming). "Basic Principles of Asset Pricing Theory: Evidence from Large-Scale Experimental Financial Markets." *Review of Finance.*

Cass, D. and Stiglitz, J.E. (1970). "The Structure of Investor Preferences and Asset Returns, and Separability in Portfolio Allocation: A Contribution to the Pure Theory of Mutual Funds." *Journal of Economic Theory* **2**, 122–160.

Coase, R. (1937). "The Nature of the Firm." *Economica* **4**, 386–405.

Coase, R. (1960). "The Problem of Social Cost." *Journal of Law and Economics* **2**, 1–44.

Cohen, R.B. (2003). "Asset Allocation Decisions of Individuals and Institutions." Harvard Business School Working Paper #03–112.

Cohen, R.N., Gompers, P.A. and Vuolteenaho, T. (2002). "Who Underreacts to Cash-flow News?: Evidence from Trading between Individuals and Institutions." *Journal of Financial Economics* **66**, 409–462.

Constantinides, G. (1986). "Capital Market Equilibrium with Transactions Costs." *Journal of Political Economy* **94**, 842–862.

Cronqvist, H. and Thaler, R.H. (2004). "Design Choices in Privatized Social Security Systems: Learning from the Swedish Experience." *American Economic Review* **94**(2).

Coval, J.D. and Moskowitz, T.J. (1999). "Home Bias at Home: Local Equity Preference in Domestic Portfolios." *Journal of Finance* **54**, 2045–2073.

Coval, D. and Thaker, A.V. (forthcoming). "Financial Intermediation as a Beliefs-Bridge Between Optimists and Pessimists." *Journal of Financial Economics.*

Crane, D., Froot, K.A., Mason, S.P., Perold, A.F., Merton, R.C., Bodie, Z., Sirri, E.R. and Tufano, P. (1995). *The Global Financial System: A Functional Perspective*. Boston: Harvard Business School Press.

Demirgüç-Kunt, A. and Levine, R. (2001). *Financial Structure and Growth: A Cross-Country Comparison of Banks, Markets, and Development*. Cambridge, MA: MIT Press.

Demirgüç-Kunt, A. and Maksimovic, V. (1998). "Law, Finance, and Firm Growth." *Journal of Finance* **53**(6), 2107–2137.

Demirgüç-Kunt, A. and Maksimovic, V. (1999). "Institutions, Financial Markets and Firm Debt Maturity." *Journal of Financial Economics* **54**(3), 295–336.

Diamond, D.W. and Dybvig, P. (1986). "Banking Theory, Deposit Insurance, and Bank Regulation." *Journal of Business* **59**(1), 55–68.

Draghi, M., Giavazzi, F. and Merton, R.C. (2003). *Transparency, Risk Management and International Financial Fragility*, Vol. 4, Geneva Reports on the World Economy, International Center for Monetary and Banking Studies.

Easterly, W. and Levine, R. (2001). "It's Not Factor Accumulation: Stylized Facts and Growth Models." *World Bank Economic Review* **15**(2), 177–219.

Fama, E. (1980). "Agency Problems and the Theory of the Firm." *Journal of Political Economy* **88**(2), 288–307.

Fama, E. (1998). "Market Efficiency, Long-Term Returns, and Behavioral Finance." *Journal of Financial Economics* **49**(3), 283–306.

Fama, E. and Jensen, M. (1983a). "Separation of Ownership and Control." *Journal of Law and Economics* **26**, 301–326.

Fama, E. and Jensen, M. (1983b). "Agency Problems and Residual Claims." *Journal of Law and Economics* **26**, 327–349.

Finnerty, J. (1988). "Financial Engineering in Corporate Finance: An Overview." *Financial Management* **17**, 14–33.

Finnerty, J. (1992). "An Overview of Corporate Securities Innovation." *Journal of Applied Corporate Finance* **4** (Winter), 23–39.

Gilson, R.J. and Kraakman, R. (2003). "The Mechanisms of Market Efficiency Twenty Years Later: The Hindsight Bias." Columbia Law Economics Working Paper No. 240 (October).

Goldman, M.B., Sossin, H.B. and Shepp, L.A. (1979). "On Contingent Claims that Insure Ex-Post Optimal Stock Market Timing." *Journal of Finance* **34**, 401–13.

Hakansson, N. (1979). "The Fantastic World of Finance: Progress and the Free Lunch." *Journal of Financial and Quantitative Analysis* **14** (Proceedings Issue), 717–34.

Hall, R.E. (2001). "Struggling to Understand the Stock Market." *American Economic Review Papers and Proceedings* **91**, 1–11.

Haugh, M.B. and Lo, A.W. (2001). "Asset Allocation and Derivatives." *Quantitative Finance* **1**(1), 45–72.

Hirshleifer, D. (2001). "Investor Psychology and Asset Pricing." *Journal of Finance* **56**(4), 1533–1597.

Hong, H., Kubik, J.D. and Stein, J.C. (2004). "The Only Game in Town: Stock-Price Consequences of Local Bias." Mimeo (June).

Huberman, G. (1999). "Familiarity Breeds Investment." *The Review of Financial Studies* **14**(3), 659–680.

Jensen, M.C. and Meckling, W.C. (1976). "Theory of the Firm: Managerial Behavior, Agency Costs and Capital Structure." *Journal of Financial Economics* **3**, 305–360.

Kahneman, D., Slovic, P. and Tversky, A. (1982). *Judgment Under Uncertainty: Heuristics and Biases.* Cambridge, UK: Cambridge University Press.

King, R.G. and Levine, R. (1993a). "Finance and Growth: Schumpeter Might Be Right." *Quarterly Journal of Economics* **153**, 717–738.

King, R.G. and Levine, R. (1993b). "Finance, Entrepreneurship, and Growth: Theory and Evidence." *Journal of Monetary Economics* **32**, 513–542.

Lamont, O.A. and Thaler, R.H. (2003). "Anomalies: The Law of One Price in Financial Markets." *Journal of Economic Perspectives* **17**(4), 191–202.

Levine, R. (2002). "Bank-Based or Market-Based Financial Systems: Which is Better?" *Journal of Financial Intermediation* **11**, 398–428.

Levine, R., Loayza, N. and Beck, T. (2000). "Financial Intermediation and Growth: Causality and Causes." *Journal of Monetary Economics* **46**, 31–77.

Lewis, K. (1998). "International Home Bias in International Finance and Business Cycles." NBER Working Paper No. W6351 (January).

Lo, A.W. and Repin, D.V. (2002). "The Psychophysiology of Real-Time Financial Risk Processing." *Journal of Cognitive Neuroscience* **14**(3), 323–339.

MacKenzie, D. (2000). "Fear in the Markets." *London Review of Books*, April 13, 13.

MacKenzie, D. (2003). "Long-Term Capital Management and the Sociology of Arbitrage." *Economy and Society* **32**(3), 349–380.

MacKenzie, D. (forthcoming). *An Engine, Not a Camera: Finance Theory and the Making of Markets.* Cambridge: MIT Press.

MacKenzie, D. (2004a). "The Big, Bad Wolf and the Rational Market: Portfolio Insurance, the 1987 Crash and the Performativity of Economics." *Economy and Society* **33**(3), 303–334.

MacKenzie, D. (2004b). "Is Economics Performative? Option Theory and the Construction of Derivatives Markets." University of Edinburgh (October).

MacKenzie, D. and Millo, Y. (2003). "Negotiating a Market, Performing Theory: The Historical Sociology of a Financial Derivatives Exchange." *American Journal of Sociology* **109**, 107–145.

Markowitz, H. (1952), "Portfolio Selection." *Journal of Finance* 7, 77–91.

Merton, R.C. (1971). "Optimum Consumption and Portfolio Rules in a Continuous-Time Model." *Journal of Economic Theory* **3**, 373–413.

Merton, R.C. (1973). "An Intertemporal Capital Asset Pricing Model." *Econometrica.* **41**, 867–887.

Merton, R.C. (1987). "A Simple Model of Capital Market Equilibrium with Incomplete Information." *Journal of Finance* **42**, 483–510.

Merton, R.C. (1989). "On the Application of the Continuous-Time Theory of Finance to Financial Intermediation and Insurance." *The Geneva Papers on Risk and Insurance* **14**(52), 225–262.

Merton, R.C. (1990). "The Financial System and Economic Performance." *Journal of Financial Services Research* **4**, 263–300.

Merton, R.C. (1992). *Continuous-Time Finance,* revised edition. Oxford: Basil Blackwell.

Merton, R.C. (1993). "Operation and Regulation in Financial Intermediation: A Functional Perspective." In: P. Englund (ed.), *Operation and Regulation of Financial Markets.* Stockholm: The Economic Council.

Merton, R.C. (1995). "Financial Innovation and the Management and Regulation of Financial Institutions." *Journal of Banking and Finance* **19**, 461–481.

Merton, R.C. (1998). "Applications of Option-Pricing Theory: 25 Years Later." *American Economic Review* **88**(3), 323–349.

Merton, R.C. (1999). "Commentary: Finance Theory and Future Trends: The Shift to Integration." *Risk* July, 48–50.

Merton, R.C. (2002). "Future Possibilities in Finance Theory and Finance Practice." In: H. Geman, D. Madan, S. Pliska and T. Vorst (eds.), *Mathematical Finance—Bachelier Congress 2000.* Berlin: Springer-Verlag.

Merton, R.C. (2003). "Thoughts on the Future: Theory and Practice in Investment Management." *Financial Analysts Journal* **59**(1), 17–23.

Merton, R.C. (2004). "On Financial Innovation and Economic Growth." *Harvard China Review* Spring, 2–3.

Merton, R.C. and Bodie, Z. (1993). "Deposit Insurance Reform: A Functional Approach," In: A. Melzer and C. Plosser (eds.), *Carnegie-Rochester Conference Series on Public Policy,* Volume 38.

Merton, R.C. and Bodie, Z. (1995). "A Conceptual Framework for Analyzing the Financial System." Chapter 1 in Crane *et al.* (1995).

Merton, R.K. (1948). "The Self-Fulfilling Prophecy." *Antioch Review* Summer, 193–210.

Merton, R.K. (1957), *Social Theory and Social Structure,* revised and enlarged edition. Glencoe, IL: Free Press.

Miller, R.M. (2002). "Can Markets Learn to Avoid Bubbles?" *The Journal of Behavioral Finance* **3**(1).

Modigliani, F. and Miller, M. (1958). "The Cost of Capital, Corporation Finance and the Theory of Investment." *American Economic Review* **48**, 261–297.

Neal, L.D. (1990). *The Rise of Financial Capitalism: International Capital Markets in the Age of Reason.* Cambridge, UK: Cambridge University Press.

North, D. (1990). *Institutions, Institutional Change, and Economic Performance.* Cambridge, UK: Cambridge University Press.

Petrosky, H. (1992). *To Engineer is Human: The Role of Failure in Successful Design.* New York: Vintage Books.

Portes, R. and Rey, H. (forthcoming). "The Determinants of Cross-Border Equity Flows." *Journal of International Economics.*

Ross, S. (1973). "The Economic Theory of Agency: The Principal's Problem." *American Economic Review* **63**(2), 134–139.

Ross, S. (2002). "A Neoclassical Look at Alternative Finance: The Case of the Closed End Funds." *European Financial Management* June, 129–135.

Ross, S. (2004). *Neoclassical Finance*, Princeton, NJ: Princeton University Press.

Rousseau, P.L. and Sylla, R. (2003). "Financial Systems, Economic Growth, and Globalization." In: M. Bordo, A. Taylor and J. Williamson (eds.), *Globalization in a Historical Perspective.* Chicago: University of Chicago Press.

Rousseau, P.L. and Wachtel, P. (1998). "Financial Intermediation and Economic Performance: Historical Evidence from Five Industrialized Countries." *Journal of Money, Credit and Banking* **30**(4), 657–678.

Rousseau, P.L. and Wachtel, P. (1999). "Equity Markets and Growth: Cross Country Evidence on Timing and Outcomes: 1980–1995." *Journal of Banking and Finance* **24**(12), 1933–1957.

Rubinstein, M. (2001). "Rational Markets: Yes or No? The Affirmative Case." *Financial Analysts Journal* **57**(3), 15–29.

Scherbina, A. (2004), "Analyst Disagreement, Forecast Bias and Stock Returns." Harvard Business School Working Paper #05-003 (June).

Scholes, M.S. (1998). "Derivatives in a Dynamic Environment." *American Economic Review* **88**(3), 350–370.

Schwert, G.W. (2003). "Anomalies and Market Efficiency." In: G.M. Constantinides, M. Harris and R. Stultz (eds.), *Handbook of the Economics of Finance.* Elsevier Science, B.V., pp. 937–972.

Sharpe, W.F. (2004). *Asset Prices and Portfolio Choice*, The Princeton Lectures in Finance, 2004, forthcoming, Princeton University Press.

Shepp, L. and Shiryaev, A.N. (1993). "The Russian Option: Reduced Regret." *The Annals of Applied Probability* **3**(3), 631–640.

Shiller, R. (1999). "Human Behavior and the Efficiency of Financial Markets," In: J.B. Taylor and M. Woodford (eds.), *Handbook of Macroeconomics*, Volume 1. Holland: Elsevier, pp. 1305–1340.

Shleifer, A. (2000). *Inefficient Markets: An Introduction to Behavioral Finance.* Oxford: Oxford University Press.

Smelser, N.J. and Swedberg, R. (eds.) (1994). *The Handbook of Economic Sociology.* Princeton: Princeton University Press.

Swedberg, R. (2003). *Principles of Economic Sociology.* Princeton: Princeton University Press.

Thaler, R.H. (ed.) (1993). *Advances in Behavioral Finance.* New York: Russell Sage Foundation.

Thaler, R.H. (2000). "From Homo Economicus to Homo Sapiens." *Journal of Economic Perspectives* **14**(1), 133–141.

Thaler, R.H. and Benartzi, S. (2004). "Save More Tomorrow: Using Behavioral Economics to Increase Employee Saving." *Journal of Political Economy* **112**(1), S164–S187.

Tobin, J. (1958). "Liquidity Preference as Behavior Towards Risk." *Review of Economic Studies* **25**, 68–85.

Weitzman, M.L. (2004). "A Unified Bayesian Theory of Equity Puzzles." Department of Economics, Harvard University (September).

Williamson, O.E. (1998). "Transaction Cost Economics: How It Works; Where It is Headed." *De Economist* **146**(3), 23–58.

Keywords: Financial system; financial structure

Journal Of Investment Management
Vol. 3, No. 1 (2005), pp. 45–59

ASSET/LIABILITY MANAGEMENT AND ENTERPRISE RISK MANAGEMENT OF AN INSURER

Thomas S. Y. Ho [a]

Risk management techniques used in banks and trading floors are generally not applicable to insurance companies. Risk measures and risk monitoring approaches must be developed to respond to the challenges to the insurance industry. This paper describes the current risk management practices for both life and general insurance businesses, and proposes the corporate model approach that extends the present approaches to provide corporate management solutions, enterprise risk management in particular, for insurers.

Recently, perhaps one of the most active areas of financial research is risk management. Extensive research has led to new risk management methods. For example, introductions of value-at-risk (VaR), earnings-at-risk, and risk adjusted performance measures are some of many innovations adopted in practice. However, the research tends to focus on risk management for trading floors or commercial banks. Few solutions apply to the insurers.

Trading floors and commercial banks share many similar characteristics in their risk management. Both businesses hold relatively short-term instruments on their balance sheets. And these instruments are often traded in the marketplace with reasonable liquidity or have acceptable model risk. Further, their gains and losses can be realized over a relatively short-term horizon and therefore the model assumptions can be verified by market reality. These attributes of their balance sheet items enable the trading floors and commercial banks to protect their capital (or equity), as measured by the assets net of the liabilities in present value terms, and use risk measures like VaR in their risk management.

However, the insurers cannot adopt these risk management methods directly, because their challenges in risk management are different. One main difference arises from the insurer's liabilities. They are in general long dated and illiquid or with no secondary markets at all. Another difference is that their risks, like mortality risk, are not market related and therefore their risks cannot be replicated or hedged. As a result, the management of the liabilities tends to be based on book value, avoiding the use of fair valuation, which may be difficult to determine. And, the management performance metrics are not based on marking-to-market value, but on a performance over a much longer time horizon. For these reasons, "enhancing the equity or increasing the

[a]Thomas Ho Company, 55 Liberty Street, New York, NY 10005-1003, USA.

shareholders' value" based on marking-to-market can no longer be used as the performance metric. The VaR approach has to be adapted to the management of insurance liability before it can be useful. To date, managing the VaR risk of the "equity" of an insurer's balance sheet is often not considered relevant in practice.

Determining an appropriate risk management approach for insurance companies is clearly an important issue for a broad range of market participants. For reasons similar to the trading floors and banks, developing a practical and effective risk management process is a concern to the practitioners in the insurance industry. Beyond the insurance industry, an understanding of the risk management process of an insurer can enable the capital market participants to better appreciate the insurers' demand for investment products. Since insurance companies are the major suppliers of funds of long-term investments, this understanding is important to develop an efficient capital market. The regulators and the securities analysts are also concerned with these issues, since the insurance industry is an integral part of the capital market.

The purpose of this paper is to first provide an overview of some of the risk management techniques used currently and then propose the corporate model approach to manage enterprise risks of the firm. Section 1 reviews the current practices, which are considered most effective in risk management for the life insurers. In a similar fashion, Section 2 describes the practices for property/casualty insurance. Section 3 discusses the challenges that these current practices face in our current environment and describes the corporate model approach to deal with these challenges. Finally, Section 4 contains the conclusions.

1 Risk Management Practice for Life Companies

There is no one standard approach to risk management for life companies in practice. Different insurers have their own methodologies and procedures in managing risks. On the one hand, there is regulation in place to ensure that insurers comply with the adequacy of their assets in supporting their liabilities. This regulation is called cash flow testing. On the other hand, some insurers have a risk management practice that deals with their positions in fair value basis. This practice is called the total return approach. We will describe these two approaches as examples to many risk management methods that are actually used and are often comprised of aspects of these two approaches.

1.1 Cash Flow Testing

To ensure the soundness of the life insurance industry in covering the potential losses of the insurance products, insurers are required to provide evidence of their financial ability to cover the liabilities. They must fulfill requirements of the solvency test annually. This test is mandated by Regulation 126 and is called cash flow testing. The rules can be summarized briefly as follows.

In the cash flow testing method, liabilities are grouped into segments by the product types that have similar characteristics. Then, some of the assets of the investment portfolio are assigned to each segment. These assets have to be qualified to support the liabilities. The value of the assets should not be less than the liability value, as measured by the reserve number, calculated by actuarial methods.

The cash flow testing method assumes that there are no new sales of the liability. The test requires the insurer to demonstrate that the assets are sufficient to cover the expected payouts. The insurer has to first determine the cash flows of both the assets and liabilities as a run-off business. And cash inflows or outflows are then re-invested or borrowed based on the assumptions made by the insurance companies. At the end of the horizon, say 30 years, the remaining asset value, after paying out all the liability cash flows, is determined. This is repeated under different market scenarios, where interest rates are assume to rise, fall, or rise and fall.

The insurer seeks to have net positive assets at the end of the time horizon under all the stochastic scenarios. In general, many insurers cannot achieve positive values in all the scenarios and regulators have to evaluate the solvency of the insurers based on the cash flow testing results.

This approach is reasonable for insurance companies because the method does not assume the insurance companies selling any assets to meet meeting the liability needs. And, therefore, it does not require any market valuation of the liabilities.

However, the cash flow testing methods require many assumptions on the asset returns. For example, the losses due to asset default have to be assumed. They also allow for a wide range of re-investment strategies. Often, these re-investment strategies are hypothetical, not implemented in practice. As a result, the method is a good measure of showing whether the assets are sufficient to support the liabilities under a set of theoretical scenarios, but not a tool for managing risks in a more active basis.

1.2 Total Return Approach

The total return approach has been described elsewhere (see Ho *et al.*, 1995). For the completeness of discussion, we will describe it briefly here. The total return approach can be used as an extension of the cash flow testing methods. The approach also uses the liability models to determine the cash flow of each product under different scenarios. The main difference between the two analyses is the use of present value measure in the total return approach versus the use of future value in the cash flow testing. By using the present value concept, the analytical results do not depend on the future re-investment strategies. This is because when assets are fairly priced, future investment strategies (buying or selling of the assets) would not affect the portfolio value today. And the present value measure for the liabilities is consistent with the market valuation of assets. Therefore, the total return approach can analyze assets and liabilities in one consistent framework. These two properties are useful to asset and liability management. The total return approach has four steps: (a) fair valuation of liabilities; (b) determination of the liability benchmark; (c) determination of the asset benchmarks; (d) establishing the return attribution process. We now describe them in turn.

1.2.1 Fair valuation of liabilities

Fair valuation of liabilities begins with the determination of a pricing curve. The pricing curve is the time value of money curve that is used to discount the liability cash flows.

The curve can be the Treasury curve or the swap curve. The cash flows of the liabilities are discounted by this curve to determine the present value of the cash flows. In the cases where the liabilities have embedded options, we use an arbitrage-free interest rate model to determine the interest rate scenarios and we determine the present value of the cash flows. In essence, the method uses the arbitrage-free valuation approach to determine the fair value of the liabilities. As a result, the liability cash flows are valued relative to those of the capital markets. Assets and liabilities are evaluated in one consistent framework. This method has been discussed extensively in other papers (Ho *et al.*, 1995; Ho, 2000; Ho and Lee, 2004).

As mentioned in the previous section, the liabilities have characteristics that are difficult to be treated like capital market assets. For example, some liabilities have a time to termination of over 30 years, beyond most of the capital market bonds. In these cases, one approach may be to assume that the yield curve is flat beyond a certain maturity to determine the fair value of these liabilities. Therefore, the assumptions of the modeling of liability have to be specified, in general.

1.2.2 Liability benchmark

When the liability is first sold to the policyholder, a constant spread is added to the pricing curve such that the present value of the liability is assured to equal the price of the liability sold. This spread is the option adjusted spread of the liability and is called the required option adjust spread (see Ho *et al.*, 1995).

The financial model of the liability becomes a representation of the actual liability. In particular, the liability model captures the simulated projected cash flow of the liability under different market scenarios. And the market scenarios are consistent with the observed interest rate levels, the interest rate volatilities, and other market parameters.

Using the liability model, we then decompose the liability to basic building blocks. For example, we can represent the liability as a portfolio of cash flows with options. These options can be caps and floors. Or they can be swaptions. Such a decomposition may allow management to manage the derivatives separately from the cash flows. This decomposition has been explained in Ho and Chen (1996). For example, Wallace (2000) describes the construction of the liability benchmark in the management of a block of business, which can be decomposed into a portfolio of cash flows and a portfolio of interest rate derivatives.

The liability benchmark captures the salient features of the liabilities in terms of their capital market risks. As a result, the method provides a systematic way to separate the market risks and the product risks, like mortality risk. The separation of these two types of risks enable us to use the capital market instruments to manage the capital market risks embedded in the liabilities and to use actuarial methods to manage the product risks. In sum, the liability benchmark may be a liability financial model or a set of financial models represented by specific cash flows and market derivatives like caps and floors. This liability benchmark replicates the liability in their projected cash flows under a broad range of scenarios. The effectiveness of the liability benchmark depends on its ability in capturing the liability cash flows under stochastic scenarios.

An insurance company may have a multiple of products and product segments. Therefore, the insurers may correspondingly have multiple liability benchmarks. These benchmarks have to be revised periodically since the actual liabilities' characteristics may change over time and the benchmarks may become less accurate in replicating the behavior of the liabilities. This revision should be conducted when the liabilities undergo significant changes.

1.2.3 Asset benchmarks

The asset benchmarks are derived from the liability benchmark. There are two types of asset benchmarks: an asset portfolio benchmark and a sector benchmark. The procedure to determine the asset benchmarks for a particular liability benchmark may follow three steps: (1) specify the investment guidelines; (2) construct the asset benchmark; (3) construct the sector benchmarks.

1.2.3.1 Investment guidelines

The procedure begins with the senior management laying out some specific guidelines about the appropriate risk that the company is willing to take. These guidelines may reflect the preferences the management and the constraints imposed on the company from outside constituents. A typical guideline may address four characteristics of an asset portfolio.

Interest rate risk exposure limit can be set by stating the maximum allowable duration mismatch, or key rate duration mismatch, between the liability benchmark and the portfolio benchmark. Further, there may be a maximum exposure of negatively convex assets that may be allowed in the benchmark.

Credit risk exposure limit may be set by the maximum allowable percentage of assets that are categorized as high yield assets. There can also be a minimum percentage of assets that are rated as "A" and above.

Liquidity in the asset portfolio is assured by the maximum allowable percentage of assets that are considered less liquid (or one could state them as illiquid assets). Assets that fall in this category, for example, are private placement bonds and commercial mortgages.

The senior management of some companies may also place overall broad guidelines on asset allocation—in the form of maximum or minimum allocation to certain specified classes of asset sectors.

Several other factors also affect the overall guidelines. For example, the insurance companies may incorporate the rating agencies' measures of risk, mimic the asset allocation of peer group companies, and taking the desired level of capital of the company into account.

1.2.3.2 Constructing the asset benchmark

The asset benchmark comprises several sector benchmarks (which are described below) with appropriate weights to each asset class (which is often referred to as the asset allocation). It represents the mix of asset classes and their weights that will meet the desired needs of the liabilities while catering to the restrictions imposed by the investment guidelines.

The design takes into account the liquidity needs, the duration (or key rate durations) and convexity profile, the interest crediting strategy, minimum guarantees, required spread over the crediting rates, and other product features. All of these attributes are not always identifiable through the liability benchmarks. And, therefore, it is important that the design incorporates the senior management's perspective on the allowable risk that the company is willing to take. The risk is defined to include the model risks as well as the market, credit, and product risks.

The portfolio managers then add specificity to the benchmark by reviewing the requirement/behavior of the liabilities, the desired minimum spread, and the guidelines specified by the senior management.

The process of refining the benchmark balances the asset allocation and the duration distribution of the assets within each asset class. The latter defines the duration of the benchmark and consequentially the targeted duration mismatch between the assets and the liabilities.

Therefore, the asset benchmark is an asset portfolio that satisfies all the constraints determined from the analysis of the liability benchmark, the investment guideline, and the asset portfolio management preferences.

1.2.3.3 The sector benchmark

The sector benchmark is specific to an asset sector or class of an asset (like investment grade domestic corporate bonds, collateralized mortgage backed securities, high yield securities, asset backed securities). The portfolio manager of each market sector manages the portfolio using the sector benchmark to measure the relative risks and returns of the portfolio. The manager's performances are then analyzed based on the sector benchmarks.

Thus far, we have described an asset benchmark that replicates the characteristics of the liability benchmark. However, if the asset and liability management process does not require immunizing the market risks, then the asset benchmark can be constructed with mismatching the asset and liability market risks. For example, some life insurers use a mean variance framework to determine their strategic asset portfolio positions. Other insurers use the distribution of the present value of the cash flows of assets net of liabilities to determine their optimal assets portfolio.

1.2.4 Return attribution

Return attribution is concerned with calculating the total returns of the assets and the liabilities and determining the components of the returns. The purpose of breaking down the returns into its components is to detect the sources of the risks and attributing the returns to decisions made in the asset and liability management process. In identifying the impact of the decisions on the insurer's asset and liability combined total return, the procedure includes a feedback effect to the management process.

The return attributions can be calculated as follows. Over a certain time horizon, say 1 month, we can determine the portfolio total return and the liability total return. The total return of an asset follows the conventional definition, and that is the change in the unrealized profit and loss plus the cash flow (dividends, coupons, and actual gain/loss from the disposition of the assets) to the insurer's portfolio over that period. The liability total return is defined analogously. It is defined as the change in the fair value of the liability plus the cash outflows of the liability over the holding period.

Both the total returns of the assets or the liabilities can be decomposed into the basic components. These components are the risk-free returns, the option adjusted spreads, the key rate duration returns, transactions, and the cheap/rich changes. Specifically, the total return of the asset portfolio is given by

$$\Delta r_{\mathrm{A}} = (r + OAS)\Delta t - \sum krd_{\mathrm{A}}(i)\Delta r(i) + e_{\mathrm{A}} \tag{1}$$

and the liability portfolio total return is given by

$$\Delta r_{\mathrm{L}} = (r + ROAS)\Delta t - \sum krd_{\mathrm{L}}(i)\Delta r(i) + e_{\mathrm{L}} \tag{2}$$

where r is the risk-free rate. OAS is the option adjusted spread of the asset portfolio. $ROAS$ is the required returns of the liability portfolio. $krd_{\mathrm{A}}(i)$ and $krd_{\mathrm{L}}(i)$ are the key rate durations of the assets and the liabilities, respectively. $\Delta r(i)$ is the shift of the ith key rate relative to the forward yield curve. Finally, e_{A} and e_{L} are the residuals of the asset total returns and the liability total returns equations, respectively. There may be other basic components depending on the asset and liability types. For clarity of exposition, I only describe some of the components here. Details are provides in Ho *et al.*, 1995.

Product risks are priced by the margins, which are the spreads incorporated in the required option adjusted spreads. And each of the product risk is measured from the historical experience. Therefore, while the asset benchmark has not incorporated the product risks explicitly, it has taken the margins for the product risks into account. The margins can then be compared with the experience of the product risks to determine the risk and return tradeoff in the pricing of the products.

Returns attribution process is becoming more important in asset management. The process relates separate departments requiring the departments to coordinate. Stabbert (1995) describes how such a coordination can be organized. Risk management considers the asset and liability management as a process in which we can measure the risks and the performance of each phase, and risk/return tradeoff analysis is conducted for each phase of the process. A more detail description of an investment cycle can be found in Ho (1995) where the management of the organization is discussed.

2 Risk Management Practice for General Insurance Companies: Dynamic Financial Analysis

General insurance is distinct from life insurance in a number of aspects. Therefore, in practice, it implements different asset liability management techniques. First, in life insurance, when the insurance is sold, the insurer knows precisely the coverage amount. When the insured dies, the death benefit is specified in the contract. It is not so with general insurance. Often, the coverage is determined after the incident has incurred. In many cases, the determination of the coverage can take many years, along with costly litigation. Therefore, the liability is often uncertain even after the incident has incurred. A related issue is the size of the payment, often called the severity risk, where it is possible that the payment can be very large. To cover these uncertainties, the assets have to be quite liquid to ensure that the insurer has the liquidity to cover the insurance losses.

Another aspect is the short-term aspect of the contract, even though the potential liability is long tail. The insurance contract is more like the 1-year term life insurance. The major part of risk in managing the liability is embedded in the persistency assumption. The end result is that the insurer tends to think in terms of all the future sales and the liabilities associated with the future insurance premiums, in their asset and liability management. In short, it is more like managing the firm's business than managing the assets and liabilities on the balance sheet, as in life insurance business. For this reason, the "asset–liability" management is more like "managing a firm as a going concern." By way of contrast, we have seen that that life insurance companies tend to view their assets and liabilities as a "run-off business," ignoring all future new sales.

One approach of managing the risk of a general insurance company is called dynamic financial analysis (DFA). DFA is a financial planning model that is designed to address a broad range of corporate issues. It is not only confined to managing the assets and liabilities on the balance sheet, but it can also incorporate future new sales, which may be the renewals resulting from persistency or sales to new customers. DFA may be used to estimate the profitability of the firm over a time horizon, to determine the likelihood of meeting the earnings target, or to manage the risk sources, which are often called the risk drivers to avoid missing the earnings target. As a result, the firm can determine its optimal actions to achieve its financial goals by means of DFA. These actions can be the change of asset allocation in its investment portfolio, the change of its sales distributions, or the change of its product pricing strategies.

DFA may be used to analyze the liquidity adequacy of the firm. When the firm may need to provide significant cash outlays under certain scenarios, DFA may be used to evaluate the ability of the firm to raise the needed cash in those scenarios. In relation to liquidity issues, DFA may be used to study the impact of adverse scenarios on the firm's credit worthiness and its debt rating. Using DFA, the firm may then simulate the business or market risks to determine a corporate financial strategy to deal with these problems.

DFA uses financial projection models to assist in the firm's financial planning. These models begin with the ability to simulate future financial statements. These proforma financial statements are based on the assumptions on the firm's future businesses and business decisions. These assumptions are provided by the users of the models. Using these assumptions, DFA entails simulating the business scenarios on the sales, expenses, business growth, and financial performance measures. At the same time, the analysis also includes simulating the interest rate, equity, and other market risks that may affect the business.

Beyond the simulations, DFA must have a tax model. While the tax codes tend to be complex with many details, a DFA approach captures the essence of these rules with a tax model to simulate the tax liabilities. Finally, DFA seeks to determine the optimal business decisions such that the firm's objective is maximized. The objective and the constraints on the decisions may depend on the simulated financial statements and the desired performance.

The inputs to the dynamic financial analysis are the initial financial statements of the firm and the business strategies that the firm contemplates in the coming years. Given this information, DFA outputs the projected financial statements at the horizon period, which may be the next quarter or several quarters hence, under multiple scenarios that reflect the market risks and the business risks. The outputs are the distributions of the performance measures of the firm.

For example, via the distributions of the earnings over a year, the system can identify the likelihood of missing the earnings forecast over a time horizon, given the market risks and business risks. Further, alternative corporate strategies can be used to see if other corporate decisions can provide a better solution.

To determine optimal decisions, objective functions have to be specified. There are alternative objective functions to meet earnings forecasts. Listed below are some examples of what firms may do:

1. *Benchmarking to the industry leader*
   One approach is to use an industry leader in the same market segment of the firm as a benchmark. The corporate management strategies are adjusted to attain the performance measures of the leading firm in the market segment. This approach may not lead to optimal corporate management strategies but it is one way for the investment community to compare the firms and determine the valuation. For example, the industry leader may have no debt, and using a zero debt ratio as a benchmark may lead its competitors to use less debt in financing their project.
2. *Average financial ratios and performance measures as the base line for comparison*
   The firm may use the industry average of financial ratios and performance measures as the base line. Then, the firm would use financial planning to ensure that the firm can outperform the industry average.
3. *Balancing the importance of the performance measures*
   Since the firm's financial performance cannot be measured by only one number, for example, the earnings number, the firm can select a number of performance measures and seek to maximize weighted performance measures with different weights.

The approach is an effective decision support tool, as it provides intuitive understanding of complex problems. The senior management can use the DFA approach to forecast the possible outcomes and suggest solutions, using their own assumptions on the business risks and market risk. However, DFA is a tool, a way to link the senior management assumptions to the outcomes, where the links are defined by accounting and tax rules, but often, not by financial theories, such as those, like the arbitrage-free pricing models, that are developed in financial research. Their objective functions in the optimization, as described above, may not be consistent with enhancing the shareholders' wealth. To the extent that some DFAs do not incorporate financial models, they have a number of limitations. More specifically, I provide three limitations below.

1. *Defining the corporate objective*
   If we take "maximizing shareholders' value" as the corporate objective, then the corporate strategies in managing earnings may not be consistent with this fundamental goal. DFA can suggest how new strategies may affect the future earnings, or benchmark the industry leaders, but also how should the senior management seek shareholders' value maximizing strategies?
   Maximizing the earnings for 1 year or over 2 years is not the same as maximizing the shareholders' value, because the shareholders' value depends on all the future corporate actions in different states of the world. The shareholders' value is a present value concept. The simulations of future outcomes do not relate to the present shareholders' value unless we know how the market discounts the future values. The determination of the appropriate market discount rate requires the understanding of the market pricing of risks and how payments are made for different outcomes. Only financial theories regarding capital markets can be used to deal with this issue.
2. *Defining optimal strategies*
   DFA can provide insights into the formulation of optimal strategies because it shows how each of the assumptions of the senior management affects the performance measure. However, the approach cannot determine the optimal strategy. All decisions are related and the optimal strategies include all future and present actions. Generally, simulating forward using some rule-based strategies are not optimal strategies that often depend on the state of the world and time in relation to the planning horizon.
   Users of DFA tend to choose the "best solution" out of a specified set of simulations. The solution does not show how the optimal strategy should be revised as the state has changed or how to discount the payoffs. As a result, DFA often fails to quantify the present value of the real option appropriately by not incorporating financial modeling.
3. *Linkages of corporate finance and capital markets*
   Corporate finance does not operate in isolation from capital markets. Corporations seek funding from capital markets, and the financing may be in the form of derivatives and other option embedded bonds. Corporations also invest in instruments that are market contingent claims. The values of these assets and liabilities must be determined by the principles of market valuation and not by the senior management's subjective view of how the securities would be priced, to maintain a coherent and objective analysis.

Financial models that have been described in the fair valuation section on the total return approach can provide these linkages. For example, we can determine the cost of borrowing by the corporate bond valuation model taking the credit risk of the firm into account. Therefore, we can appropriately incorporate the change in the firm risk to calculate the cost of borrowing.

3 The Corporate Model

Thus far, we have discussed the current practices and their natural extensions in managing the life and general insurance businesses. However, these approaches are now being challenged to be more effective and relevant to the changing market environment. The challenges arise from the changing market environment, regulatory pressure, and the competitive nature of the business.

As insurers seek to gain the economy of scale, they become holding companies of both life and general insurance companies, and they sell a broad spectrum of products. In practice, no longer can we dichotomize the world into life insurance and general insurance. Insurers can have both life and general businesses.

Further, new products are introduced that do not fall into the usual genre of a spread product, where the product risk is less significant or can be managed by controlling the market risk, or a going concern business, where the product risks are significant. For example, the long-term heath care insurance in life insurance is more like the general insurance where the potential product liability is significant and difficult to estimate.

Another challenge is to relate the risk management to the shareholders' value. For the shareholders' value, lowering the risks of the asset and liability return may not be desirable. There is no direct relationship between managing the total returns of the assets and liabilities to the shareholders' value, the capitalization of the firm. Therefore, in both the total return approach and the DFA approach, we do not have a well-specified objective function in formulating the strategies to the shareholders' value. Certainly, there is no specific reason to justify the optimization.

All these questions suggest that we need to combine the total return approach and the DFA approach in one consistent framework. On the one hand, we need to extend the total return approach to incorporate the new sales and product pricing strategies. On the other hand, the DFA approach should incorporate the appropriate valuation models of the financial products to determine the fair market valuation of the assets and liabilities.

The model that brings the two approaches together in one consistent framework is called the corporate model. The corporate model is described in more detail in Ho and Lee (2004). In the corporate model approach, we determine all the assets and liabilities by arbitrage-free relative valuation models. We calibrate all the assets and liabilities to the observed securities prices. We then specify the model of the new sales. From these models, we can determine the free cash flow generated by the product sales and the asset and liability management. The present value of the free cash flow is then related to the market capitalization via relative valuation approaches. The optimal risk management is determined to maximize the market capitalization of the insurer subject to the market constraints, like the rating agencies' measure of credit risks, the stock analysts' demand on the performance metrics.

The extension of the approach based on incorporating the following features of modeling:

3.1 *The Sales Volume*

Similar to the DFA approach, we use the stochastic distributions of the sales volume as inputs to the model. Financial models of new sales are used to determine the projected free cash flows and the reported gross earnings. Specifically, the sales projections are estimated from the budgeting process and the uncertainties of the sales volume are determined using historical data. The sales model for the next quarter is given by

$$v_{n+1} = gv_n + v_n\sigma Z + \sigma_\mathrm{T} W \tag{3}$$

where v is the sales volume measured in \$ of the face value of the product and g is the growth rate of the product. The term $v_n\sigma Z$ represents the multiplicative random walk process and Z is the unit normal distribution. The term $\sigma_\mathrm{T} W$ represents the transient uncertainty of the sales. For example, in auto insurance, g may be tied to the growth of the population of drivers and the inflation rate. For term insurance, the growth rate may be the change in demographics and the inflation. σ is the standard deviation of a unit of sales. This model suggests that the sales follow a particular trend in growth, but the sales are uncertain. The uncertainties are modeled by the random walk process and the transient uncertain movements from one period to another.

Sales projections are important to risk management in a number of ways. First, the risk of future sales and the risk of the inforce business are often highly related. For example, when a product experience shows that the product has been significantly adversely mispriced, the industry tends to improve the profit margin of the product in future sales. Therefore, the losses on the balance sheet tend to be mitigated by the increased profits of the future sales. The converse is also true. When insurers' products are shown to be profitable, then the competitive pressure would decrease the profit margin. Via market competitive forces, there is a natural time diversification of the risks of sales and the risk of the inforce business.

Notice also that the stochastic process of the sales is different to that of the stock. Sales tend to fluctuate around a fundamental market trend, while equity takes on a random walk. In GAAP accounting, profits are released over time, using reserve accounting. This approach in essence allows for time diversification of the sales risks. Therefore, while there is significant sales uncertainty from one quarter to another, the risk is often diversified over the life of the product, leading to a more stable income.

The corporate model should capture these effects, not only for the general insurance products but also for the life insurance products. While the life insurance products may have significant embedded options with market risks, such distinctive features should not affect the concept of incorporating a model of new sales and the modeling of the reserves of these products.

3.2 Asset Economic Value and the GAAP Balance Sheet Statements

Insurance products by and large are reported in book value in the GAAP financial statements. The values are reported as a form of amortization of the historical cost, not affected by the changes in the market realities, like the changes in the interest rate levels. However, for the insurance assets, most insurers choose to categorize their assets as "ready for sales." Therefore, the assets are marked to market, and the unrealized gains and losses are reported. The fair valuation of the asset portfolio should therefore be consistent with the book value accounting for the most part, other than those assets classified under "hold till maturity" where the fair values are not reported.

Given the relationship between the fair value accounting and the book value accounting of the assets, we can now determine the reconciliation of the total returns of the assets and the net investment income of the assets in the income statements. Specifically, based on the asset portfolio, we can determine the interest and dividend incomes. Further, we can develop a model of the realized gain, and therefore we can determine the reported net investment income. The residuals between the total returns of the assets and the net investment income can be reconciled with the items in the comprehensive income of the income statement.

Specifically, let A_n and F_n be the asset fair value and the face value, respectively, at time n reported in the financial statements. For simplicity assume that there is no change in the face value from period n to $n + 1$. Then according to GAAP accounting,

$$\Delta r_A A_n = \Delta G_n + R_n + I_n \tag{4}$$

where ΔG_n is the change of the unrealized gain/loss and from period n to $n + 1$. R_n X_n, and I_n are the realized gain/loss and the net cash inflows and outflows to the asset portfolio, and the interests income respectively. $\Delta r_A A_n$ is the total return, according to Eq. (1).

Now allowing for inflow and outflows to the asset portfolio, we have

$$A_{n+1} - A_n = \Delta r_A A_n - X_n \tag{5}$$

Finally, by definition of the net investment income (NII) in the income statement, we have

$$NII_n = R_n + I_n \tag{6}$$

These equations relate the financial statement numbers to the fair valuation of the assets.

In this modeling, we can show the impact of the embedded options in the investment portfolio on the reported income of the firm. To the extent that the market risk may affect the insurance product sales, this model relates the futures sales to the fair value of the assets and the reported investment income. For example, variable annuities sales are found to be significantly related to the equity market performance, and the fixed annuities sales are related to both the equity market performance and the interest rate level. Since the fair values of the assets are also related to these market risks, this model enables us to extend our asset and liability management decisions to incorporate the sales volume.

We have discussed extensively above in using the fair value of liabilities to manage the asset and liabilities in the total return approach. The corporate model can then extend this asset and liability concept to that for an ongoing concern.

3.3 *Modeling the Discount Rate of the Businesses*

We have discussed the use of the arbitrage-free model and the required option adjusted spread to determine the fair value of the liabilities. In maximizing the shareholders' value, we cannot just focus on the value of the inforce business but must also take the future sales and the franchise value of the going concern of a block of business into account. Therefore, we need to evaluate the value of a block of business as a contingent claim on the sales opportunities of the business. Ho and Lee (2004) have shown that the block of business can be modeled as a real option on the business risk. This real option can incorporate the growth options of the business and can also determine the appropriate discount rate of the free cash flows, where the discount rate can be inferred from the businesses of the other firms.

Our corporate model approach differs from the traditional discounting free cashflow in the following ways: (1) We separate the risks of the inforce business from the business risks of the future sales and operations. The present value of the cash flows from the inforce business are captured by the fair value models. Our model recognizes that the risks of the future sales and other operational risks require a discount rate appropriately determined, not derived from the cost of capital of the firm nor from that used for the inforce business. (2) The value of a block of business can be valued as an option modeling the uncertainties of the future opportunities, enabling us to incorporate the franchise value in our risk management process.

Valuation of a block of business begins with the valuation of the liability for \$1 face value, assuming the required option adjusted spread (ROAS) to be zero as described in Section 2.1. Now we can define the gain-on-sale (p) to be the premium or present value of all future premiums net of the present value of the liability based on zero ROAS. p is, therefore, the present value of the profits. Instead of releasing the profit over time, we capture the profit at the time of sale. This number varies from one product to another. It follows that the total dollar profit is vp. Given the volume stochastic process of Eq. (7), we now have a stochastic process of the future gain-on-sale.

Ho and Lee (2004) then show that the present value of the gain-on-sale can be modeled as an "underlying security" where we can model the growth option in acquiring more inforce business. The same framework can also model the fixed costs and expenses incurred in managing the business. Using this option pricing framework, we can then determine the value of the block of business. We now have a model of the value of the business:

$$V = V(pv, \text{growth options, expenses}) \qquad (7)$$

3.4 *The Objective of Risk Management*

The corporate model provides us the quantification of the goal of risk management. Risk management is not simply minimizing risks nor does risk management focuses only on measuring and monitoring risks. Risk management is a quality control process, ensuring that functioning of the businesses is consistent with the design of the business model. Indeed, enterprise risk management has the responsibility to assure that the business processes are functioning as expected and can detect any flaws in the design of the business model. In so doing, the action of the enterprise risk management always enhances the shareholders' value.

We have shown how we determine the economic or fair value of the assets and liabilities. Further, corporate model relates the fair value measures to the financial statements. Finally, the corporate model assigns the values to the block of businesses taking the franchise value into consideration.

In sum, we need to determine the maximal value by changing the investment strategies, product sales strategies, and other corporate choice variables:

$$\text{Max } V(vp, \text{growth options, expenses}) \tag{8}$$

subject to constraints that may be related to the target net income and the risk of net income in a multiperiod context. The projected net income can be modeled using the sales stochastic process, Eq. (3), and net investment income of Eq. (6), and the financial statement identities.

Enterprise risk management can monitor the inputs to the corporate model which are the observed changes in the market parameters, the sales volume, the expenses, and the reported insurance losses. We can also observe the output of the corporate model, which are the financial statements and the economic values of the assets and liabilities. Therefore, the corporate model can be tested for its validity over time. Further, the model can detect any changes in the input data and the output data that are not consistent with the model. These deviations can then alert the management of the enterprise risk management process. The end result is that the enterprise risk management can detect defects in the business model when the defects are small and we can remedy the problems ahead of time.

This approach has many applications. Perhaps, the most relevant application for the senior management is the specification of the quality of the reported net income number. The model shows precisely how the business risks are transformed to the risk of the net income. The sales risks are transformed by diversification across businesses and by the inforce businesses. Also, the reported sales risks are diversified over time. The risk of the total returns of the asset and liability portfolio is diversified by the sales of different products. But some fair value risks may not be properly accounted for by GAAP accounting. For example, the embedded options in assets and liabilities, and some equity risks in structured investments are often reported not in a way consistent with the fair valuation approach. But by specifying the quality of the net income numbers and depicting the business processes responsible for the risk transform, we can identify the strategies in managing the enterprise risks.

These strategies enable insurers to offer more transparency of the business model to investors, regulators, and rating agencies alike. As a result, enterprise risk management enables the firm to maximize the market capitalization of the insurer subject to the market constraints, like the rating agencies' measure of credit risks, the stock analysts' demand on the performance metrics.

4 Conclusions

While all insurance companies are engaged in selling insurance products, they differ significantly in their approaches in managing their assets and liabilities and in managing their risks. Indeed, asset liability management and risk management in practice is in fact quite fragmented within the industry. The methods used depend on the product within the company or depend on the business units. The approach is clearly different between the life companies and the general insurance companies and from one company to another within the same sector.

We have shown that the life insurance companies' risk management practice focuses on the inforce business. They seek to manage the assets and the liabilities on their balance sheets. By way of contrast the general insurance companies tend to manage the assets and liabilities as a going concern, taking future sales and pricing strategies into account.

The fragmentation limits the usefulness of the asset/liability and the risk management processes. As a result, insurer's risk management practice may be limited to determine whether a product's risk can be appropriately managed or a business unit satisfies a solvency test. But we cannot determine how each business unit should be optimally managed. Methodologies have been proposed to answer these questions.

We describe the corporate model as one solution to the problem. In essence, the corporate model combines the DFA model and the total return approach. Further, we develop a valuation model of a block of business. Using a consistent framework tying the financial statements and the fair value accounting, we can develop an enterprise risk management process that can analyze the risk prospectively and retrospectively. The proposed method therefore enables us to monitor and manage enterprise risks.

Acknowledgments

The author would like to thank Mark Abbott, Marlys Appleton, Edwin Betz, Ashok Chawla, Robert Lally, Alex Scheitlin, Gerd Stabbert, Kin Tam, and Marsha Wallace for their helpful comments and suggestions. Any errors are the responsibilities of the author.

References

Ho, T. (1992). "Key Rate Durations: Measure of Interest Rate Risk." *Journal of Fixed Income* 2(2).

Ho, T. (1995). "Quality-Based Investment Cycle." *Journal of Portfolio Management* 22(1).

Ho, T. (2000). "Market Valuation of Liabilities: Transfer Pricing, Profit Release, and Credit Spread." In: Vanderhoof, I. and Altman, E. (eds.), *The Fair Value of Insurance Business*. Dordrecht: Kluwer Academic Publisher.

Ho, T. and Chen, M. (1996). "Arbitrage-Free Bond Canonical Decomposition." In: Ho, T. (ed.), *Fixed Income Solutions*. Irwin Professional Publishing, pp. 283–298.

Ho, T. and Lee, S.B. (2004). *The Oxford Guide to Financial Modeling*. Oxford: Oxford University Press.

Ho, T., Scheitlin, A. and Tam, K. (1995). "Total Return Approach to Performance Measurements." In: Altman, E. and Vanderhoof, I. (eds.), *The Financial Dynamics of the Insurance Industry.* Irwin Professional Publishing, pp. 341–377.

Lally, R. (1993). "Managing Fixed-Income Assets Within a Multi-Asset Class Insurance Portfolio." In: Ho, T. (ed.), *Fixed-Income Portfolio Management.* Business One Irwin, pp. 87–100.

Stabbert, G. (1995). "An Analytical Approach to Asset/Liability Performance Measurement." In: Ho, T. (ed.), *Fixed Income Investment.* Irwin Professional Publishing, pp. 205–229.

Wallace, M. (2000). "Fair-Value Accounting for Financial Liabilities." In: Vanderhoof, I. and Altman, E. (eds.), *The Fair Value of Insurance Business.* Dordrecht: Kluwer Academic Publisher.

Keyword: Risk management

Journal Of Investment Management
Vol. 1, No. 1 (2003), pp. 55–93

IT'S 11 PM—DO YOU KNOW WHERE YOUR LIQUIDITY IS? THE MEAN–VARIANCE–LIQUIDITY FRONTIER

Andrew W. Lo[a], *Constantin Petrov*[b], *and Martin Wierzbicki*[c]

We introduce liquidity into the standard mean–variance portfolio optimization framework by defining several measures of liquidity and then constructing three-dimensional mean–variance–liquidity frontiers in three ways: liquidity filtering, liquidity constraints, and a mean–variance–liquidity objective function. We show that portfolios close to each other on the traditional mean–variance efficient frontier can differ substantially in their liquidity characteristics. In a simple empirical example, the liquidity exposure of mean–variance efficient portfolios changes dramatically from month to month, and even simple forms of liquidity optimization can yield significant benefits in reducing a portfolio's liquidity-risk exposure without sacrificing a great deal of expected return per unit risk.

1 Introduction

Liquidity has long been recognized as one of the most significant drivers of financial innovation, and the collapse of several high-profile hedge funds such as Askin Capital Management in 1994 and Long Term Capital Management in 1998 has only intensified the financial industry's focus on the role of liquidity in the investment management process. Many studies—in both academic journals and more applied forums—have made considerable progress in defining liquidity, measuring the cost of immediacy and price impact, deriving optimal portfolio rules in the presence of transactions costs, investigating the relationship between liquidity and arbitrage, and estimating liquidity risk premia in the context of various partial and general equilibrium asset-pricing models.[1] However, relatively little attention has been paid to the more practical problem of integrating liquidity directly into the portfolio construction process.[2]

In this paper, we attempt to remedy this state of affairs by modeling liquidity using simple measures such as trading volume and percentage bid/offer spreads, and then introducing these measures into the standard mean–variance portfolio optimization process to yield optimal mean–variance–liquidity portfolios. We begin by proposing several measures of the liquidity ℓ_i of an individual security, from which we define the liquidity ℓ_p of a portfolio $\omega_p \equiv [\omega_{p1}\omega_{p2}\cdots\omega_{pn}]'$ as the weighted average $\sum_i \ell_i\omega_{pi}$ of the individual securities' liquidities. Using these liquidity measures, we can construct

[a]Harris & Harris Group Professor, MIT Sloan School of Management, and Chief Scientific Officer, AlphaSimplex Group, LLC, 50 Memorial Drive, Cambridge, MA 02142-1347, USA (corresponding author).

[b]Research Analyst, Fidelity Management and Research Co., 82 Devonshire Street, Boston, MA 02109, USA.

[c]838 Green Street, San Francisco, CA 94133, USA.

three types of "liquidity-optimized" portfolios: (a) a mean–variance-efficient portfolio subject to a liquidity filter that each security in the portfolio have a minimum level of liquidity ℓ_0; (b) a mean–variance-efficient portfolio subject to a constraint that the portfolio have a minimum level of liquidity ℓ_0; and (c) a mean–variance–liquidity-efficient portfolio, where the optimization problem has three terms in its objective function: mean, variance, and liquidity. Using three different definitions of liquidity—turnover, percentage bid/offer spread, and a nonlinear function of market capitalization and trade size—we show empirically that liquidity-optimized portfolios have some very attractive properties, and that even simple forms of liquidity optimization can yield significant benefits in terms of reducing a portfolio's liquidity-risk exposure without sacrificing a great deal of expected return per unit risk.

In Section 2, we describe our simple measures of liquidity, and we define our three liquidity-optimized portfolios in Section 3. We provide an empirical example of liquidity-optimized portfolios in Section 4 for a sample of 50 US stocks using monthly, daily, and transactions data from January 2, 1997 to December 31, 2001, and we conclude in Section 5.

2 Liquidity Metrics

The natural starting point of any attempt to integrate liquidity into the portfolio optimization process is to develop a quantitative measure of liquidity, i.e., a liquidity metric. Liquidity is a multi-faceted concept, involving at least three distinct attributes of the trading process—price, time, and size—hence a liquid security is one that can be traded quickly, with little price impact, and in large quantities. Therefore, we are unlikely to find a single statistic that summarizes all of these attributes. To represent these distinct features, we start with the following five quantities on which our final liquidity metrics will be based:

$$\text{Trading volume} \equiv \text{Total number of shares traded at time } t \tag{1}$$

$$\text{Logarithm of trading volume} \equiv \log\,(\text{Trading volume}) \tag{2}$$

$$\text{Turnover} \equiv \frac{\text{Trading volume}}{\text{Shares outstanding}} \tag{3}$$

$$\text{Percentage bid/ask spread} \equiv \frac{\text{Ask} - \text{Bid}}{(\text{Ask} + \text{Bid})/2} \tag{4}$$

$$\text{Loeb price impact function} \equiv f\,(\text{Trade size, Market cap}) \tag{5}$$

where the first three variables measure the amount of trading and the last two measure the cost.[3]

Perhaps the most common measure of the liquidity of a security is its trading volume. It is almost tautological to say that a security is more liquid if it is traded more frequently and in greater quantities. Both trading volume and turnover capture this aspect of liquidity, and because these two variables are so highly correlated (see Tables 3 and 4), we will use only one of the three measures of trading activity (1)–(3) in our empirical analysis. Given Lo and Wang's (2000) motivation for turnover in the context of modern asset-pricing models such as the Capital Asset Pricing Model and the Arbitrage Pricing Theory, we shall adopt turnover (3) as our measure of trading activity.

Another popular measure of the liquidity of a security is the cost of transacting in it, either as buyer or seller, hence the bid/ask spread is a natural candidate. Smaller bid/ask spreads imply lower costs of trading, whereas larger bid/ask spreads are partly attributable to a liquidity premium demanded by market-makers for making markets in illiquid securities.[4]

Finally, market capitalization—the market value of total outstanding equity—has also been proposed as an important proxy for liquidity. Larger amounts of outstanding equity tend to be traded more frequently, and at a lower cost because there will be a larger market for the stock. Of course, even a large amount of outstanding equity can be distributed among a small number of major shareholders, yielding little liquidity for the stock, but this seems to be the exception rather than the rule. We adopt the specification proposed by Loeb (1983) in which he provides estimates of the percentage round-trip total trading cost including: (a) the market-maker's spread; (b) the price concession; and (c) the brokerage commission. The total trading cost is an array with nine capitalization categories and nine block sizes (see Table II in Loeb, 1983). This matrix provides a good approximation for liquidity, but to account for the continuous nature of market capitalization and block sizes beyond his original specification, we interpolate and extrapolate Loeb's table using a two-dimensional spline.[5] Figure 1 contains a graphical representation of our parametrization of Loeb's specification, and

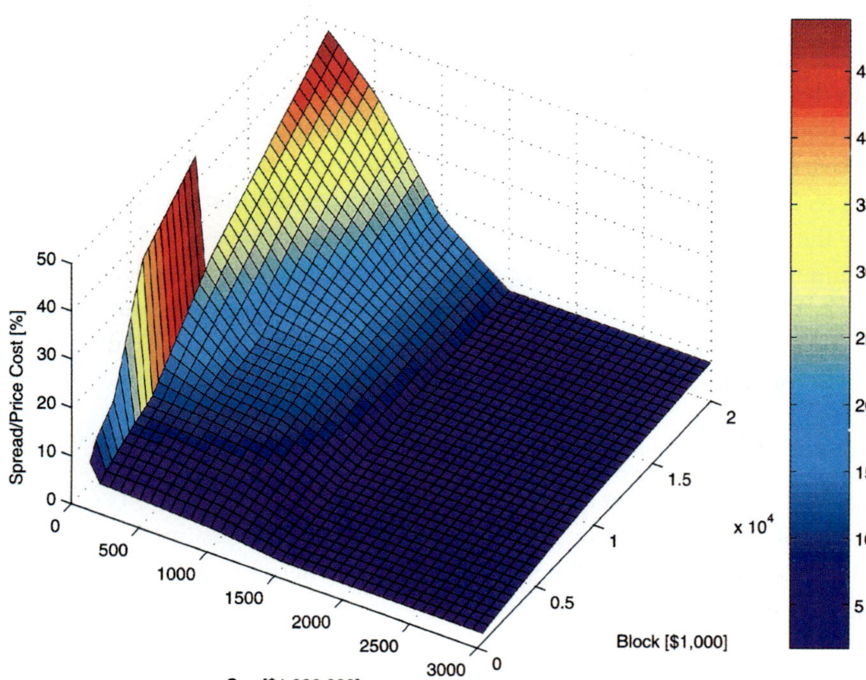

Figure 1 Loeb's (1983) price impact function which gives the percentage total cost as a function of block size and market capitalization, with spline interpolation and linear extrapolation.

our Matlab sourcecode is provided in Appendix A.I. To minimize the impact of *ad hoc* extrapolation procedures such as the one we use to extend Loeb (1983) (see footnote 5), we assumed a fixed block size of \$250,000 in all our calculations involving Loeb's liquidity metric, and for this size, the extrapolation/capping of the trading cost is used rather infrequently.

2.1 *Liquidity Metrics for Individual Securities*

To construct liquidity metrics, we begin by computing (1)–(5) with daily data and then aggregating the daily measures to yield monthly quantities. Monthly trading volume is defined as the sum of the daily trading volume for all the days within the month, and monthly log-volume is simply the natural logarithm of monthly trading volume. Monthly turnover is defined as the sum of daily turnover for all the days within the month (see Lo and Wang, 2000 for further discussion). The monthly bid/ask spread measure is defined as a mean of the daily bid/ask spreads for all the days within the month. And finally, the average monthly Loeb price impact measure is defined as a mean of the corresponding daily measures for all days within the month.

Having defined monthly counterparts to the daily variables (l)–(5), we renormalize the five monthly measures to yield quantities that are of comparable scale. Let $\tilde{\ell}_{it}$ represent one of our five liquidity variables for security i in month t. Then the corresponding *liquidity metric* ℓ_{it} is defined as:

$$\ell_{it} \equiv \frac{\tilde{\ell}_{it} - \min_{k,\tau} \tilde{\ell}_{k\tau}}{\max_{k,\tau} \tilde{\ell}_{k\tau} - \min_{k,\tau} \tilde{\ell}_{k\tau}} \tag{6}$$

where the maximum and minimum in (6) are computed over all stocks k and all dates in the sample so that each of the five normalized measures—which we now refer to as a liquidity metric to distinguish it from the unnormalized variable—takes on values strictly between 0 and 1. Therefore, if the turnover-based liquidity metric for a given security is 0.50 in a particular month, this implies that the level of turnover exceeds the minimum turnover by 50% of the difference between the maximum and minimum turnover for all securities and across all months in our sample. Note that for consistency, we use the *reciprocal* of the monthly bid/ask spread measure in defining ℓ_{it} for bid/ask spreads so that larger numerical values imply more liquidity, as do the other four measures.

2.2 *Liquidity Metrics for Portfolios*

Now consider a portfolio p of securities defined by the vector of portfolio weights $\omega_p \equiv [\omega_{p1}\omega_{p2}\cdots\omega_{pn}]'$ where $\omega_p'\iota = 1$ and $\iota \equiv [1\cdots 1]'$. Assume for the moment that this is a long-only portfolio so that $\omega_p \geq 0$. Then a natural definition of the liquidity ℓ_{pt} of this portfolio is simply:

$$\ell_{pt} \equiv \sum_{i=1}^{n} \omega_{pi}\ell_{it} \tag{7}$$

which is a weighted average of the liquidities of the securities in the portfolio.

For portfolios that allow short positions, (7) is not appropriate because short positions in illiquid securities may cancel out long positions in equally illiquid securities, yielding a very misleading picture of the overall liquidity of the portfolio. To address this concern, we propose the following definition for the liquidity metric of a portfolio with short positions, along the lines of Lo and Wang's (2000) definition of portfolio turnover:

$$\ell_{pt} \equiv \sum_{i=1}^{n} \frac{|\omega_{pi}|}{\sum_{j=1}^{n} |\omega_{pj}|} \ell_{it} \tag{8}$$

In the absence of short positions, (8) reduces to (7), but when short positions are present, their liquidity metrics are given positive weight as with the long positions, and then all the weights are renormalized by the sum of the absolute values of the weights.

2.3 Qualifications

Although the liquidity metrics described in Sections 2.1 and 2.2 are convenient definitions for purposes of mean–variance portfolio optimization, they have a number of limitations that should be kept in mind. First, (7) implicitly assumes that there are no interactions or cross-effects in liquidity among securities, which need not be the case. For example, two securities in the same industry might have similar liquidity metrics individually, but may become somewhat more difficult to trade when combined in a portfolio because they are considered close substitutes by investors. This assumption can be relaxed by specifying a more complex "liquidity matrix" in which ℓ_{it} are the diagonal entries but where interaction terms ℓ_{ijt} are specified in the off-diagonal entries. In that case, the liquidity metric for the portfolio p is simply the quadratic form:

$$\ell_{pt} \equiv \sum_{i=1}^{n} \sum_{j=1}^{n} \omega_{pi}\omega_{pj}\ell_{ijt} \tag{9}$$

The off-diagonal liquidity metrics are likely to involve subtleties of the market microstructure of securities in the portfolio as well as more fundamental economic links among the securities, hence for our current purposes, we assume that they are zero.

Second, because (7) is a function only of the portfolio weights and not of the dollar value of the portfolio, ℓ_{pt} is scale independent. While this also holds true for mean–variance analysis as a whole, the very nature of liquidity is dependent on scale to some degree. Consider the case where IBM comprises 10% of two portfolios p and q. According to (7), the contribution of IBM to the liquidity of the overall portfolio would be the same in these two cases: 10% times the liquidity metric of IBM. However, suppose that the dollar value of portfolio p is $100,000 and the dollar value of portfolio q is $100 million—is a $10,000 position in IBM identical to a $10 million position in terms of liquidity?

At issue is the fact that, except for Loeb's measure of price impact, the liquidity metrics defined by the variables (1)–(4) are not functions of trade size, hence are scale-independent. Of course, this is easily remedied by reparametrizing the liquidity metric ℓ_{it} so that it varies with trade size, much like Loeb's price impact function, but this creates at least three additional challenges: (a) there is little empirical evidence to determine the appropriate functional specification[6]; (b) trade size may not be the only variable that affects liquidity; and (c) making ℓ_{it} a function of trade size complicates the portfolio optimization problem considerably, rendering virtually all of the standard mean–variance results scale-dependent. For these reasons, we shall continue to assume scale-independence for ℓ_{it} throughout this study (even for Loeb's price impact function, for which we fix the trade size at \$250,000), and leave the more challenging case for future research.

More generally, the liquidity variables (1)–(5) are rather simple proxies for liquidity, and do not represent liquidity premia derived from dynamic equilibrium models of trading behavior.[7] Therefore, these variables may not be stable through time and over very different market regimes. However, given their role in influencing the price, time, and size of transactions in equity markets, the five liquidity metrics defined by (1)–(5) are likely to be highly correlated with equilibrium liquidity premia under most circumstances and should serve as reasonable local approximations to the liquidity of a portfolio.

Finally, because our liquidity metrics are *ad hoc* and not the by-product of expected utility maximization, they have no objective interpretation and must be calibrated to suit each individual application. Of course, we might simply assert that liquidity is a sufficiently distinct characteristic of a financial security that investors will exhibit specific preferences along this dimension, much like for a security's mean and variance. However, unlike mean and variance, it is difficult to identify plausible preference rankings for securities of varying liquidity levels. Moreover, there are approximation theorems that derive mean–variance preferences from expected utility theory (see, e.g., Levy and Markowitz, 1979), and corresponding results for our liquidity metrics have yet to be developed.

Nevertheless, liquidity is now recognized to be such a significant factor in investment management that despite the qualifications described above, there is considerable practical value in incorporating even *ad hoc* measures of liquidity into standard mean–variance portfolio theory. We turn to this challenge in Section 3.

3 Liquidity-Optimized Portfolios

Armed with quantitative liquidity metrics $\{\ell_{it}\}$ for individual securities and portfolios, we can now incorporate liquidity directly into the portfolio construction process. There are at least three methods for doing so: (a) imposing a liquidity "filter" for securities to be included in a portfolio optimization program; (b) constraining the portfolio optimization program to yield a mean–variance efficient portfolio with a minimum level of liquidity; and (c) adding the liquidity metric into the mean–variance objective function directly. We describe each of these methods in more detail in Sections 3.1–3.3, and refer to portfolios obtained from these procedures as "mean–variance-liquidity (MVL) optimal" portfolios.[8]

3.1 *Liquidity Filters*

In this formulation, the portfolio optimization process is applied only to those securities with liquidity metrics greater than some threshold level ℓ_0. Denote by U the universe of all securities to be considered in the portfolio optimization process, and let U_0 denote the subset of securities in U for which $\ell_{it} \geq \ell_0$:

$$\mathrm{U}_0 \equiv \{i \in \mathrm{U} : \ell_{it} \geq \ell_0\} \tag{10}$$

The standard mean–variance optimization process can now be applied to the securities in U_0 to yield mean–variance-efficient liquidity-filtered portfolios:

$$\min_{\{\omega\}} \frac{1}{2}\omega' \Sigma_0 \omega \quad \text{subject to} \tag{11a}$$

$$\mu_p = \omega' \mu_0 \tag{11b}$$

$$1 = \omega' \iota \tag{11c}$$

where μ_0 is the vector of expected returns of securities in U_0, Σ_0 is the return covariance matrix of securities in U_0, and as μ_p is varied, the set of ω_p^* that solve (11) yields the ℓ_0-liquidity-filtered mean–variance efficient frontier.

3.2 *Liquidity Constraints*

An alternative to imposing a liquidity filter is to impose an additional constraint in the mean–variance optimization problem:

$$\min_{\{\omega\}} \frac{1}{2}\omega' \Sigma \omega \quad \text{subject to} \tag{12a}$$

$$\mu_p = \omega' \mu \tag{12b}$$

$$\ell_0 = \begin{cases} \omega' \ell_t & \text{if } \omega \geq 0 \\ \sum_{i=1}^{n} \frac{|\omega_{pi}|}{\sum_{j=1}^{n} |\omega_{pj}|} \ell_{it} & \text{otherwise} \end{cases} \tag{12c}$$

$$1 = \omega' \iota \tag{12d}$$

where μ is the vector of expected returns of securities in the unconstrained universe U, Σ is the return covariance matrix of securities in U, $\ell_t \equiv [\ell_{1t} \cdots \ell_{nt}]'$ is the vector of liquidity metrics for securities in U, and as μ_p is varied, the set of ω_p^* that solve (12) yields the ℓ_0-liquidity-constrained mean–variance-efficient frontier. Note that the liquidity constraint (12c) is in two parts, depending on whether ω is long-only or long-short. For simplicity, we impose a non-negativity restriction on ω in our empirical example so that the constraint reduces to $\ell_0 = \omega' \ell_t$.

3.3 *Mean–Variance–Liquidity Objective Function*

Perhaps the most direct method of incorporating liquidity into the mean–variance portfolio optimization process is to include the liquidity metric in the objective function:[9]

$$\max_{\{\omega\}} \omega'\mu - \frac{\lambda}{2}\omega'\Sigma\omega + \phi\omega'\ell_t \quad (13a)$$

$$\text{subject to } 1 = \omega'\iota, 0 \leq \omega \quad (13b)$$

where λ is the risk tolerance parameter, ϕ determines the weight placed on liquidity, and we have constrained ω to be non-negative so as to simplify the expression for the liquidity of the portfolio.

4 An Empirical Example

To illustrate the practical relevance of liquidity metrics for investment management, we construct the three types of liquidity-optimized portfolios described in Section 3 using historical data for 50 US stocks selected from the University of Chicago's Center for Research in Securities Prices (CRSP) and the New York Stock Exchange's Trades and Quotes (TAQ) database for the sample period from January 2, 1997 to December 31, 2001. These 50 stocks are listed in Table 1, and were drawn randomly from 10 market capitalization brackets, based on December 31, 1996 closing prices. These stocks were chosen to provide a representative portfolio with sufficiently diverse liquidity characteristics, and Appendix A.2 provides a more detailed description of our sampling procedure.[10]

In Section 4.1 we review the basic empirical characteristics of our sample of stocks and define the mean and covariance estimators that are the inputs to the liquidity-optimized portfolios described in Sections 3.1–3.3. Section 4.2 contains results for liquidity-filtered portfolios, Section 4.3 contains corresponding results for liquidity-constrained portfolios, and Section 4.4 contains results for portfolios obtained by optimizing a mean–variance–liquidity objective function.

4.1 Data Summary

Table 2 reports summary statistics for the daily prices, returns, turnovers, volume, bid/ask spreads and Loeb measures for the 50 stocks listed in Table 1. Table 2 shows that the average price generally increases with market capitalization, and the minimum and maximum average prices of \$1.72 and \$72.72 correspond to stocks in the first and tenth brackets, respectively. Average daily returns were generally positive, with the exception of a small negative return for GOT. The lower-bracket stocks exhibit very high historical average returns and volatilities, while the top-bracket stocks displayed the opposite characteristics. For example, the average daily returns and volatilities of the stocks in the first and tenth brackets were 0.27% and 7.13%, and 0.06% and 2.4%, respectively.

The relation between daily turnover and market capitalization is less clear due to the fact that turnover is volume normalized by shares outstanding. In general, the mid-tier stocks exhibited the highest turnover, up to 2.13% a day, whereas the daily turnover of bottom-tier and top-tier stocks were only 0.3%–0.4%. However, a clearer pattern emerges from the raw volume numbers. From the first to the fifth bracket, average

Table 1 50 US stocks selected randomly within 10 market capitalization brackets, based on December 31, 1996 closing prices. For comparison, market capitalizations based on December 31, 2002 closing prices are also reported.

Ticker	Name	1996 Market Cap ($MM)	2001 Marker Cap ($MM)	Marker Cap Bracket
MANA	MANATRON INC	4.30	13.37	1
SPIR	SPIRE CORP	6.80	21.48	1
WTRS	WATES INSTRUMENTS INC	7.13	12.57	1
CTE	CARDIOTECH INTERNATIONAL INC	9.02	15.38	1
NCEB	NORTH COAST ENERGY INC	9.09	51.86	1
ALDV	ALLIED DEVICES CORP	12.11	4.85	2
RVEE	HOLIDAY R V SUPERSTORES INC	12.32	10.36	2
DAKT	DAKTRONICS INC	16.76	153.23	2
ANIK	ANIKA RESEARCH INC	18.49	9.93	2
GMCR	GREEN MOUNTAIN COFFEE INC	20.93	183.21	2
EQTY	EQUITY OIL CO	39.05	22.84	3
STMI	S T M WIRELESS INC	40.94	10.14	3
LTUS	GARDEN FRESH RESTAURANT CORP	42.07	37.60	3
DISK	IMAGE ENTERTAINMENT INC	45.18	37.99	3
ISKO	ISCO INC	48.17	56.91	3
DWCH	DATAWATCH CORP	52.33	3.33	4
LASE	LASERSIGHT INC	53.85	16.39	4
KVHI	K V H INDUSTRIES INC	54.20	65.00	4
GOT	GOTTSCHALKS INC	54.98	32.87	4
MIMS	M I M CORP	60.21	382.31	4
URS	U R S CORP NEW	77.43	490.28	5
AEOS	AMERICAN EAGLE OUTFITTERS INC	77.99	1,881.07	5
DSPG	D S P GROUP INC	81.09	623.53	5
QDEL	QUIDEL CORP	98.21	218.47	5
EFCX	ELECTRIC FUEL CORP	99.30	42.60	5
AEIS	ADVANCED ENERGY INDUSTRIES INC	114.32	847.71	6
ADVS	ADVENT SOFTWARE INC	223.07	1,689.06	6
MOND	ROBERT MONDAVI CORP THE	269.15	348.92	6
NABI	N A B I	302.87	392.91	6
LAMR	LAMAR ADVERTISING CO	427.07	3,496.69	6
HNCS	H N C SOFTWARE INC	597.69	727.84	7
ART	APTARGROUP INC	632.42	1,255.76	7
GGC	GEORGIC GULF CORP	928.16	586.73	7
CMVT	COMVERSE TECHNOLOGY INC	935.52	4,163.84	7
AHG	APRIA HEALTHCARE GROUP INC	959.10	1,361.88	7
BEC	BECKMAN INSTRUMENTS INC NEW	1,113.07	2,699.91	8
ATG	A G L RESOURCES INC	1,173.01	1,270.66	8
ACXM	ACXIOM CORP	1,229.33	1,518.49	8
EAT	BRINKER INTERNATIONAL INC	1,236.62	2,922.79	8
XRAY	DENTSPLY INTERNATIONAL INC NEW	1,277.75	2,605.33	8
BCR	BARD C R INC	1,596.78	3,296.27	9
HIB	HIBERNIA CORP	1,621.76	2,829.27	9
CTL	CENTURY TELEPHONE ENTRPRS INC	1,846.76	4,628.18	9

Table 1 (*Continued*)

Ticker	Name	1996 Market Cap ($MM)	2001 Marker Cap ($MM)	Marker Cap Bracket
NI	N I P S C O INDUSTRIES INC	2,399.93	4,768.67	9
LIZ	LIZ CLAIBORNE INC	2,759.02	2,617.30	9
ATML	ATMEL CORP	3,271.16	3,431.05	10
EMN	EASTMAN CHEMICAL CO	4,292.65	3,008.64	10
CLX	CLOROX CO	5,181.06	9,198.42	10
AEP	AMERICAN ELECTRIC POWER INC	7,708.26	14,026.89	10
GIS	GENERAL MILLS INC	9,970.67	18,947.03	10

daily trading volume is typically less than 100 million shares, but a discrete shift occurs starting in the fifth bracket, where daily volume jumps to 300 million shares or more and generally remains at these higher levels for the higher market-cap brackets.

The opposite pattern is observed with the distribution of the percentage bid/ask spread. For small-cap stocks, the average bid/ask spread varies between 1% and 8%. High bid/ask spreads are observed between the first and fifth brackets, but starting with the fifth bracket, the spread falls rapidly to values as low as 0.19%. For mid- and top-tier stocks, differences in bid/ask spreads are very small. Loeb's (1983) liquidity metric exhibits the same general patterns—for small-cap stocks, the metric is as high as 28%, but by the fourth bracket, the metric stabilizes between 3% and 1.3%. The standard deviation of this metric for the top-tier stocks is close to zero.

Table 3 contains correlation matrices for the average price, market capitalization, return, turnover, volume and Loeb's metric using daily data from January 2, 1997 to December 31, 2001. The three sub-panels correspond to correlation matrices for the combined portfolio of 50 stocks, the large-cap sub-portfolio (the 26th to 50th stocks in Table 1), and the small-cap subportfolio (the 1st to 25th stocks in Table 1), respectively.[11] Some of the correlations in Table 3 are unusually high by construction and need not concern us. For example, since turnover is defined as the ratio of volume to shares outstanding, where the latter is generally a slowly varying function through time, the correlation between the volume and the turnover is higher than 90% in each of the three correlation matrices in Table 3. The same is true for the high negative correlation between Loeb's metric and market capitalization.

The correlations between market capitalization, price, and turnover are more significant, confirming the general trends observed in Table 2. In each subportfolio, higher market capitalization corresponds to higher average prices, and higher turnover and volume. The correlations are the strongest in the small-cap subportfolio where the gradients of all the underlying variables are the highest. For example, the correlations between the market capitalization and the turnover in the combined, large- and small-cap subportfolios are 11.94%, 4.01% and 19.87%, respectively. At 90%, the correlation between the market capitalization and average price in the small-cap subportfolio is particularly strong. The relationship between turnover, volume, and

Table 2 Summary statistics for daily prices, returns, turnover, volume bid/ask spreads, and Loeb measures for 50 US stocks selected randomly within 10 market capitalization brackets. Statisics for prices, returns, turnover, volume, and the Loeb measure are based on daily data from January 2, 1997 to December 31, 2001. Statistics for bid/ask spreads are based on tick data from January 3, 2000 to December 31, 2001. Trading volume is measured in units of millions of shares per day, and the Loeb measure is computed for a fixed block size of $250,000.

	Average	Return (%)		Turnover (%)		Volume		Bid/Ask (%)		Loeb (%)	
Stock	Price ($)	Mean	SD	Mean	SD	Mean	SD	Mean	SD	Mean	SD
MANA	4.43	0.26	6.33	0.29	0.57	9	18	4.98	2.91	24.17	5.56
SPIR	6.44	0.39	8.28	0.53	1.90	19	63	5.15	3.66	19.29	5.06
WTRS	5.38	0.20	5.69	0.31	1.41	5	21	5.13	2.38	28.11	2.44
CTE	1.73	0.29	8.27	0.44	1.43	28	95	6.63	3.57	26.67	4.62
NCEB	2.30	0.23	7.07	0.13	0.49	13	32	8.29	8.07	18.57	7.18
ALDV	2.17	0.15	6.85	0.32	0.68	15	32	5.50	2.90	25.84	4.14
RVEE	3.04	0.11	5.36	0.20	0.36	15	27	5.57	3.96	19.44	3.29
DAKT	10.92	0.28	4.74	0.43	0.69	36	79	1.63	1.03	9.90	6.64
ANIK	5.68	0.09	5.88	0.73	1.91	62	177	5.30	3.01	14.09	7.48
GMCR	13.56	0.28	4.65	0.56	0.86	25	45	1.48	1.07	13.76	6.72
EQTY	2.35	0.11	5.58	0.27	0.39	34	50	3.97	3.25	16.93	3.83
STMI	6.25	0.17	8.05	0.82	2.52	57	177	3.74	2.25	14.19	6.42
LTUS	12.62	0.02	3.25	0.51	0.83	26	43	2.21	1.28	8.26	3.73
DISK	4.60	0.13	5.97	0.57	1.01	84	141	2.50	1.56	8.07	3.59
ISKO	6.74	0.14	5.06	0.10	0.18	5	10	5.34	2.79	14.19	3.48
DWCH	1.92	0.18	9.96	1.09	4.97	100	457	6.32	5.02	23.22	6.27
LASE	5.46	0.05	7.00	1.07	1.44	158	228	2.72	1.80	9.01	4.99
KVHI	5.08	0.19	6.73	0.34	0.95	25	69	2.85	1.70	14.15	6.47
GOT	6.57	−0.01	2.88	0.14	0.32	16	40	2.12	1.19	6.41	3.40
MIMS	5.14	0.33	6.95	1.02	1.80	186	361	3.20	2.75	8.24	4.51
URS	17.75	0.13	2.84	0.27	0.29	41	47	0.81	0.50	3.22	0.30
AEOS	34.97	0.35	4.54	2.13	1.96	931	1,225	0.31	0.17	2.16	0.97
DSPG	29.62	0.26	4.96	2.04	2.43	300	328	0.52	0.24	2.97	0.55
QDEL	4.35	0.17	5.17	0.50	0.70	121	169	1.94	1.16	4.87	2.23
EFCX	5.01	0.18	8.11	1.35	4.10	236	648	1.40	0.71	8.53	5.49
AEIS	27.22	0.28	5.47	1.02	1.51	280	450	0.45	0.22	2.74	0.58
ADVS	46.29	0.24	4.80	1.02	1.08	208	331	0.52	0.36	2.49	0.81
MOND	38.98	0.04	2.69	0.97	1.28	79	104	0.51	0.28	3.15	0.01
NABI	5.40	0.19	6.09	0.66	0.91	236	321	1.57	0.88	3.30	0.62
LAMR	37.91	0.13	3.30	0.68	0.84	340	425	0.34	0.18	1.90	0.77
HNCS	37.57	0.25	5.46	1.55	1.76	404	448	0.54	0.31	2.63	0.54
ATR	35.80	0.09	2.38	0.24	0.23	74	71	0.51	0.28	2.62	0.24
GGC	21.11	0.01	2.74	0.47	0.54	148	169	0.49	0.23	2.94	0.18
CMVT	68.65	0.15	4.45	2.01	1.78	2,065	3,095	0.15	0.07	1.61	0.52
AHG	16.16	0.10	3.99	0.61	0.72	318	376	0.55	0.36	2.66	0.52
BEC	49.48	0.09	1.93	0.48	0.34	170	130	0.25	0.11	1.56	0.34
ATG	19.76	0.04	1.46	0.21	0.17	117	93	0.47	0.23	2.39	0.24
ACXM	22.29	0.07	4.27	0.93	1.17	719	1,005	0.35	0.14	1.89	0.63
EAT	23.90	0.12	2.64	0.60	0.60	451	493	0.33	0.15	1.66	0.54
XRAY	34.75	0.08	2.09	0.52	0.54	256	275	0.37	0.19	1.55	0.30

Table 2 (*Continued*)

Stock	Average Price ($)	Return (%) Mean	Return (%) SD	Turnover (%) Mean	Turnover (%) SD	Volume Mean	Volume SD	Bid/Ask (%) Mean	Bid/Ask (%) SD	Loeb (%) Mean	Loeb (%) SD
BCR	43.38	0.10	2.11	0.60	0.81	314	418	0.22	0.11	1.30	0.00
HIB	14.91	0.06	2.23	0.30	0.24	449	381	0.51	0.30	1.30	0.02
CTL	39.95	0.09	2.11	0.37	0.34	428	459	0.31	0.13	1.30	0.00
NI	29.05	0.04	1.61	0.39	0.54	503	692	0.33	0.18	1.30	0.00
LIZ	42.34	0.05	2.36	0.64	0.48	385	282	0.23	0.12	1.30	0.00
ATML	22.94	0.11	4.86	2.13	1.42	4,177	3,514	0.28	0.15	1.41	0.35
EMN	50.82	0.01	2.05	0.40	0.28	313	220	0.23	0.12	1.30	0.00
CLX	72.72	0.07	2.37	0.42	0.34	708	690	0.23	0.11	1.30	0.00
AEP	42.15	0.04	1.43	0.26	0.18	595	454	0.19	0.10	1.30	0.00
GIS	58.42	0.06	1.29	0.35	0.27	791	781	0.22	0.11	1.30	0.00

Table 3 Correlation matrices (in %) for average price, market capitalization, average return, turnover, volume, and the Loeb measure for the combined sample of 50 randomly selected securities (five from each of 10 market capitalization brackets), and large- and small-capitalization subportfolios (the 25 largest and 25 smallest market capitalization securities, respectively, of the 50), using daily data from January 2, 1997 to December 31, 2001. The Loeb measure is computed for a fixed block size of $250,000.

	Price	Market Cap	Return	Turnover	Volume	Loeb
			Combined Sample			
Price	100.0	79.1	6.0	10.5	6.4	−63.1
Market Cap	79.1	100.0	4.8	11.9	19.0	−70.4
Return	6.0	4.8	100.0	7.4	6.2	−4.1
Turnover	10.5	11.9	7.4	100.0	95.0	−8.8
Volume	6.4	19.0	6.2	95.0	100.0	−12.4
Loeb	−63.1	−70.4	−4.1	−8.8	−12.4	100.0
			Large Capitalization Stocks			
Price	100.0	67.5	5.5	0.1	−6.8	−43.3
Market Cap	67.5	100.0	4.1	4.0	14.3	−52.4
Return	5.5	4.1	100.0	−0.4	−1.6	−2.9
Turnover	0.1	4.0	−0.4	100.0	92.9	−2.8
Volume	−6.8	14.3	−1.6	92.9	100.0	−7.4
Loeb	−43.3	−52.4	−2.9	−2.8	−7.4	100.0
			Small Capitalization Stocks			
Price	100.0	90.7	6.5	20.8	19.6	−82.9
Market Cap	90.7	100.0	5.5	19.9	23.7	−88.4
Return	6.5	5.5	100.0	15.3	13.9	−5.3
Turnover	20.8	19.9	15.3	100.0	97.1	−14.9
Volume	19.6	23.7	13.9	97.1	100.0	−17.4
Loeb	−82.9	−88.4	−5.3	14.9	−17.4	100.0

Loeb's metric is particularly important because each metric represents an alternate measure of liquidity. With the notable exception of the correlation between Loeb's metric and turnover in the large-cap subportfolio, all correlations have the correct signs and are statistically significant at a 5% level. For example, for the combined portfolio, the turnover-Loeb and volume-Loeb correlations are −8.83% and −12.40%, respectively. The corresponding correlations for the small-cap subportfolio are −14.91% and −17.37%, respectively. The weak correlation between turnover and Loeb's metric for the large-cap subportfolio can be explained by the lack of variation in Loeb's metric at higher capitalization levels, a feature evident in Table 2. High positive return-volume and return-turnover correlations in the small-cap subportfolio—13.92% and 15.29%, respectively—are also noteworthy, and is not observed in the large-cap subportfolio.

Table 4 is similar to Table 3 except for the addition of another liquidity metric, the percentage bid/ask spread. Because our source of bid/ask spread data was available only

Table 4 Correlation matrices (in %) for average price, market capitalization, average return, turnover, volume, the Loeb measure, and bid/ask spreads for the combined sample of 50 randomly selected securities (five from each of 10 market capitalization brackets), and large- and small-capitalization subportfolios (the 25 largest and 25 smallest market capitalization securities, respectively, of the 50), using daily data from January 3, 2000 to December 31, 2001. The Loeb measure is computed for a fixed block size of $250,000, and bid/ask spreads are daily averages based on intradaily tick data.

	Price	Market Cap	Return	Turnover	Volume	Loeb	Bid/ask
			Combined Sample				
Price	100.0	87.9	7.9	14.3	10.2	−60.6	−31.0
Market Cap	87.9	100.0	7.0	11.0	12.6	−66.7	37.9
Return	7.9	7.0	100.0	6.6	6.0	−5.0	−0.4
Turnover	14.3	11.0	6.6	100.0	97.7	−8.6	−8.6
Volume	10.2	12.6	6.0	97.7	100.0	−9.2	−10.6
Loeb	−60.6	−66.7	−5.0	−8.6	−9.2	100.0	27.5
Bid/ask	−31.0	−37.9	−0.4	−8.6	−10.6	27.5	100.0
			Large Capitalization Stock				
Price	100.0	84.4	7.2	2.0	−4.1	−39.6	−26.0
Market Cap	84.4	100.0	6.6	−1.1	0.9	−44.4	−34.8
Return	7.2	6.6	100.0	0.1	−0.5	−3.5	−1.0
Turnover	2.0	−1.1	0.1	100.0	96.8	0.7	−5.4
Volume	−4.1	0.9	−0.5	96.8	100.0	0.6	−8.1
Loeb	−39.6	−44.4	−3.5	0.7	0.6	100.0	14.7
Bid/ask	−26.0	−34.8	−1.0	−5.4	−8.1	14.7	100.0
			Small Capitalization Stocks				
Price	100.0	91.4	8.7	26.7	24.5	−81.6	−36.0
Market Cap	91.4	100.0	7.4	23.0	24.2	−89.1	−41.0
Return	8.7	7.4	100.0	13.1	12.6	−6.6	0.2
Turnover	26.7	23.0	13.1	100.0	98.6	−18.0	−11.8
Volume	24.5	24.2	12.6	98.6	100.0	−19.0	−13.2
Loeb	−81.6	−89.1	−6.6	−18.0	−19.0	100.0	40.3
Bid/ask	−36.0	−41.0	0.2	−11.8	−13.2	40.3	100.0

starting on January 3, 2000, all the correlations were re-estimated with the more recent two-year sample from January 3, 2000 to December 31, 2001.[12] The patterns in Table 4 are similar to those in Table 3. Market capitalization is positively correlated with average price, turnover, and volume, and is negatively correlated with Loeb's metric and the bid/ask spread. For the combined portfolio, the turnover-Loeb and the volume-Loeb correlations as well as the turnover-bid/ask and the volume-bid/ask correlations are of the order of -10%, that is, they have the correct sign and are statistically significant. For the large-cap subportfolio, turnover-Loeb, volume-Loeb, turnover-bid/ask, and volume-bid/ask correlations are all statistically insignificant. For the combined portfolio, and large- and small-cap subportfolios, the bid/ask-Loeb correlations are strong and equal to 27.48%, 14.68% and 40.29%, respectively.

Tables 3 and 4 confirm that the correlations between the various liquidity measures—turnover, volume, Loeb's metric, and the bid/ask spread—are generally consistent with each other, yet are not all perfectly correlated, hence each measure seems to capture certain aspects of liquidity not reflected in the others. The single exception is volume and turnover, which are extremely highly correlated, so we eliminate volume and log-volume from consideration and confine our attention to the following three liquidity measures in our empirical analysis: turnover, bid/ask spreads, and Loeb's metric.

To compute mean–variance–liquidity frontiers, we require estimates of the expected return μ and covariance matrix Σ of the 50 stocks in our sample. Using daily returns data from January 2, 1997 to December 31, 2001, we compute the following standard estimators:

$$\hat{\mu} = \frac{1}{T}\sum_{t=1}^{T} \mathbf{R}_t \tag{14a}$$

$$\hat{\Sigma} = \frac{1}{T-1}\sum_{t=1}^{T} (\mathbf{R}_t - \hat{\mu})(\mathbf{R}_t - \hat{\mu})' \tag{14b}$$

where $\mathbf{R}_t \equiv [R_{1t} \cdots R_{50t}]'$ is the vector of date-t returns of the 50 stocks in our sample. We convert these estimates to a monthly frequency by multiplying by 21, the number of trading days per month. Liquidity-optimized portfolios may then be constructed with these estimates and any one of the liquidity metrics defined in Section 2.

To underscore the fact that liquidity can vary considerably from one month to the next, in Sections 4.2–4.4 we will construct liquidity-optimized portfolios for the months listed in Table 5, which include the start and end of our sample as controls, as well as months that contain significant liquidity events such as the default of Russian government debt in August 1998 and the terrorist attacks of September 11, 2001.

4.2 The Liquidity-Filtered Frontier

Given estimates $\hat{\mu}$ and $\hat{\Sigma}$ of the mean and covariance matrix of the 50 stocks in our sample, we can readily extract the filtered counterparts μ_0 and Σ_0 with which to construct the liquidity-filtered mean–variance frontier according to Section 3.1. For expositional

Table 5 Significant months during the sample period from December 1996 to December 2001 for which liquidity-optimized portfolios are constructed.

Date	Event
December 1996	Beginning of sample
August 1998	Russian default/LTCM
October 1998	Fall of 1998
March 2000	First peak of S&P 500
July 2000	Second peak of S&P 500
April 2001	First bottom of S&P 500
September 2001	9/11 terrorist attacks, second bottom of S&P 500
December 2001	End of sample

convenience, we focus only on one of the three liquidity metrics—turnover—in this section, and will consider the other two liquidity metrics in Section 4.3.[13]

In Table 6 we report the means and standard deviations of two benchmark portfolios—the global minimum-variance portfolio, and the tangency portfolio—and the Sharpe ratio of the tangency portfolio for various levels of the liquidity filter for each of the months listed in Table 5.[14] For each set of portfolios of a given month, the first row—with "Liquidity Metric" set to 0.00—corresponds to portfolios with no liquidity filters imposed, hence these refer to the usual mean–variance benchmark portfolios. Subsequent rows of a given month correspond to portfolios with increasingly stricter liquidity filters imposed at fixed increments until the liquidity filter yields too few securities to construct a meaningful efficient frontier (four securities or less).

Consider the first group of rows in Table 6, for December 1996, the start of our sample period. Without any liquidity filtering, the tangency portfolio has an expected monthly return of 4.13% and a monthly return standard deviation of 5.72%, implying a monthly Sharpe ratio of 0.65.[15] However, with a liquidity filter of 2.29 imposed—only stocks with liquidity metrics greater than or equal to 2.29 are included in the portfolio—the tangency portfolio changes to one with an expected return of 4.23%, a standard deviation of 8.20%, and a Sharpe ratio of 0.46. Although the expected return increases, the standard deviation increases more than proportionally so as to yield a Sharpe ratio that is only 71% of the unfiltered portfolio's Sharpe ratio. As the liquidity filter threshold ℓ_0 in (10) is increased, the Sharpe ratio of the tangency portfolio will continue to decrease since it represents the best risk/reward trade-off available for a given set of securities, and portfolios with lower values of ℓ_0 include all the securities of portfolios with higher values of ℓ_0 but not vice-versa. For the month of December 1996, a liquidity filter of 9.15 yields a Sharpe ratio for the tangency portfolio of 0.39, almost half the value of the unfiltered portfolio's Sharpe ratio.

However, the trade-off between liquidity and the risk/reward profile of the efficient frontier is quite different during March 2000, the height of the bull market when the first peak of the S&P 500 is attained. For the same level of liquidity, 2.29, the Sharpe ratio of the tangency portfolio is 0.64, virtually identical to that of the unfiltered portfolio.[16] In contrast to December 1996, liquidity seems to be less problematic in

Table 6 Monthly means and standard deviations of tangency and minimum-variance portfolios of liquidity-filtered MVL-efficient frontiers for 50 randomly selected stocks (five from each of 10 market capitalization brackets), based on a monthly normalized turnover liquidity metric for the months of December 1196, August 1998, October 1998, March 2000, July 2000, April 2001, September 2001, and December 2001. Expected returns and covariances of the 50 individual securities are estimated with daily returns data from January 2, 1997 to December 31, 2001 and do not vary from month to month.

		Tangency		Min Var		
Date	Liquidity Metric	Mean	SD	Mean	SD	Sharpe
1996-12	0.00	4.13	5.72	1.53	3.37	0.65
1996-12	2.29	4.23	8.20	1.49	4.91	0.46
1996-12	4.57	5.72	13.04	2.49	8.58	0.40
1996-12	6.86	6.32	15.10	2.51	9.71	0.39
1996-12	9.15	6.41	15.36	5.29	14.14	0.39
1998-08	0.00	4.13	5.72	1.53	3.37	0.65
1998-08	2.29	4.22	6.94	1.60	4.29	0.55
1998-08	4.57	5.96	13.69	1.84	7.69	0.40
1998-08	6.86	6.36	15.28	2.47	9.61	0.39
1998-08	9.15	6.36	16.21	4.06	12.77	0.37
1998-10	0.00	4.13	5.72	1.53	3.37	0.65
1998-10	2.29	3.53	6.52	1.48	3.86	0.48
1998-10	4.57	4.13	8.59	1.79	5.38	0.43
1998-10	6.86	6.07	13.96	2.42	9.27	0.40
1998-10	9.15	6.07	13.96	2.80	9.60	0.40
1998-10	11.43	6.18	14.75	2.70	9.68	0.39
2000-03	0.00	4.13	5.72	1.53	3.37	0.65
2000-03	2.29	4.25	6.02	1.60	3.57	0.64
2000-03	4.57	4.31	6.90	1.69	4.20	0.56
2000-03	6.86	4.98	8.86	2.44	6.36	0.51
2000-03	9.15	5.71	10.63	4.25	9.41	0.50
2000-03	11.43	5.69	10.61	4.53	9.58	0.50
2000-03	13.72	6.01	11.54	5.07	10.72	0.48
2000-03	16.00	6.09	12.60	4.92	11.41	0.45
2000-03	18.29	6.11	12.64	5.13	11.69	0.45
2000-03	20.58	6.14	14.44	4.86	12.80	0.40
2000-03	22.86	6.14	14.44	4.86	12.80	0.40
2000-03	25.15	4.32	16.00	3.68	14.62	0.24
2000-07	0.00	4.13	5.72	1.53	3.37	0.65
2000-07	2.29	3.88	6.43	1.53	3.79	0.54
2000-07	4.57	4.98	10.55	2.33	7.50	0.43
2000-07	6.86	5.94	13.17	3.90	11.14	0.42
2000-07	9.15	6.34	15.69	4.85	13.80	0.38
2001-04	0.00	4.13	5.72	1.53	3.37	0.65
2001-04	2.29	4.40	6.88	1.52	3.90	0.58
2001-04	4.57	6.45	11.67	2.47	7.70	0.52
2001-04	6.86	6.36	13.61	2.73	9.54	0.44
2001-04	9.15	6.46	15.33	4.19	12.84	0.39
2001-04	11.43	6.68	16.79	3.97	13.26	0.37
2001-09	0.00	4.13	5.72	1.53	3.37	0.65
2001-09	2.29	4.27	6.84	1.70	4.19	0.56

Table 6 (*Continued*)

Date	Liquidity Metric	Tangency Mean	Tangency SD	Min Var Mean	Min Var SD	Sharpe
2001-09	4.57	5.34	11.02	1.54	6.39	0.44
2001-09	6.86	5.30	11.09	2.32	7.22	0.44
2001-09	9.15	6.50	14.49	5.55	13.41	0.41
2001-12	0.00	4.13	5.72	1.53	3.37	0.65
2001-12	2.29	3.84	6.46	1.47	3.75	0.53
2001-12	4.57	5.04	10.17	1.50	5.94	0.45
2001-12	6.86	5.37	11.53	2.26	8.30	0.43
2001-12	9.15	6.50	14.51	4.43	12.40	0.42

March 2000, with little or no material impact of liquidity filtering on the Sharpe ratio. In fact, even in the extreme case of a filter of 9.15, the resulting Sharpe ratio is 0.50 in March 2000, which is higher than the Sharpe ratio of the December 1996 filtered tangency portfolio with a filter of 2.29. In fact, a filter level of 22.86 is required in March 2000 to yield a Sharpe of 0.40, which is approximately the risk/reward profile of the portfolio with the most extreme liquidity filter in December 1996, a filter of 9.15.

The results in Table 6 are more readily appreciated via graphical representation since we have now expanded the focus from two dimensions (mean and variance) to three (mean, variance, and liquidity). Figures 2 and 3 display liquidity-filtered mean–variance–liquidity (MVL) efficient frontiers for each of the dates in Table 5. At the "ground level" of each of the three-dimensional coordinate cubes in Figures 2 and 3, we have the familiar expected-return and standard-deviation axes. The liquidity threshold ℓ_0 of (10) is measured along the vertical axis. In the plane of ground level, the liquidity level is zero hence the efficient frontier is the standard Markowitz mean–variance efficient frontier, and this frontier will be identical across all the months in our sample since the estimated mean $\hat{\mu}$ and covariance matrix $\hat{\Sigma}$ are based on the entire sample of daily data from January 2, 1997 to December 31, 2001 and do not vary over time. However, as the liquidity metric is used to filter the set of securities to be included in constructing the mean–variance-efficient frontier, the risk/reward profile of the frontier will change, as depicted by the color of the surface. By construction, the liquidity of a filtered portfolio is always greater than or equal to the liquidity threshold ℓ_0, and since the normalization of all liquidity metrics is performed cross-sectionally as well as through time, the color and the height of the frontiers at different dates have the same meaning and can be compared to one another.

Figures 2 and 3 show that as the liquidity filter is imposed, the frontier located at ground level rises steeply—implying relatively little impact on the risk/reward trade-off—until the liquidity threshold reaches the level of the least liquid stock in the portfolio. When the threshold ℓ_0 is incremented further, some of the illiquid stocks fail to satisfy the liquidity filter and are eliminated from the filtered portfolio. As the number of stocks in the portfolio is reduced in this fashion, the MVL frontier becomes less efficient and the frontier surface shifts inward, in the north-east direction.[17] For

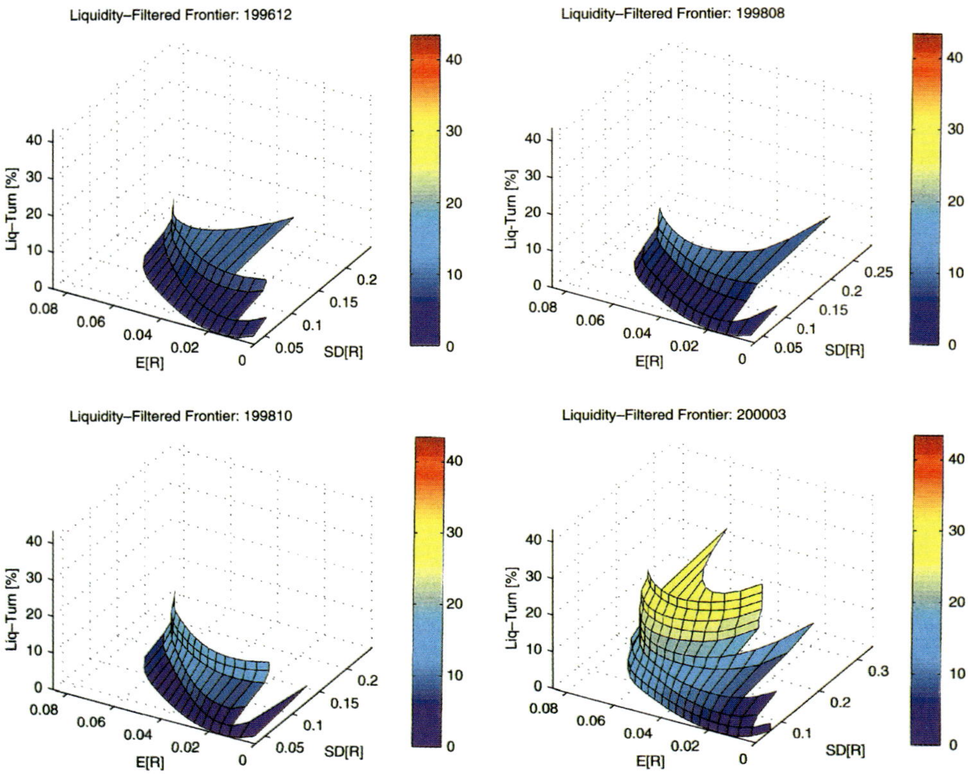

Figure 2 Liquidity-filtered MVL-efficient frontiers for 50 randomly selected stocks (five from each of 10 market capitalization brackets), based on a monthly normalized turnover liquidity metric for the months of December 1996, August 1998, October 1998, and March 2000. Expected returns and covariances of the 50 individual securities are estimated with daily returns data from January 2, 1997 to December 31, 2001 and do not vary from month to month. Color strips to the right of each figure provide the correspondence between liquidity levels and the spectrum.

sufficiently high liquidity thresholds, too few securities satisfy the filter and it becomes impossible to compute a non-degenerate MVL frontier, hence the graph ends beyond these levels.[18]

The evolution of the MVL-efficient frontier is highly dependent on the underlying trends in the liquidity distribution. During our 5-year sample period, the average monthly turnover of our randomly selected portfolio of 50 stocks grew steadily from 0.56% in 1997 to 0.90% in 2000, along with the level of the market. In 2001, the market declined dramatically and the average turnover decreased to 0.70%. The higher moments of turnover—the standard deviation, skewness, and kurtosis—followed similar but somewhat more dramatic trends. At 0.17% and 0.16% in 1997 and 1998, respectively, the standard deviation of turnover was almost unchanged as the market rallied. In 2000, when average turnover peaked at 0.90%, the standard deviation of turnover also peaked at 0.42%, i.e., the distribution of turnover expanded. At the same time, extremely high skewness and kurtosis during the boom years of 1999 and 2000 indicated that a small number of stocks enjoyed very active trading. As

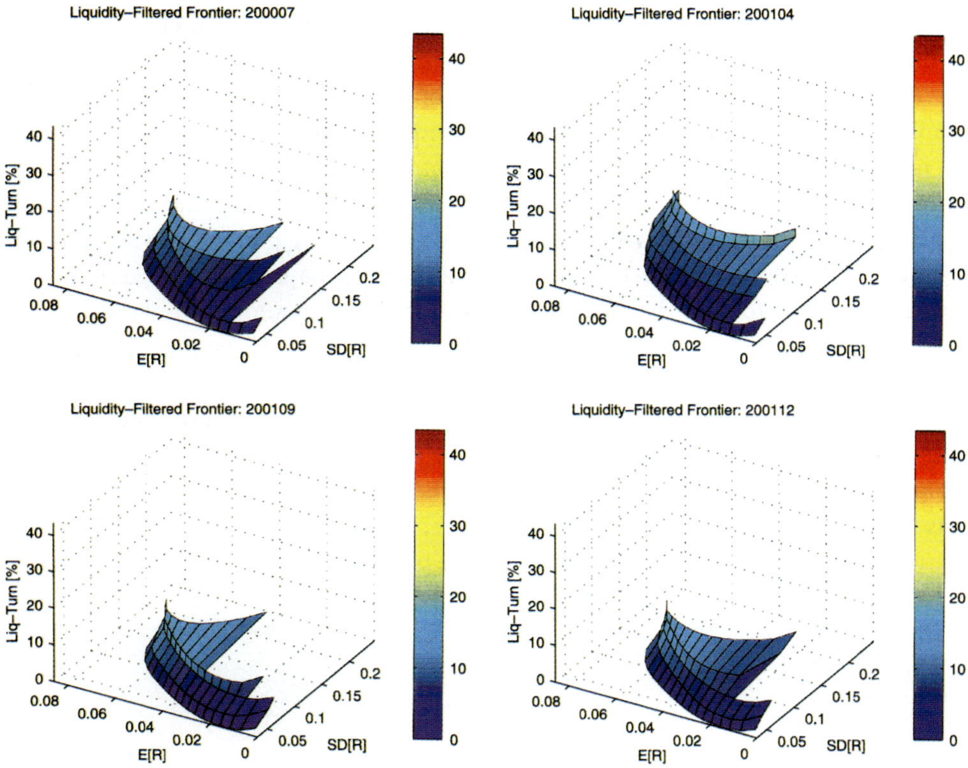

Figure 3 Liquidity-filtered MVL-efficient frontiers for 50 randomly selected stocks (five from each of 10 market capitalization brackets), based on a monthly normalized turnover liquidity metric for the months of July 2000, April 2001, September 2001, and December 2001. Expected returns and covariances are estimated with daily returns data from January 2, 1997 to December 31, 2001. Color strips to the right of each figure provide the correspondence between liquidity levels and the spectrum.

markets declined in 2001, the moments of the distribution of turnover returned to their 1997 levels.

These patterns are borne out by the graphs in Figures 2 and 3. The upper left subplot in Figure 2 shows the MVL-efficient frontier calculated using turnover in December 1996. At this point in time, the turnover distribution was quite compressed by historical standards and its mean was relatively low. When the liquidity filter is raised, the frontier shifts to the northeast and its risk/return profile deteriorates. Similar patterns are observed in the upper right and lower left subplots in Figure 2, corresponding to August 1998 and October 1998, respectively. Although the levels of the S&P 500 in both months were similar, the liquidity conditions were apparently more favorable in October 1998, which is depicted by a brighter color and steeper MVL surface in the latter case. In March 2000 (lower right subplot of Figure 2), the market reached its peak. During that time, the mean and standard deviation of turnover were both very high, making the liquidity filter almost irrelevant up to a very high liquidity threshold. However, during the bear market of late 2000 and 2001 (Figure 3), liquidity deteriorated considerably and the MVL-efficient frontier flattens out to levels comparable with 1996.

An alternative to describing the evolution of the MVL surface is to select a small number of characteristic points on this surface and to plot the trajectories of these points in mean–standard deviation–liquidity space through time. For any mean–variance-efficient frontier, the most relevant point is, of course, the tangency portfolio. In Figures 4 and 5, the *trajectories* of the tangency portfolio are plotted for various levels of the liquidity filter and over time. Each point along the trajectory corresponds to the tangency portfolio of the efficient frontier for a given liquidity threshold ℓ_0. The numerical value of the threshold (in %) is displayed next to the tangency point, and the position of each point is projected onto the ground-level plane for visual clarity. In addition, two sets of lines are drawn on the ground-level plane: a straight line connecting the riskless portfolio to each tangency portfolio (whose slope is the Sharpe ratio of the tangency portfolio), and curved lines which are MVL frontiers for various levels of the liquidity filter. For each figure, the trajectory of the tangency point starts at the same location on the ground-level plane. In the absence of any liquidity

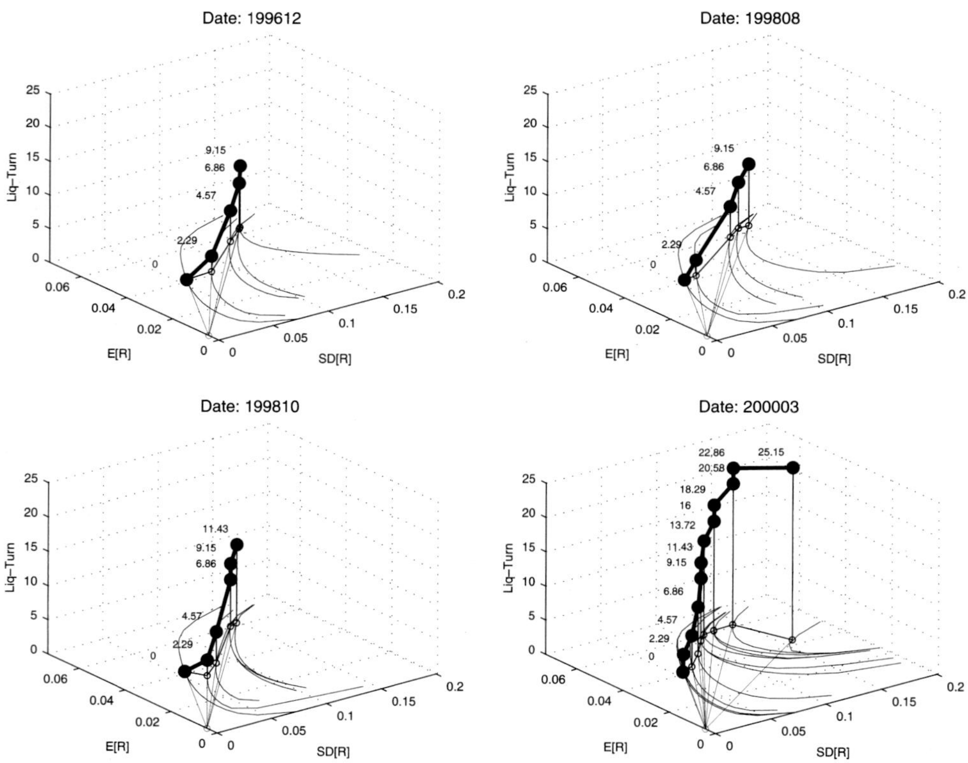

Figure 4 Trajectories of the tangency portfolio for liquidity-filtered MVL-efficient frontiers for 50 randomly selected stocks (five from each of 10 market capitalization brackets), based on a monthly normalized turnover liquidity metric for the months of December 1996, August 1998, October 1998, and March 2000. Expected returns and covariances of the 50 individual securities are estimated with daily returns data from January 2, 1997 to December 31, 2001 and do not vary from month to month.

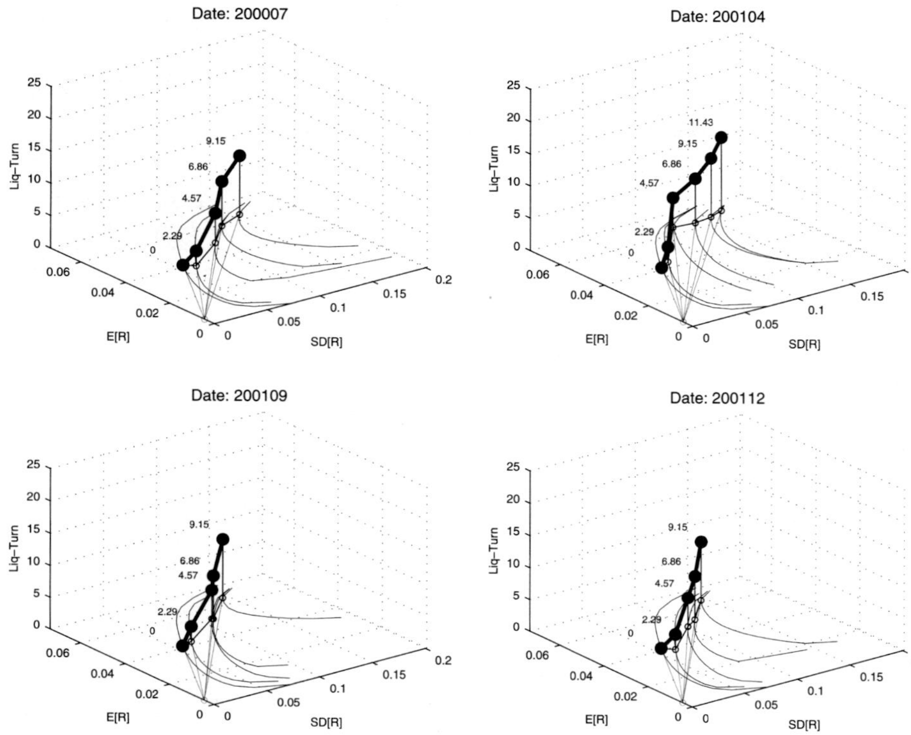

Figure 5 Trajectories of the tangency portfolio for liquidity-filtered MVL-efficient frontiers for 50 randomly selected stocks (five from each of 10 market capitalization brackets), based on a monthly normalized turnover liquidity metric for the months of July 2000, April 2001, September 2001, and December 2001. Expected returns and covariances of the 50 individual securities are estimated with daily returns data from January 2, 1997 to December 31, 2001 and do not vary from month to month.

effects, the trajectory of the tangency portfolio would be vertical and its projection onto the ground-level plane would coincide with its starting point, but because the liquidity filter does have an impact in filtering out certain securities, as the threshold increases, the trajectory of the tangency portfolio moves eastward and away from the viewer. The ground-level projection of the tangency trajectory moves initially in the east/northeast direction but always yielding less desirable Sharpe ratios. In some cases, as the liquidity threshold increases, the ground-level projection of the tangency portfolio turns southeast, yielding tangency portfolios with higher volatility and lower expected return, but with higher levels of liquidity (see, for example, the lower right subplot, for March 2000, in Figure 4). At some point, when it becomes impossible for any of the 50 randomly selected securities to satisfy the liquidity filter, the trajectory terminates. The dynamics of the trajectory of the tangency portfolio is a qualitative alternative to assessing the impact of liquidity on the characteristics of a mean–variance optimal portfolio.

The graphs in Figures 4 and 5 show that for successively higher liquidity filters, the risk/reward profile of the efficient frontier—as measured by the tangency portfolio—worsens, but at different rates for different months. Figure 6 depicts the time variation

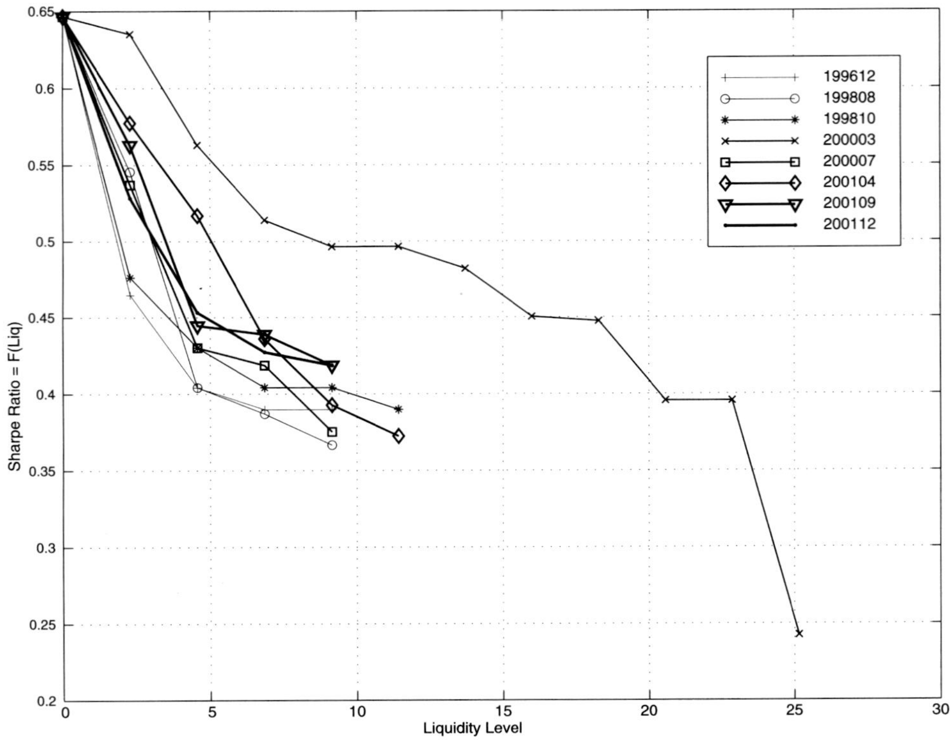

Figure 6 Sharpe ratio trajectories of tangency portfolios of liquidity-filtered MVL-efficient frontiers for 50 randomly selected stocks (five from each of 10 market capitalization brackets), based on a monthly normalized turnover liquidity metric, as a function of the liquidity filter, for the months of December 1996, August 1998, October 1998, March 2000, July 2000, April 2001, September 2001, and December 2001. Expected returns and covariances of the 50 individual securities are estimated with daily returns data from January 2, 1997 to December 31, 2001 and do not vary from month to month. Thicker lines represent trajectories from more recent months.

of this trade-off more explicitly by graphing the trajectories of Sharpe ratios as a function of the liquidity filter for each of the months in Table 5. This two-dimensional representation of a three-dimensional object is a simple way to highlight the trade-off between liquidity and investment performance. When the level of liquidity is high (March 2000), the Sharpe ratio declines rather slowly in response to rising levels of liquidity filtering, but when liquidity conditions are poor (September 2001), the Sharpe ratio falls precipitously as the liquidity threshold is increased. For liquidity-filtered portfolios, the decline in performance takes the form of discrete jumps because the liquidity threshold changes the composition of the portfolio by filtering out illiquid stocks. We shall see in Section 4.3 that imposing liquidity constraints can smooth out these jumps.

4.3 The Liquidity-Constrained Frontier

The liquidity-filtered portfolios described in Section 4.2 illustrate the potential value of incorporating simple notions of liquidity into the portfolio construction process, but a more direct approach is to impose liquidity constraints directly into the optimization problem as described in Section 3.2. Table 7 summarizes the characteristics of liquidity-constrained portfolios for the same 50 stocks considered in Section 4.2 using the same liquidity metric, monthly normalized turnover.

In contrast to the liquidity-filtered portfolios of Table 6, the results in Table 7 show that the performance of liquidity-constrained portfolios is considerably more attractive, with generally higher Sharpe ratios for the same liquidity thresholds and smoother transitions as the threshold is increased. For example, for the month of December 1996, an increase in the liquidity threshold from 0.00 to 2.29 yields a drop in the Sharpe atio from 0.65 to 0.46 for the liquidity-filtered portfolios in Table 6, but Table 7 shows no decline in the Sharpe ratio for the liquidity-constrained portfolios. In fact, for every month in Table 5, imposing a liquidity constraint of 2.29 has virtually no impact on the Sharpe ratio, and in some months, e.g., March 2000, the threshold can be increased well beyond 2.29 without any loss in performance for the tangency portfolio.

The intuition for these improvements lies in the fact that in contrast to liquidity filtering—which eliminates securities that fall below the liquidity threshold—liquidity-constrained portfolios generally contain all 50 securities and the portfolio weights are adjusted accordingly so as to achieve the desired liquidity threshold. Rather than simply dropping securities that fall below the liquidity threshold, the liquidity-constrained portfolios underweight them and overweight the more liquid securities, yielding Sharpe ratios that are larger than those of liquidity-filtered portfolios for the same liquidity threshold, and smoother functions of the liquidity threshold.

The intuition for the advantages of liquidity constraints over liquidity filtering is not tied to the turnover liquidity metric, but carries over to the other two metrics as well. Table 8 summarizes the characteristics of liquidity-constrained portfolios for all three liquidity metrics—turnover, Loeb, and bid/ask spread—during March 2000 and December 2001. For all three metrics, and during both months, it is clear that the Sharpe ratios of the tangency portfolio are generally unaffected by the first few levels of liquidity constraints, in contrast to the behavior of the liquidity-filtered portfolios of Table 6.[19] However, Table 8 does show that the three metrics behave somewhat differently as market conditions change. During the height of the market in March 2000, the turnover and Loeb metrics yield a larger number of feasible liquidity-constrained efficient portfolios than the bid/ask metric, but in the midst of the bear market in December 2001, it is the Loeb and bid/ask metrics that yield more feasible efficient portfolios. While this may seem to suggest that the Loeb metric is the most robust of the three, the comparison is not completely fair since we have fixed the block size for the Loeb metric at $250,000, and the price impact of such a transaction is likely to be quite different between March 2000 and December 2001.[20] The three liquidity metrics capture distinct—albeit overlapping—aspects of liquidity, and which metric is most useful depends intimately on the nature of the application at hand.

A graphical representation of the turnover-constrained MVL frontier renders an even clearer illustration of the difference between liquidity-filtered and liquidity-constrained portfolios. Figures 7 and 8 contain the liquidity-constrained counterparts

Table 7 Monthly means and standard deviations of tangency and minimum-variance portfolios of liquidity-constrained MVL-efficient frontiers for 50 randomly selected stocks, (five from each of 10 market capitalization brackets), based on a monthly normalized turnover liquidity metric for the months of December 1996, August 1998, October 1998, March 2000, July 2000, April 2001, September 2001, and December 2001. Expected returns and covariances of the 50 individual securities are estimated with daily returns data from January 2, 1997 to December 31, 2001 and do not vary from month to month.

	Liquidity	Tangency		Min Var		
Date	Threshold	Mean	SD	Mean	SD	Sharpe
1996-12	0.00	4.13	5.72	1.53	3.37	0.65
1996-12	2.29	4.13	5.72	1.53	3.39	0.65
1996-12	4.57	4.99	7.36	1.69	4.15	0.62
1996-12	6.86	5.71	9.53	1.98	5.69	0.55
1996-12	9.15	5.78	11.18	2.26	7.66	0.48
1996-12	11.43	5.65	13.03	2.61	9.88	0.40
1996-12	13.72	5.28	14.86	2.83	12.39	0.33
1998-08	0.00	4.13	5.72	1.53	3.37	0.65
1998-08	2.29	4.13	5.72	1.53	3.38	0.65
1998-08	4.57	4.81	6.93	1.76	4.09	0.63
1998-08	6.86	5.90	9.44	2.14	5.57	0.58
1998-08	9.15	6.11	10.97	2.60	7.56	0.52
1998-08	11.43	6.12	12.69	3.16	9.84	0.45
1998-08	13.72	6.13	14.95	3.81	12.38	0.38
1998-10	0.00	4.13	5.72	1.53	3.37	0.65
1998-10	2.29	4.13	5.72	1.53	3.37	0.65
1998-10	4.57	4.13	5.72	1.55	3.42	0.65
1998-10	6.86	4.46	6.33	1.66	3.75	0.64
1998-10	9.15	4.98	7.42	1.76	4.33	0.61
1998-10	11.43	5.52	8.69	1.90	5.09	0.59
1998-10	13.72	5.62	9.38	2.02	5.98	0.55
1998-10	16.00	5.66	10.10	2.25	6.98	0.52
1998-10	18.29	5.63	10.85	2.45	8.03	0.48
1998-10	20.58	5.56	11.67	2.65	9.13	0.44
1998-10	22.86	5.51	12.62	2.84	10.27	0.40
1998-10	25.15	5.37	13.51	3.02	11.46	0.37
1998-10	27.44	4.96	13.97	3.17	12.70	0.32
2000-03	0.00	4.13	5.72	1.53	3.37	0.65
2000-03	2.29	4.13	5.72	1.53	3.37	0.65
2000-03	4.57	4.13	5.72	1.53	3.37	0.65
2000-03	6.86	4.13	5.72	1.73	3.48	0.65
2000-03	9.15	4.12	5.70	1.97	3.82	0.65
2000-03	11.43	4.54	6.41	2.24	4.33	0.64
2000-03	13.72	5.06	7.38	2.52	4.98	0.63
2000-03	16.00	5.61	8.47	2.79	5.73	0.61
2000-03	18.29	5.77	9.04	3.06	6.55	0.59
2000-03	20.58	5.87	9.64	3.33	7.43	0.57
2000-03	22.86	5.93	10.26	3.60	8.35	0.54
2000-03	25.15	5.96	10.95	3.87	9.31	0.51

Table 7 (*Continued*)

Date	Liquidity Threshold	Tangency		Min Var		Sharpe
		Mean	SD	Mean	SD	
2000-03	27.44	5.98	11.74	4.14	10.29	0.47
2000-03	29.72	6.00	12.64	4.42	11.31	0.44
2000-03	32.01	6.01	13.62	4.67	12.36	0.41
2000-03	34.29	6.01	14.74	4.84	13.44	0.38
2000-03	36.58	6.03	16.08	4.84	14.66	0.35
2000-03	38.87	6.03	17.61	4.86	16.08	0.32
2000-03	41.15	6.00	19.33	4.85	17.70	0.29
2000-03	43.44	5.83	20.85	4.76	19.45	0.26
2000-07	0.00	4.13	5.72	1.53	3.37	0.65
2000-07	2.29	4.13	5.72	1.53	3.37	0.65
2000-07	4.57	4.12	5.70	1.73	3.62	0.65
2000-07	6.86	4.96	7.23	1.97	4.42	0.63
2000-07	9.15	5.92	9.38	2.33	5.61	0.59
2000-07	11.43	6.14	10.61	2.70	7.06	0.54
2000-07	13.72	6.17	11.78	3.09	8.67	0.49
2000-07	16.00	6.24	13.25	3.50	10.37	0.44
2000-07	18.29	6.36	15.08	3.91	12.15	0.39
2000-07	20.58	6.51	17.26	4.32	14.00	0.35
2001-04	0.00	4.13	5.72	1.53	3.37	0.65
2001-04	2.29	4.13	5.72	1.53	3.37	0.65
2001-04	4.57	4.16	5.77	1.63	3.66	0.65
2001-04	6.86	5.33	7.95	1.69	4.45	0.61
2001-04	9.15	5.90	9.53	1.94	5.59	0.57
2001-04	11.43	5.92	10.45	2.09	6.95	0.53
2001-04	13.72	5.80	11.48	2.31	8.48	0.47
2001-04	16.00	5.55	12.63	2.55	10.10	0.40
2001-04	18.29	5.28	14.19	2.78	11.80	0.34
2001-09	0.00	4.13	5.72	1.53	3.37	0.65
2001-09	2.29	4.13	5.72	1.53	3.37	0.65
2001-09	4.57	4.13	5.72	1.79	3.65	0.65
2001-09	6.86	4.63	6.57	2.10	4.42	0.64
2001-09	9.15	5.49	8.23	2.50	5.52	0.61
2001-09	11.43	6.05	9.65	2.92	6.86	0.58
2001-09	13.48	6.34	10.87	3.40	8.36	0.54
2001-09	16.00	6.44	11.99	4.04	10.01	0.50
2001-09	18.29	6.55	13.48	4.75	11.83	0.45
2001-12	0.00	4.13	5.72	1.53	3.37	0.65
2001-12	2.29	4.13	5.72	1.53	3.37	0.65
2001-12	4.57	4.11	5.70	1.67	3.64	0.65
2001-12	6.86	4.96	7.19	1.91	4.52	0.63
2001-12	9.15	5.88	9.14	2.33	5.81	0.59
2001-12	11.43	6.35	10.68	2.87	7.35	0.55
2001-12	13.72	6.55	12.02	3.47	9.06	0.51
2001-12	16.00	6.69	13.49	4.24	10.97	0.46
2001-12	18.29	6.80	15.13	5.07	13.11	0.42

Table 8 Monthly means and standard deviations of tangency and minimum-variance portfolios of liquidity-constrained MVL-efficient frontiers for 50 randomly selected strocks (five from each of 10 market capitalization brackets), for three liquidity metrices—turnover, Loeb's (1983) price impact measure, and bid/ask spread—for March 2000 and December 2001. Expected returns and covariances for the 50 individual securities are estimated with daily returns data from January 2, 1997 to December 31, 2001 and do not vary from month to month.

Liquidity Threshold	Tangency Mean	Tangency SD	Min Var Mean	Min Var SD	Sharpe
		March 2000			
		Turnover-Constrained Portfolios			
0.00	4.13	5.72	1.53	3.37	0.65
2.29	4.13	5.72	1.53	3.37	0.65
4.57	4.13	5.72	1.53	3.37	0.65
6.86	4.13	5.72	1.73	3.48	0.65
9.15	4.12	5.70	1.97	3.82	0.65
11.43	4.54	6.41	2.24	4.33	0.64
13.72	5.06	7.38	2.52	4.98	0.63
16.00	5.61	8.47	2.79	5.73	0.61
18.29	5.77	9.04	3.06	6.55	0.59
20.58	5.87	9.64	3.33	7.43	0.57
22.86	5.93	10.26	3.60	8.35	0.54
25.15	5.96	10.95	3.87	9.31	0.51
27.44	5.98	11.74	4.14	10.29	0.47
29.72	6.00	12.64	4.42	11.31	0.44
32.01	6.01	13.62	4.67	12.36	0.41
34.29	6.01	14.74	4.84	13.44	0.38
36.58	6.03	16.08	4.84	14.66	0.35
38.87	6.03	17.61	4.86	16.08	0.32
41.15	6.00	19.33	4.85	17.70	0.29
43.44	5.83	20.85	4.76	19.45	0.26
		Loeb-Constrained Portfolios			
0.00	4.13	5.72	1.53	3.37	0.65
4.95	4.13	5.72	1.53	3.37	0.65
9.90	4.13	5.72	1.53	3.37	0.65
14.85	4.13	5.72	1.53	3.37	0.65
19.81	4.13	5.72	1.53	3.37	0.65
24.76	4.13	5.72	1.53	3.37	0.65
29.71	4.13	5.72	1.53	3.37	0.65
34.66	4.13	5.72	1.53	3.37	0.65
39.61	4.13	5.72	1.53	3.37	0.65
44.56	4.13	5.72	1.53	3.37	0.65
49.51	4.15	5.75	1.53	3.37	0.65
54.46	4.06	5.62	1.54	3.37	0.65
59.42	3.88	5.36	1.54	3.37	0.64
64.37	3.73	5.18	1.54	3.37	0.64
69.32	3.60	5.06	1.54	3.37	0.63
74.27	3.49	5.01	1.53	3.38	0.61
79.22	3.38	4.99	1.49	3.42	0.59
84.17	3.29	5.09	1.45	3.48	0.56

Table 8 (*Continued*)

Liquidity Threshold	Tangency Mean	Tangency SD	Min Var Mean	Min Var SD	Sharpe
89.12	3.22	5.28	1.42	3.58	0.53
94.08	3.18	5.63	1.39	3.71	0.49
		Bid/Ask-Constrained Portfolios			
0.00	4.13	5.72	1.53	3.37	0.65
2.46	4.13	5.72	1.53	3.37	0.65
4.91	4.13	5.72	1.53	3.37	0.65
7.37	4.13	5.72	1.53	3.37	0.65
9.82	3.94	5.45	1.54	3.37	0.64
12.28	3.60	5.09	1.54	3.37	0.62
14.73	3.29	5.01	1.45	3.47	0.57
17.19	3.10	5.45	1.35	3.75	0.49
19.65	3.24	7.06	1.36	4.16	0.40
22.10	3.98	11.23	1.24	5.20	0.32
		December 2001			
		Turnover-Constrained Portfolios			
0.00	4.13	5.72	1.53	3.37	0.65
2.29	4.13	5.72	1.53	3.37	0.65
4.57	4.11	5.70	1.67	3.64	0.65
6.86	4.96	7.19	1.91	4.52	0.63
9.15	5.88	9.14	2.33	5.81	0.59
11.43	6.35	10.68	2.87	7.35	0.55
13.72	6.55	12.02	3.47	9.06	0.51
16.00	6.69	13.49	4.24	10.97	0.46
18.29	6.80	15.13	5.07	13.11	0.42
		Loeb-Constrained Portfolios			
0.00	4.13	5.72	1.53	3.37	0.65
4.95	4.13	5.72	1.53	3.37	0.65
9.90	4.13	5.72	1.53	3.37	0.65
14.85	4.13	5.72	1.53	3.37	0.65
19.81	4.13	5.72	1.53	3.37	0.65
24.76	4.13	5.72	1.53	3.37	0.65
29.71	4.13	5.72	1.53	3.37	0.65
34.66	4.13	5.72	1.53	3.37	0.65
39.61	4.13	5.72	1.53	3.37	0.65
44.56	4.13	5.72	1.53	3.37	0.65
49.51	4.13	5.72	1.53	3.37	0.65
54.46	4.12	5.71	1.54	3.37	0.65
59.42	4.00	5.53	1.54	3.37	0.65
64.37	3.81	5.27	1.53	3.37	0.64
69.32	3.64	5.08	1.54	3.37	0.63
74.27	3.52	5.00	1.54	3.38	0.62
79.22	3.38	4.95	1.52	3.41	0.59
84.17	3.27	5.00	1.46	3.48	0.57
89.12	3.17	5.16	1.42	3.57	0.53
94.08	3.07	5.44	1.39	3.70	0.48

Table 8 (*Continued*)

Liquidity Threshold	Tangency		Min Var		Sharpe
	Mean	SD	Mean	SD	
		Bid/Ask-Constrained Portfolios			
0.00	4.13	5.72	1.53	3.37	0.65
2.46	4.13	5.72	1.53	3.37	0.65
4.91	4.13	5.72	1.53	3.37	0.65
7.37	4.13	5.72	1.53	3.37	0.65
9.82	4.13	5.72	1.53	3.37	0.65
12.28	4.13	5.72	1.53	3.37	0.65
14.73	4.13	5.72	1.53	3.37	0.65
17.19	4.13	5.72	1.53	3.37	0.65
19.65	4.12	5.71	1.54	3.37	0.65
22.10	4.13	5.73	1.54	3.37	0.65
24.56	4.17	5.78	1.547	3.37	0.65
27.01	4.08	5.64	1.54	3.37	0.65
29.47	3.97	5.48	1.54	3.37	0.65
31.92	3.84	5.30	1.54	3.37	0.64
34.38	3.72	5.16	1.54	3.37	0.64
36.84	3.60	5.01	1.54	3.37	0.63
39.29	3.49	4.91	1.54	3.37	0.62
41.75	3.38	4.83	1.53	3.37	0.61
44.20	3.29	4.79	1.51	3.38	0.60
46.66	3.19	4.77	1.46	3.40	0.58

to Figures 2 and 3. In the upper left subplot of Figure 7, which contains the MVL frontier for December 1996, the period when the distribution of average turnover was at its historically low mean and standard deviation, the sail-like surface is rather flat and covers relatively little surface area. The infeasibility of the constrained portfolio optimization problem at higher liquidity thresholds is responsible for the tattered edges of the surface starting at the fourth liquidity level (note that the size of the liquidity increments is identical across all months and all the axes have the same scale). At the highest levels of liquidity, only the most liquid segments of the MVL frontier appear in Figure 7. Because of the generally positive correlation between liquidity and market capitalization, and the fact that the large-cap stocks in our sample have modest expected returns and volatilities as compared to the smaller-cap stocks, at higher liquidity threshold levels portfolios on the MVL frontier consist mostly of defensive large-cap equities.

In the upper right sub-plot of Figure 7 (August 1998), liquidity conditions have improved—the MVL frontier rises up from the ground-level plane almost vertically, and up to the third liquidity threshold, the shape of the frontier remains almost unaffected by the liquidity constraint. In the lower left sub-plot of Figure 7 we observe a dramatic increase in liquidity—the MVL frontier is twice as tall as the December 1996 frontier, and the level of liquidity at which the surface starts bending to the right is significantly higher than in the previous figures. In the lower right subplot of Figure 7,

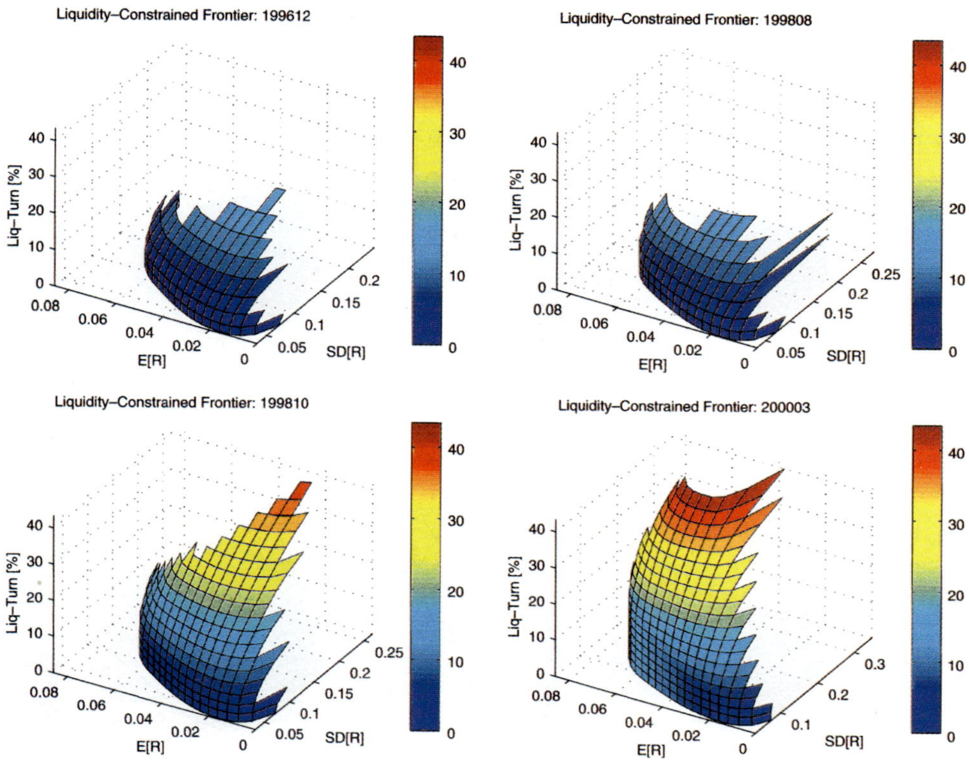

Figure 7 Liquidity-constrained MVL-efficient frontiers for 50 randomly selected stocks (five from each of 10 market capitalization brackets), based on a monthly normalized turnover liquidity metric for the months of December 1996, August 1998, October 1998, and March 2000. Expected returns and covariances of the 50 individual securities are estimated with daily returns data from January 2, 1997 to December 31, 2001 and do not vary from month to month. Color strips to the right of each figure provide the correspondence between liquidity levels and the spectrum.

corresponding to the first peak in the S&P 500 (March 2000), the MVL frontier is at its tallest and it is apparent that the liquidity constraint is irrelevant up to a very high liquidity threshold.

Figure 8 tells a very different story. The shape and height of the MVL frontier change dramatically starting with the upper left subplot for July 2000 (the second peak of the S&P 500) and moving clockwise to April 2001 (the first bottom of the S&P 500), September 2001 (the terrorist attacks on 9/11) and December 2001 (the last month of the simulation). In the face of the bear market of 2000–2001, liquidity conditions have clearly deteriorated, and Figure 8 provides a detailed roadmap of the dynamics of this trend.

The dynamics of liquidity-constrained MVL frontiers can also be seen through the trajectories of the tangency portfolio, contained in Figures 9–11. As with the liquidity-filtered trajectories in Figures 4–6, the trajectories in Figures 9 and 10 originate at the same point on the ground-level plane because the lowest-level frontier is unaffected by the liquidity constraint, and the trajectories remain vertical until the first liquidity threshold, at which point they begin to move initially in the northeast direction and,

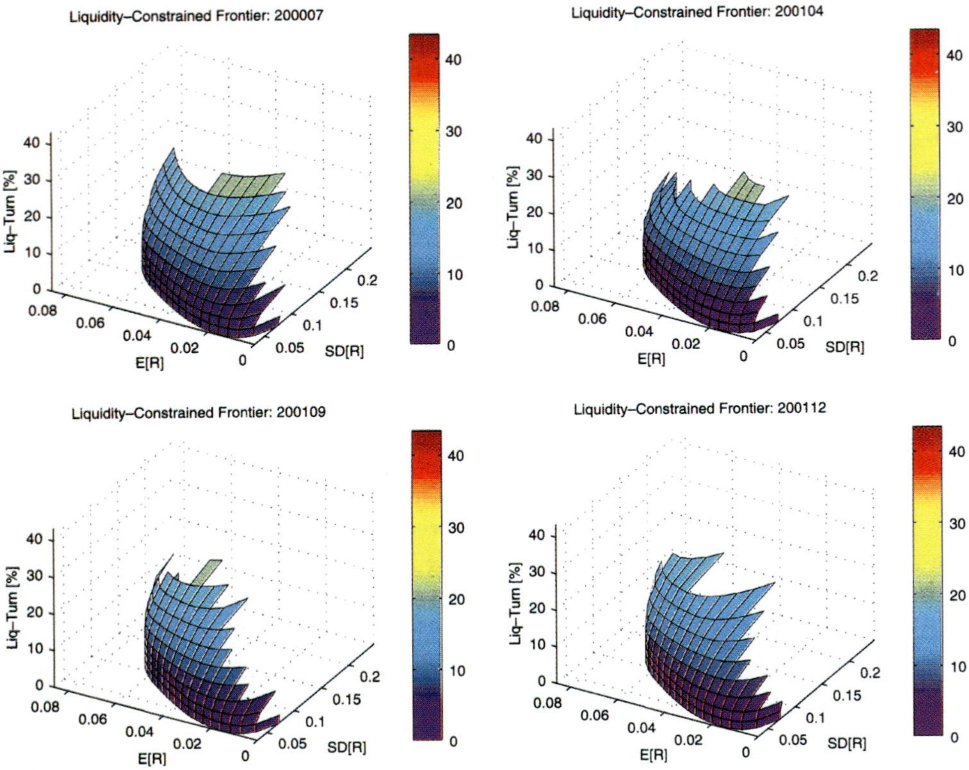

Figure 8 Liquidity-constrained MVL-efficient frontiers for 50 randomly selected stocks (five from each of 10 market capitalization brackets), based on a monthly normalized turnover liquidity metric for the months of July 2000, April 2001, September 2001, and December 2001. Expected returns and covariances are estimated with daily returns data from January 2, 1997 to December 31, 2001. Color strips to the right of each figure provide the correspondence between liquidity levels and the spectrum.

in some cases, eventually turning towards the southeast direction, until they reach a sufficiently high liquidity threshold where the tangency portfolios no longer exist.

Figure 11 summarizes the trajectories of Figures 9 and 10 by plotting the Sharpe ratio as a function of the liquidity threshold for each of the months in Table 5. In contrast to the liquidity-filtered trajectories of Figure 6, the liquidity-constrained trajectories of Figure 11 are all concave, and each trajectory is comprised of three distinct segments. The first segment—beginning at the left boundary of the graph—is parallel to the liquidity axis, indicating that liquidity constraints have no effect on the tangency portfolio's Sharpe ratio. The second segment is decreasing and concave, implying Sharpe ratios that decline at increasingly faster rates as the liquidity threshold is increased. The third segment is decreasing but linear, implying Sharpe ratios that decline with increasing liquidity thresholds, but at a constant rate.

Intuitively, an optimal MVL portfolio—one that balances all three characteristics in some fashion—should be located somewhere along the second segments of the Sharpe ratio curves in Figure 11. It is along these segments that marginal increases

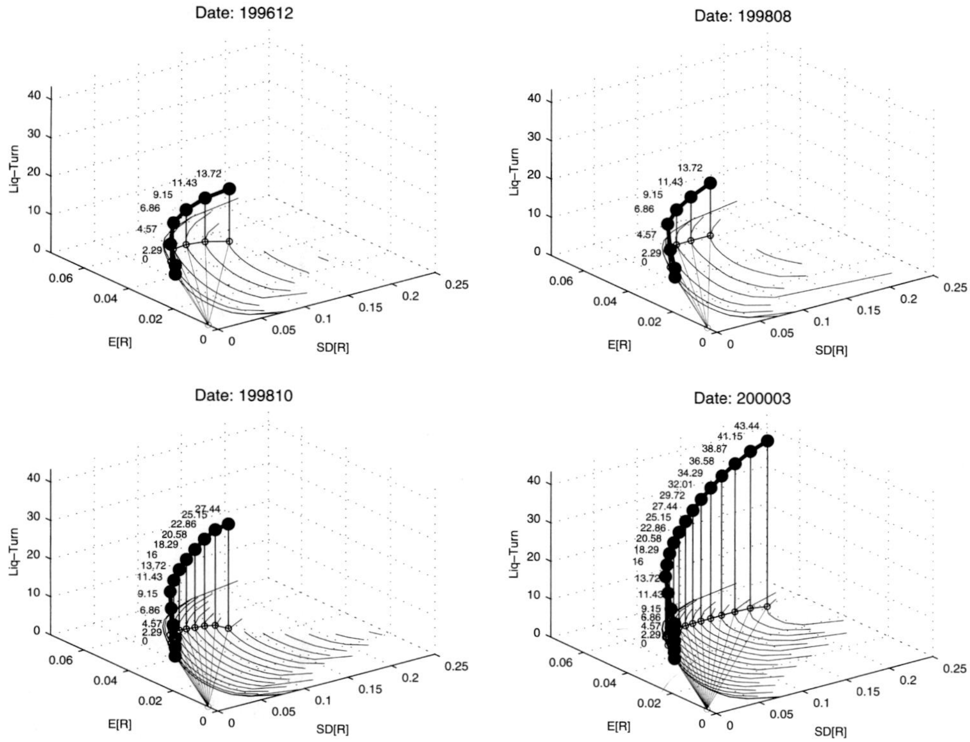

Figure 9 Trajectories of the tangency portfolio for liquidity-constrained MVL-efficient frontiers for 50 randomly selected stocks (five from each of 10 market capitalization brackets), based on a monthly normalized turnover liquidity metric for the months of December 1996, August 1998, October 1998, and March 2000. Expected returns and covariances of the 50 individual securities are estimated with daily returns data from January 2, 1997 to December 31, 2001 and do not vary from month to month.

in the liquidity threshold yield increasingly higher costs in terms of poorer Sharpe ratios, hence there should be some liquidity threshold along this segment that balances an investor's preference for liquidity and the risk/reward profile of the tangency portfolio. Of course, turning this heuristic argument into a formal procedure for construction MVL-optimal portfolios requires the specification of preferences for mean, variance, and liquidity, which is precisely the approach developed in Section 3.3 and implemented in Section 4.4.

4.4 The Mean–Variance–Liquidity Frontier

Although the most direct method for incorporating liquidity into the portfolio construction process is to specify an objective function that includes liquidity as in Section 3.3, this assumes that investors are able to articulate their preferences for liquidity. This may not be true given that liquidity has only recently become an explicit factor in the investment process of many individual and institutional investors. However, by

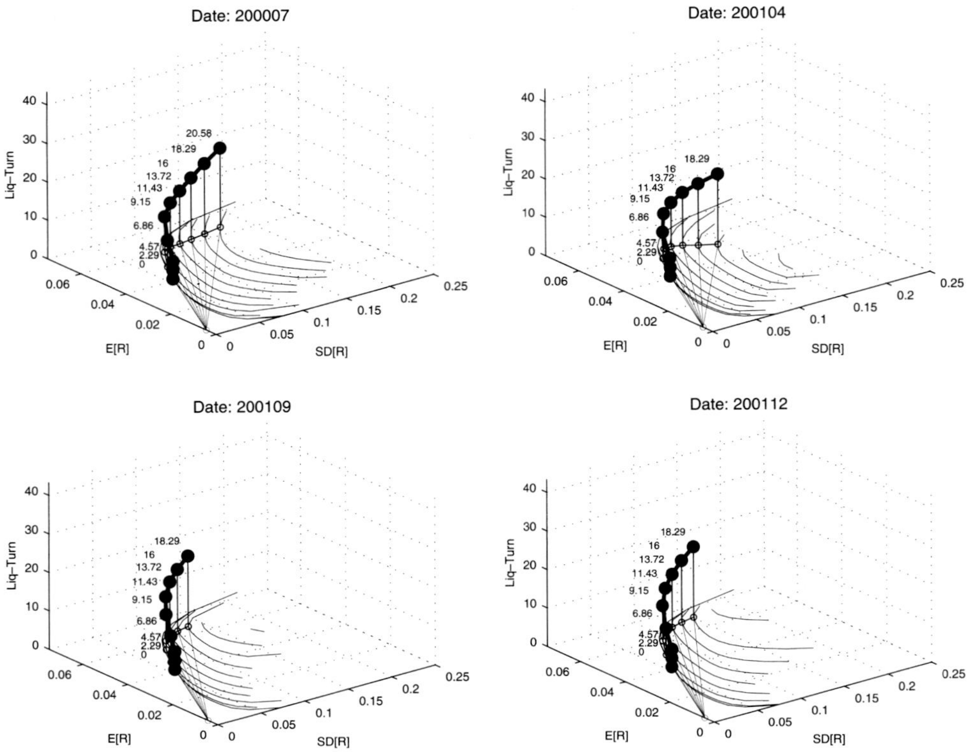

Figure 10 Trajectories of the tangency portfolio for liquidity-constrained MVL-efficient frontiers for 50 randomly selected stocks (five from each of 10 market capitalization brackets), based on a monthly normalized turnover liquidity metric for the months of July 2000, April 2001, September 2001, and December 2001. Expected returns and covariances of the 50 individual securities are estimated with daily returns data from January 2, 1997 to December 31, 2001 and do not vary from month to month.

providing various calibrations of the MVL objective function (13) and their empirical implications for our sample of 50 stocks, we hope to develop a more formal understanding of liquidity preferences in the mean–variance context.

Recall from (13) of Section 3.3 that the MVL objective function is given by:

$$\max_{\{\omega\}} \; \omega'\mu - \frac{\lambda}{2}\omega'\Sigma\omega + \phi\omega'\ell_t$$

$$\text{subject to } 1 = \omega'\iota, \quad 0 \leq \omega$$

where ϕ represents the weight placed on liquidity. Figure 12 contains four graphs—the expected return, standard deviation, liquidity, and Sharpe ratio of the optimal portfolio—each as a function of the risk aversion parameter λ, and for various values of the liquidity parameter ϕ where the liquidity metric used is monthly normalized turnover. When $\phi \equiv 0$, (13) reduces to the standard Markowitz–Tobin mean–variance portfolio optimization problem. As the risk aversion parameter λ increases along the horizontal axis in Figure 12, both the expected return and the standard deviation of the optimal portfolio decline as the investor places increasingly higher penalties on the

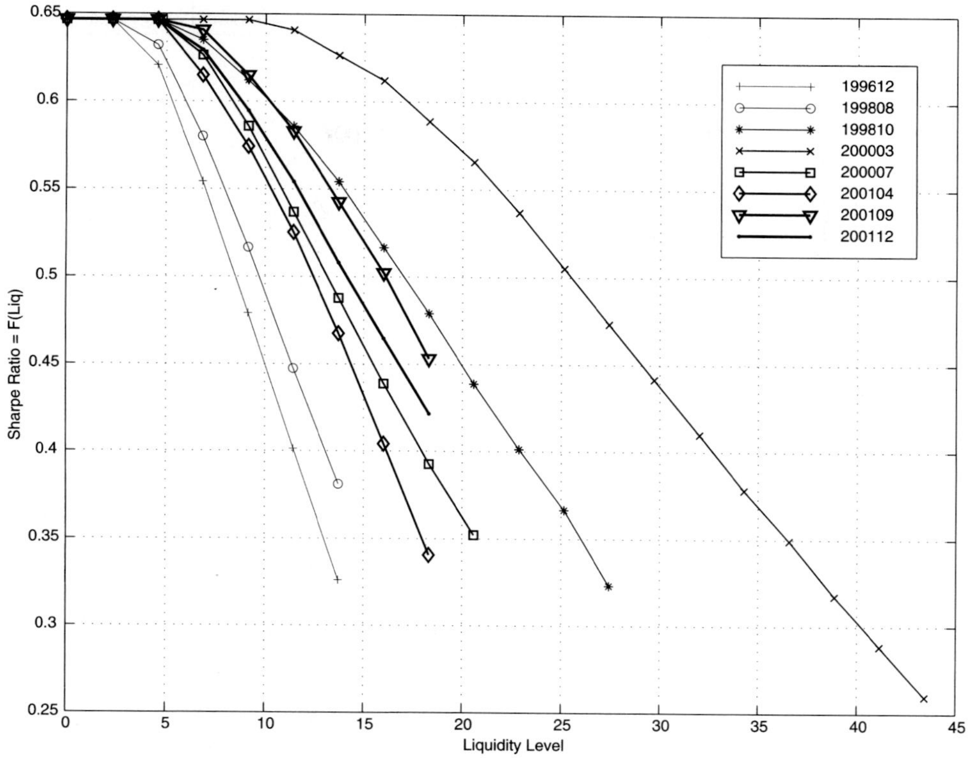

Figure 11 Sharpe-ratio trajectories of tangency portfolios of liquidity-constrained MVL-efficient frontiers for 50 randomly selected stocks (five from each of 10 market capitalization brackets), based on a monthly normalized turnover liquidity metric, as a function of the liquidity threshold, for the months of December 1996, August 1998, October 1998, March 2000, July 2000, April 2001, September 2001, and December 2001. Expected returns and covariances of the 50 individual securities are estimated with daily returns data from January 2, 1997 to December 31, 2001 and do not vary from month to month. Thicker lines represent trajectories from more recent months.

portfolio's risk. Up to $\lambda = 10$, the standard deviation declines faster than the expected return, leading to a rising Sharpe ratio curve. After reaching its peak at $\lambda = 10$, the Sharpe ratio begins to decline.

Once liquidity is allowed to enter the objective function, i.e., $\phi > 0$, the dynamics of the optimal portfolio become more complex. For expositional convenience, we focus our comments exclusively on the Sharpe ratio of the optimal portfolio. The interaction between the penalty for risk and the payoff for liquidity in (13) depends on the interaction between the cross-sectional distributions of liquidity and volatility in our sample. Typically, a security's liquidity metric and volatility are both correlated with market capitalization, e.g., large-cap stocks usually exhibit lower volatility and higher liquidity than smaller-cap counterparts. In this case, when a MVL objective function is optimized, the risk and liquidity components act in the same direction—an increment in either λ or ϕ, apart from differences in scale, has the same qualitative impact on the optimal portfolio's characteristics. On the other hand, if the correlations between the liquidity metric and volatility are weak, then the interactions between the second and

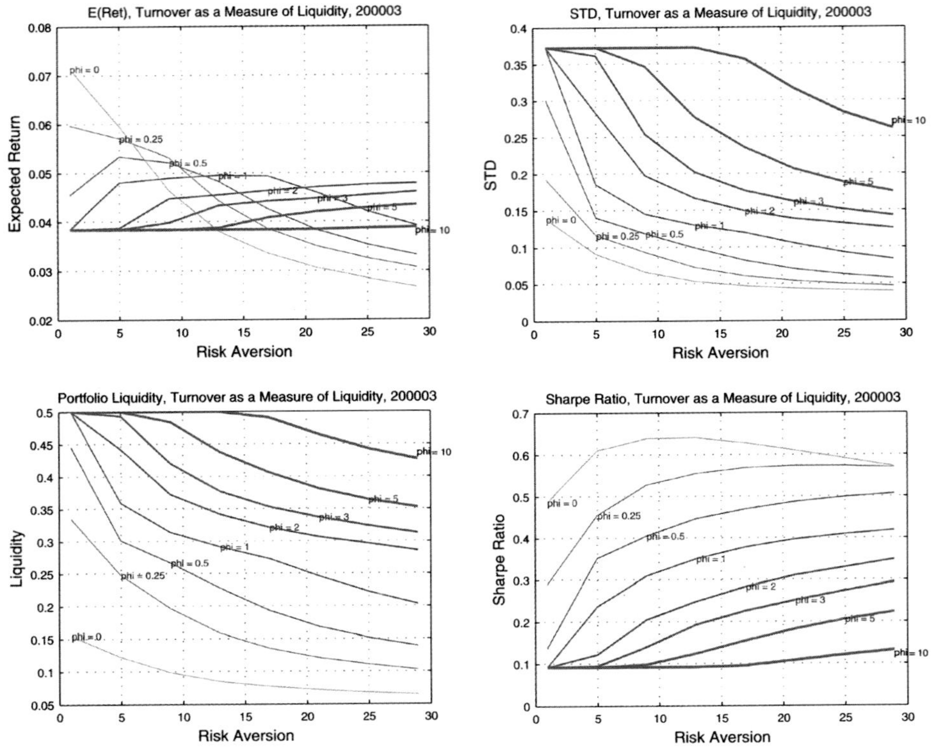

Figure 12 Properties of optimal MVL portfolios using a monthly normalized turnover liquidity metric for 50 randomly selected stocks (five from each of 10 market capitalization brackets), for the month of March 2000. Expected returns and covariances of the 50 individual securities are estimated with daily returns data from January 2, 1997 to December 31, 2001, and "phi" denotes the liquidity parameter where a value of 0.00 implies that liquidity is not included in the portfolio optimization problem.

third terms in the objective function (13) are more complicated. Figure 13 plots daily cross-sectional correlations between raw turnover and rolling 20-day return standard deviations for the sample of 50 stocks, and with the notable exception of the year 2000, the correlation between liquidity and volatility is weak, hence there are indeed three distinct components in optimizing (13): expected return, risk, and liquidity. This is confirmed in Figure 12 for cases where $\phi > 0$. The addition of liquidity in the mean–variance objective function results in lower Sharpe ratios for all values of λ, and ϕ, and risk aversion and liquidity act as countervailing forces in the objective function.

It should be emphasized that the specific interactions between λ and ϕ are quite sensitive to the liquidity metric used. For example, Figure 14 displays the same relations as in Figure 12 but using the bid/ask spread as the liquidity metric instead of turnover. A comparison of the two figures shows some significant differences in the dynamics of the Sharpe ratio for the MVL-optimal portfolio. With the bid/ask liquidity metric, the tightening of both risk aversion and liquidity thresholds shifts the optimal portfolio qualitatively in the same direction—towards larger-cap, less risky stocks. An increase in the liquidity preference parameter ϕ accelerates the migration of portfolio toward

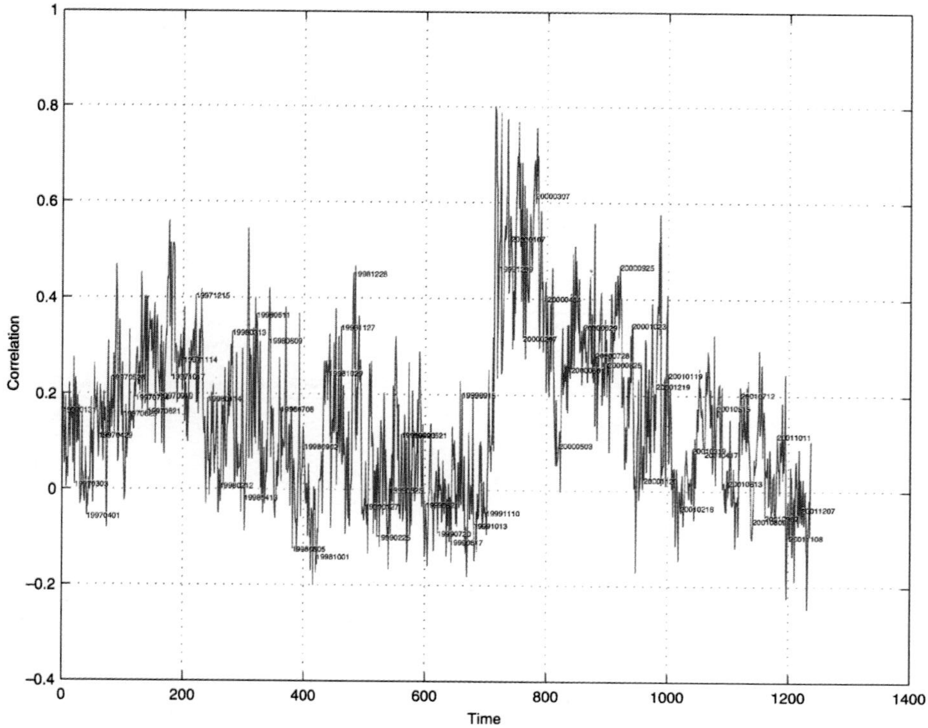

Figure 13 Daily cross-sectional correlations between raw turnover and rolling 20-day standard deviations for 50 randomly selected stocks (five from each of 10 market capitalization brackets) from January 2, 1997 to December 31, 2001.

larger-cap stocks driven by an increase in the risk aversion parameter, λ. This is due to the fact that during our sample period, the cross-sectional correlation between individual bid/ask spreads and volatilities is quite high and positive, and since liquidity is inversely proportional to bid/ask spread, the correlation between liquidity and volatility in this case is strong and negative.

5 Conclusions

In this paper, we have proposed several measures of liquidity for individual securities and their portfolios, and have developed the implications of these measures for standard mean–variance portfolio analysis. In particular, there are at least three ways to integrate liquidity into the investment process once a liquidity metric is defined—through liquidity filtering, liquidity constraints, and a direct optimization of a mean–variance–liquidity objective function. In a simple empirical example of 50 randomly selected securities, we have shown that in many cases, even the simplest liquidity-based portfolio optimization procedures can yield mean–variance-efficient portfolios that are considerably more liquid than their standard counterparts. More importantly, because liquidity varies so much over time, the mean–variance–liquidity landscape is a highly dynamic surface that contains pitfalls and opportunities, and which should be managed carefully and purposefully.

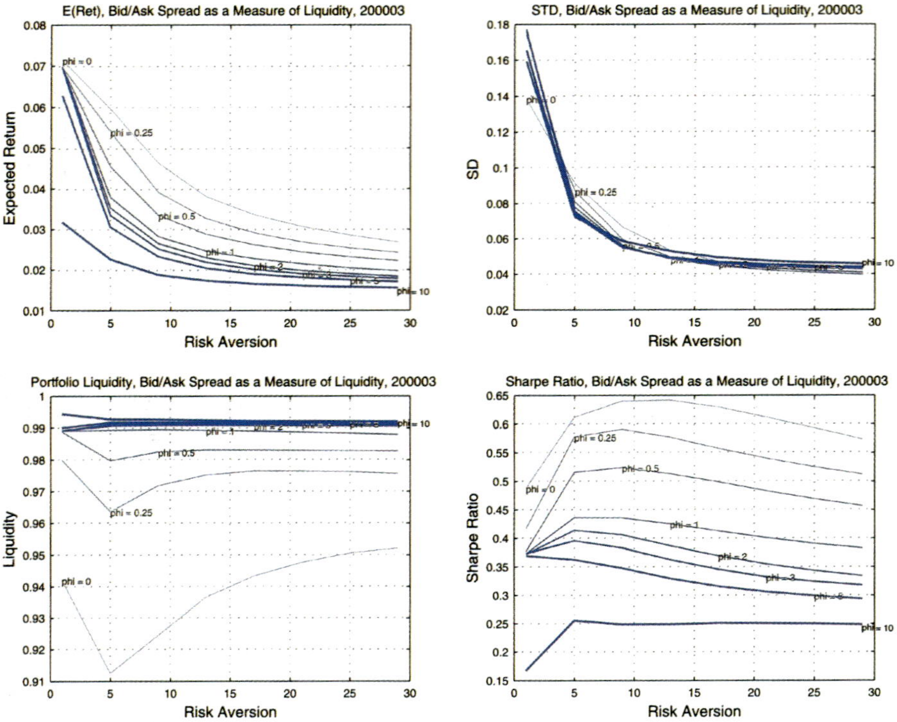

Figure 14 Properties of optimal MVL portfolios using a monthly normalized bid/ask spread liquidity metric for 50 randomly selected stocks (five from each of 10 market capitalization brackets), for the month of March 2000. Expected returns and covariances of the 50 individual securities are estimated with daily returns data from January 2, 1997 to December 31, 2001, and "phi" denotes the liquidity parameter where a value of 0.00 implies that liquidity is not included in the portfolio optimization problem.

Because the integration of liquidity directly into portfolio management processes has not yet become standard practice, many aspects of our analysis can be improved upon and extended. Our liquidity metrics are clearly simplistic and not based on any equilibrium considerations, and our definition of portfolio liquidity as the weighted average of individual securities' liquidity measures may not be the best definition in all contexts. Better methods of measuring liquidity will obviously lead to better MVL portfolios.[21] The dynamics of liquidity should also be modeled explicitly, in which case static mean–variance optimization may no longer be appropriate but should be replaced by dynamic optimization methods such as stochastic dynamic programming. Preferences for liquidity must be investigated in more detail—do such preferences exist, and if so, are they stable and how should they best be parametrized? Finally, we have ignored estimation error in the portfolio construction process, and just as sampling variation affects mean and covariance matrix estimators, liquidity estimators will also be subject to sampling variation and this may have significant impact on the empirical properties of MVL portfolios.[22]

We believe we have only begun to explore the many practical implications of liquidity for investment management, and our framework adds an important new dimension—literally as well as figuratively—to the toolkit of quantitative portfolio managers. In particular, with three dimensions to consider, portfolio management can no longer operate within a purely numerical paradigm, and three- and four-dimensional visualization techniques will become increasingly central to industrial applications of portfolio optimization. We plan to explore these issues in ongoing and future research, and hope to have provided sufficient "proof-of-concept" in this paper for the benefits of incorporating liquidity into the investment process.

Appendix A

In this appendix we provide Matlab sourcecode for our extension of Loeb's (1983) price impact function in A.I, and the details of our sample selection procedure in A.2.

A.1 Matlab Loeb Function `tloeb`

```
function tloeb
% the default value for the Loeb (1983)
spread/price cost b = 50;

% cap range

xi = [ 0.01 10 25 50 75 100 500 1000 1500 3000 ];

% block size range, in $1,000's

yi = [ 0.01 5 25 250 500 1000 2500 5000 10000 20000 ]

% original Loeb (1983) measure of liquidity
% (Table II)

Zi = [

17.3  17.3  27.3  43.8  NaN   NaN   NaN   NaN   NaN   NaN   ;
 8.9   8.9  12.0  23.8  33.4  NaN   NaN   NaN   NaN   NaN   ;
 5.0   5.0   7.6  18.8  25.9  30.0  NaN   NaN   NaN   NaN   ;
 4.3   4.3   5.8   9.6  16.9  25.4  31.5  NaN   NaN   NaN   ;
 2.8   2.8   3.9   5.9   8.1  11.5  15.7  25.7  NaN   NaN   ;
 1.8   1.8   2.1   3.2   4.4   5.6   7.9  11.0  16.2  NaN   ;
 1.9   1.9   2.0   3.1   4.0   5.6   7.7  10.4  14.3  20.0  ;
 1.9   1.9   1.9   2.7   3.3   4.6   6.2   8.9  13.6  18.1  ;
 1.1   1.1   1.2   1.3   1.7   2.1   2.8   4.1   5.9   8.0   ;
 1.1   1.1   1.2   1.3   1.7   2.1   2.8   4.1   5.9   8.0 ] ;
```

```
nx = size(xi,2); ny = size(yi,2);

% array of indices of last non-NaN points in Zi
matrix along mcap dimension nonnan = [ 4 4 5 6 7
8 9 ];

% deal with NaN's in zi matrix

% loop over rows
for i = 1: size(xi,2) -3

  % last non-nan point
  f = nonnan(i);
  for j=f+1:1:ny
    % Loeb cost based on simple linear extra-
    % polation starting from the end points
    zi(i,j) = zi(i,f)+(zi(i,f)-zi(f-1))*(yi(j)-
    yi(f))/(yi(f) - y(f-1));

    % cap the cost zi by b = 50% if cost >50%;
    if zi(i,j) > 50; zi(i,j) = b;
    end;

    % If trade size > 20% of market cap (not
    % T. Loeb's original 5% ), zi is still NaN
    if (yi(j)/1000) > 0.2*xi(i); zi(i,j) = NaN;
    end;
        end
    end
    zi

    % produce arrays acceptable by MATLAB for 3D
    % graphics
    for i = 1:ny
        for j = 1:nx
            x(i,j) = (xi(j));
            y(i,j) = (yi(i));
            z(i,j) = zi(j,i);
        end
    end
```

```
% determine max-min for interpolation
maxx = max(xi); minx = min(xi); maxy = max(yi);
miny = min(yi);

% the number of nodes in each direction
N = 40; dx = (maxx - minx)/N;
dy = (maxy - miny)/N;
% interpolated arrays

for i=1:N
    for j=1:N
      x1(i,j)=xi(1)+dx*j;
      y1(i,j)=yi(1)+dy+i;
    end
end

% plot extended Loeb function

mesh((x1), (y1), interp2(x, y, z, x1, y1,
'linear') ) view(30,50); colormap(jet); grid on;
xlabel('Cap [$1,000,000]', 'Fontsize', 8);
ylabel('Block [$1000]', 'Fontsize, 8)
zlabel('Spread/Price Cost [%]');
% title ('Loeb (1983) Total Spread/ Price Cost');

print -depsc p:\\msl\\tloeb.eps
```

A.2 Sampling Procedure

The process by which we selected our sample of 50 stocks and constructed our dataset for the empirical example consisted of the following five steps:

1. Using CRSP, we selected all ordinary common stocks having CRSP share code, SHRCD, equal to 11 or 10 for December 1996, the last pre-sample month, and for December 2001, the last in-sample month. ADRs, SBIs, units, certificates, closed-end funds and REITs were excluded. From these two sets of stocks, one for December 1996 and one for December 2001, we selected a common subset.
2. From this common subset we selected stocks with valid daily returns which have never been delisted during the in-sample period. For each stock, we calculated the initial market capitalization as of the last trading day, December 31, 1996, of the pre-sample period.

Table A.1 Data items extracted from CRSP Daily Master File.

Variable	Definition
CUSIP	CUSIP identifier
PERMNO	CRSP permanent number
PERMCO	CRSP permanent company number
TICKER	Exchange ticker symbol
COMNAM	Company name
SHRCD	Share code
SICCD	Standard industrial classification code
DATE	Trading date
BIDLO	Bid or low price
ASKHI	Ask or high price
PRC	Actual close (positive number) or the average between BIDLO and ASHKI (negative number)
VOL	Trading volume, units of one share
RET	Daily total return, including dividends
SHROUT	Number of shares outstanding, in thousands

3. We split the final subset of stocks into 10 capitalization categories, in millions US dollars (see Loeb, 1983):

$$0.1\ 10\ 25\ 50\ 75\ 100\ 500\ 1,000\ 1,500\ 3,000 \geq 3,000$$

   The filtering is concluded by random selection of five stocks from each capitalization category.
4. For each stock in our randomly selected portfolio, we downloaded the data items listed in Table A.1 from the daily CRSP database, and calculated the daily market capitalization, in thousands of dollars, by multiplying the absolute value of price, |PRC|, by number of shares outstanding, SHROUT, and daily turnover, TURN, by dividing the daily trading volume, VOL, by the current number of shares outstanding, SHROUT.
5. For each randomly selected stock, using the CRSP TICKER symbol as the key, we downloaded from the TAQ database the tick-by-tick BID and ASK prices, calculated tick-by-tick bid/ask spreads, averaged the spreads for each day, and combined them with the remaining CRSP data set. The TAQ data, which are used exclusively for bid/ask spread calculations, start in January 2000, while the CRSP data start in January 1997. Missing daily bid/ask spreads in the 2000–2001 period (this problem is particularly acute for small cap stocks) were backfilled with valid ex-post values. For example, if a valid bid/ask spread at t_1 is $s(t_1)$, and the bid/ask spreads at t_2 and t_3 are missing because there were no quotes in the TAQ database, then we assign $s(t_2) = s(t_3) = s(t_1)$.

Acknowledgments

Research support from the MIT Laboratory for Financial Engineering and Undergraduate Research Opportunities Program is gratefully acknowledged. We thank Simon Lee for excellent research assistance, and Gifford Fong, Svetlana Sussman, and a referee for helpful comments.

Notes

1 See, for example, Acharya and Pedersen (2002), Aiyagari and Gertler (1991), Atkinson and Wilmott (1995), Amihud and Mendelson (1986b), Bertsimas and Lo (1998), Boyle and Vorst (1992), Chordia, Roll and Subrahmanyam (2000, 2001a,b, 2002), Chordia, Subrahmanyam, and Anshuman (2001), Cohen *et al.* (1981), Constandnides (1986), Davis and Norman (1991), Dumas and Luciano (1991), Epps (1976), Garman and Ohlson (1981), Gromb and Vayanos (2002), Grossman and Laroque (1990), Grossman and Vila (1992), Heaton and Lucas (1994, 1995), Hodges and Neuberger (1989), Holmstrom and Tirole (2001), Huang (2002), Litzenberger and Rolfo (1984), Leland (1985), Liu and Longstaff (2000), Lo, Mamaysky, and Wang (2001), Magill and Constandnides (1976), Morton and Pliska (1995), Pastor and Stambaugh (2002), Sadka (2003), Shleifer and Vishny (1997), Tuckman and Vila (1992), Vayanos (1998), Vayanos and Vila (1999), and Willard and Dybvig (1999).

2 Of course, many studies have considered the practical significance of trading costs or "slippage" in investment management, e.g., Arnott and Wagner (1990), Bertsimas and Lo (1998), Bodurtha and Quinn (1990), Brinson, Hood, and Beebower (1986, 1991), Chan and Lakonishok (1993, 1995), Collins and Fabozzi (1991), Cuneo and Wagner (1975), Gammill and Pérold (1989), Hasbrouck and Schwartz (1988), Keim and Madhavan (1997), Leinweber (1993, 1994), Loeb (1983), Pérold (1988), Schwartz and Whitcomb (1988), Stoll (1993), Treynor (1981), Wagner and Banks (1992), Wagner and Edwards (1993), and the papers in Sherrerd (1993). None of these studies focuses squarely on the quantitative trade-off between expected return, risk, and liquidity. However, Michaud (1989) observes that standard mean–variance portfolio optimization does not take liquidity into account, and proposes liquidity constraints and quadratic penalty functions in a mean–variance framework in Michaud (1998, Chapter 12).

3 The third dimension of liquidity—time to completion of a purchase or sale—is obviously missing from this list, but only because of lack of data. With access to time-stamped orders of a large institutional trading desk, time-based measures of liquidity can easily be constructed as well.

4 See, for, example, Amihud and Mendelson (1986a,b), Glosten and Milgrom (1985), Lo, Mamaysky, and Wang (2001), Tiniç (1972), and Vayanos (1998).

5 Loeb's original matrix does not allow for a block sizes in excess of 5% of a stock's total market capitalization which, in our sample, would imply a maximum block size of $5\% \times \$2.84$ MM $=$ \$0.142 MM, a relatively small number. To relax this restriction, we extrapolate the total cost function to allow for block sizes of up to 20% of market capitalization, where the extrapolation is performed linearly by fixing the capitalization level and using the last two available data points along the block-size dimension. The maximum total cost is capped at 50%, an arbitrary large number. For example, for the \$0–10 MM capitalization sector (see Table II in Loeb, 1983) and block sizes of \$5,000, \$25,000 and \$250,000 the total spread/price costs are 17.3%, 27.3% and 43.8%, respectively. The cost at the next block size of \$500,000 is computed as:

$$\min[50\%, 43.8\% + (\$500,000 - \$250,000)(43.8\% - 27.3\%)/(\$50,000 - \$25,000)] = 50\%$$

[6] However, see Bertsimas and Lo (1998), Chan and Lakon-ishok (1993, 1995), Hausman, Lo, and MacKinlay (1992), Kraus and Stoll (1972), Lillo, Farmer, and Mantegna (2003), and Loeb (1983) for various approximations in a number of contexts.

[7] This literature is vast, and overlaps with the literature on financial asset-pricing models with transactions costs. Some of the more relevant examples include Amihud and Mendelson (1986b), Bagehot (1971), Constantinides (1986), Demsetz (1968), Gromb and Vayanos (2002), Lo, Mamaysky and Wang (2001), Tiniç (1972), Vayanos (1998), and Vayanos and Vila (1999). For a more complete list of citations, see the references contained in Lo, Mamaysky and Wang (2001).

[8] For expositional convenience, all of our tables and graphs use standard deviations in place of variances as risk measures. Nevertheless, we shall continue to refer to graphs of efficient frontiers as "mean–variance–liquidity efficient frontiers" despite the fact that standard deviation is the x-axis, not variance. We follow this convention because the objective function on which our efficient frontiers are based are mean–variance objective functions, and because "mean–standard deviation–liquidity" is simply too cumbersome a phrase to use more than once.

[9] See, for example, Michaud (1998, Chapter 12).

[10] For comparison, Table 1 also reports market capitalizations based on December 31, 2001 prices. From December 31, 1996 to December 31, 2001, the average portfolio market capitalization increased twofold, with mid-tier market-capitalization stocks—those in the 5th, 6th and 7th brackets—experiencing the biggest gains. The market capitalization of the top-tier stocks increased less dramatically. By the end of the sample, the original capitalization-based ranking was generally well preserved—the correlation between the 1996 and 2001 year-end market capitalizations was over 95%.

[11] Since 1,256 observations were used to calculate the correlation coefficients, the 95% confidence interval under the null hypothesis of zero correlation is $[-5.6\%, 5.6\%]$.

[12] For this 2-year sample, the 95% confidence interval under the null hypothesis of zero correlation is $[-8.9\%, 8.9\%]$.

[13] Results for the Loeb and bid/ask metrics are qualitatively identical to those for turnover, hence we omit them to conserve space. However, they are available upon request.

[14] Throughout this study, we assume a fixed value of 0.4308% per month for the riskless return R_f.

[15] These values may seem rather high, especially in the context of current market conditions. There are two explanations: (a) our sample period includes the tail end of the remarkable bull market of the 1990s, and contains some fairly spectacular high-flyers such as North Coast Energy (571% 5-year return from 1996 to 2001), Daktronics (914% 5-year return), and Green Mountain Coffee (875% 5-year return); (b) we are using a relatively small sample of 50 stocks, which is considerably less well-diversified than other well-known portfolios such as the S&P 500 or the Russell 2000, and the lack of diversification will tend to yield higher expected returns (especially given the small-cap component in our portfolio) and higher standard deviations.

[16] Recall that the only difference between the December 1996 and March 2000 portfolio inputs is the liquidity metrics for each stock; the estimated means and covariance matrix are the same for both months, i.e., the values obtained by applying (14) to the entire sample of daily returns from January 2, 1997 to December 31, 2001.

[17] Within each liquidity plane (planes that are parallel to ground level), portfolios to the north have higher expected return, and portfolios to the east have higher standard deviation.

[18] We refrain from computing MVL frontiers when the number of securities falls below 5.

[19] Recall that each of the liquidity metrics has been normalized to take on values strictly between 0 and 1, hence liquidity thresholds are comparable across metrics and are denominated in units of percent of the range of the original liquidity measure.

[20] In fact, this observation suggests that the Loeb function—as well as any other realistic measure of price impact—varies with market conditions, and such dependencies should be incorporated directly into the specification of the price impact function, i.e., through the inclusion of "state variables" that capture the salient features of the market environment at the time of the transactions. See Bertsimas and Lo (1998) and Bertsimas, Hummel, and Lo (2000) for examples of such specifications.

[21] See, for example, Chordia, Roll, and Subrahmanyam (2000, 2001, 2002), Getmansky, Lo, and Makarov (2003), Glosten and Harris (1988), Lillo, Farmer, and Mantegna (2003), Lo, Mamaysky, and Wang (2001), Pastor and Stambaugh (2002), and Sadka (2003) for alternate measures of liquidity.

[22] See, for example, Jobson and Korkie (1980, 1981), Klein and Bawa (1976, 1977), and Michaud (1998).

References

Acharya, V. and Pedersen, L. (2002). "Asset Pricing with Liquidity Risk." Unpublished working paper, London Business School.

Aiyagari, R. and Gertler, M. (1991). "Asset Returns with Transaction Costs and Uninsured Individual Risk." *Journal of Monetary Economics* **27**, 311–331.

Amihud, Y. and Mendelson, H. (1986a). "Asset Pricing and the Bid-Asked Spread." *Journal of Financial Economics* **17**, 223–249.

Amihud, Y. and Mendelson, H. (1986b). "Liquidity And Stock Returns." *Financial Analysts Journal* **42**, 43–48.

Arnott, R. and Wagner, W. (1990). "The Measurement And Control of Trading Costs." *Financial Analysts Journal* **46**, 73–80.

Atkinson, C. and Wilmott, P. (1995). "Portfolio Management with Transaction Costs: An Asymptotic Analysis of the Morton and Pliska Model." *Mathematical Finance*, 357–367.

Bagehot, W. (a.k.a. Jack Treynor), (1971). "The Only Game in Town." *Financial Analysts Journal* **22**, 12–14.

Bertsimas, D. and Lo, A. (1998). "Optimal Control of Execution Costs." *Journal of Financial Markets* **1**, 1–50.

Bertsimas, D., Hummel, P. and Lo, A. (2000). "Optimal Control of Execution Costs for Portfolios." *Computing in Science & Engineering* **1**, 40–53.

Bodurtha, S. and Quinn, T. (1990). "Does Patient Program Trading Really Pay?" *Financial Analysts Journal* **46**, 35–42.

Brinson, G., Hood, R. and Beebower, G. (1986). "Determinants of Portfolio Performance." *Financial Analysts Journal* **42**, 39–44.

Brinson, G., Singer, B. and Beebower, G. (1991). "Determinants of Portfolio Performance II: An Update." *Financial Analysts Journal* **47**, 40–48.

Chan, L. and Lakonishok, J. (1993). "Institutional Trades and Intra-Day Stock Price Behavior." *Journal of Financial Economics* **33**, 173–199.

Chan, L. and Lakonishok, J. (1995). "The Behavior of Stock Prices Around Institutional Trades." *Journal of Finance* **50**, 1147–1174.

Chordia, T., Roll, R. and Subrahmanyam, A. (2000). "Commonality in Liquidity." *Journal of Financial Economics* **56**, 3–28.

Chordia, T., Roll, R. and Subrahmanyam, A. (2001). "Market Liquidity and Trading Activity Source." *Journal of Finance* **56**, 501–530.

Chordia, T., Roll, R. and Subrahmanyam, A. (2002). "Order Imbalance, Liquidity, and Market Returns." *Journal of Financial Economics* **65**, 111–130.

Chordia, T., Subrahmanyam, A. and Anshuman, V. (2001). "Trading Activity and Expected Stock Returns." *Journal of Financial Economics* **59**, 3–32.

Cohen, K., Maier, S., Schwartz, R. and Whitcomb, D. (1981). "Transaction Costs, Order Placement Strategy and Existence of the Bid-Ask Spread." *Journal of Political Economy* **89**, 287–305.

Collins, B. and Fabozzi, F. (1991). "A Methodology for Measuring Transaction Costs." *Financial Analysts Journal* **47**, 27–36.

Constantinides, G. (1986). "Capital Market Equilibrium with Transaction Costs." *Journal of Political Economy* **94**, 842–862.

Cuneo, L. and Wagner, W. (1975). "Reducing the Cost of Stock Trading." *Financial Analysts Journal* **26**, 35–44.

Davis, M. and Norman, A. (1990). "Portfolio Selection with Transactions Costs." *Mathematics of Operations Research* **15**, 676–713.

Demsetz, H. (1968). "The Cost of Transacting." *Quarterly Journal of Economics* **82**, 35–53.

Dumas, B. and Luciano, E. (1991). "An Exact Solution to a Dynamic Portfolio Choice Problem under Transactions Costs." *Journal of Finance* **46**, 577–595.

Epps, T. (1976). "The Demand For Brokers' Services: The Relation Between Security Trading Volume And Transaction Cost." *Bell Journal of Economics* 7, 163–196.

Gammill, J. and Perold, A. (1989). "The Changing Character Of Stock Market Liquidity." *Journal of Portfolio Management* **15**, 13–18.

Garman, M. and Ohlson, J. (1981). "Valuation Of Risky Assets In Arbitrage-Free Economies With Transactions Costs." *Journal of Financial Economics* **9**, 271–280.

Getmansky, M., Lo, A. and Makarov, I. (2003). "Econometric Models of Serial Correlation and Illiquidity in Hedge Fund Returns." Unpublished working paper, MIT Sloan School of Management.

Glosten, L. and Harris, L. (1988). "Estimating the Components of the Bid/Ask Spread." *Journal of Financial Economics* **21**, 123–142.

Glosten, L. and Milgrom, P. (1985). "Bid, Ask, and Transaction Prices in a Specialist Market with Heterogeneously Informed Traders." *Journal of Financial Economics* **13**, 71–100.

Gromb, D. and Vayanos, D. (2002). "Equilibrium and Welfare in Markets with Financially Constrained Arbitrageurs." *Journal of Financial Economics* **66**, 361–407.

Grossman, S. and Laroque, G. (1990). "Asset Pricing and Optimal Portfolio Choice in the Presence of Illiquid Durable Consumption Goods." *Econometrica* **58**, 25–52.

Hasbrouck, J. and Schwartz, R. (1988). "Liquidity and Execution Costs in Equity Markets." *Journal of Portfolio Management* **14**, 10–16.

Hausman, J., Lo, A. and MacKinlay, C. (1992). "An Ordered Probit Analysis of Transaction Stock Prices." *Journal of Financial Economics* **31**, 319–379.

Heaton, J. and Lucas, D. (1996). "Evaluating the Effects of Incomplete Markets on Risk Sharing and Asset Pricing." *Journal of Political Economy* **104**, 443–487.

Holmstrom, B. and Tirole, J. (2001). "LAPM: A Liquidity-Based Asset Pricing Model." *Journal of Finance* 57, 1837–1867.

Huang, M. (forthcoming). "Liquidity Shocks and Equilibrium Liquidity Premia." *Journal of Economic Theory*.

Jobson, J. and Korkie, R. (1980). "Estimation for Markowitz Efficient Portfolios." *Journal of the American Statistical Association* 75, 544–554.

Jobson, J. and Korkie, R. (1981). "Performance Hypothesis Testing with the Sharpe and Treynor Measures." *Journal of Finance* **36**, 889–908.

Keim, D. and Madhavan, A. (1997). "Transactions Costs and Investment Style: An Inter-Exchange Analysis of Institutional Equity Trades." *Journal of Financial Economics* **46**, 265–292.

Klein, R. and Bawa, V. (1976). "The Effect of Estimation Risk on Optimal Portfolio Choice." *Journal of Financial Economics* **3**, 215–231.

Klein, R. and Bawa, V. (1977). "The Effect of Limited Information and Estimation Risk on Optimal Portfolio Diversification." *Journal of Financial Economics* **5**, 89–111.

Kraus, A. and Stoll, H. (1972). "Price Impacts of Block Trading on the New York Stock Exchange." *Journal of Finance* **27**, 569–588.

Leinweber, D. (1993). "Using Information From Trading in Trading and Portfolio Management." In Sherrerd, K. (ed.) *Execution Techniques, True Trading Costs, and the Microstructure of Markets.* Charlottesville, VA: Association for Investment Management and Research.

Leinweber, D. (1994). "Careful Structuring Reins In Transaction Costs." *Pensions and Investments,* July 25, 19.

Lillo, F., Farmer, D. and Mantegna, R. (2003). "Master Curve for Price-Impact Function." *Nature* **421**, 129–130.

Liu, J. and Longstaff, F. (2000). "Losing Money on Arbitrages: Optimal Dynamic Portfolio Choice in Markets with Arbitrage Opportunities." Unpublished working paper, Anderson Graduate School of Management, UCLA.

Lo, A., Mamaysky, H. and Wang, J. (2001). "Asset Prices and Trading Volume Under Fixed Transactions Costs." NBER Working Paper No. W8311.

Lo, A. and Wang, J. (2000). "Trading Volume: Definitions, Data Analysis, and Implications of Portfolio Theory." *Review of Financial Studies* **13**, 257–300.

Loeb, T. (1983). "Trading Cost: The Critical Link Between Investment Information and Results." *Financial Analysts Journal* **39**, 39–44.

Michaud, R. (1989). "The Markowitz Optimization Enigma: Is 'Optimized' Optimal?" *Financial Analysts Journal* **45**, 31–42.

Michaud, R. (1998). *Efficient Asset Management: A Practical Guide to Stock Portfolio Optimization and Asset Allocation.* Boston, MA: Harvard Business School Press.

Morton, A. and Pliska, S. (1995). "Optimal Portfolio Management with Fixed Transaction Costs." *Mathematical Finance* **5**, 337–356.

Pastor, L. and Stambaugh, R. (forthcoming). "Liquidity Risk and Expected Stock Returns." *Journal of Political Economy.*

Perold, A. (1988). "The Implementation Shortfall: Paper Versus Reality." *Journal of Portfolio Management* **14**, 4–9.

Sadka, R. (2003). "Momentum, Liquidity Risk, and Limits to Arbitrage." Unpublished working paper, Kellogg Graduate School of Management, Northwestern University.

Schwartz, R. and Whitcomb, D. (1988). "Transaction Costs and Institutional Investor Trading Strategies." In: *Monograph Series in Finance and Economics 1988–2/3.* New York: Salomon Brothers Center for the Study of Financial Institutions, New York University.

Sherrerd, K., ed. (1993). *Execution Techniques, True Trading Costs, and the Microstructure of Markets.* Charlottesville, VA: Association for Investment Management and Research.

Shleifer, A. and Vishny, R. (1997). "The Limits of Arbitrage." *Journal of Finance* **52**, 35–55.

Stoll, H. (1993). *Equity Trading Costs.* Charlottesville, VA: Association for Investment Management and Research.

Tiniç, S. (1972). "The Economics of Liquidity Services." *Quarterly Journal of Economics* **86**, 79–93.

Tuckman, B. and Vila, J. (1992). "Arbitrage With Holding Costs: A Utility-Based Approach." *Journal of Finance* **47**, 1283–1302.

Vayanos, D. (1998). "Transaction Costs and Asset Prices: A Dynamic Equilibrium Model." *Review of Financial Studies* **11**, 1–58.

Vayanos, D. and Vila, J. (1999). "Equilibrium Interest Rate and Liquidity Premium With Transaction Costs." *Econometric Theory* **13**, 509–539.

Wagner, W. (1993). "Defining and Measuring Trading Costs." In: Sherrerd, K. (ed.) *Execution Techniques, True Trading Costs, and the Microstructure of Markets.* Charlottesville, VA: Association for Investment Management and Research.

Wagner, W. and Banks, M. (1992). "Increasing Portfolio Effectiveness Via Transaction Cost Management." *Journal of Portfolio Management* **19**, 6–11.

Wagner, W. and Edwards, M. (1993). "Best Execution." *Financial Analysts Journal* **49**, 65–71.

Willard, G. and Dybvig, P. (1999). "Empty Promises and Arbitrage." *Review of Financial Studies* **12**, 807–834.

Journal Of Investment Management
Vol. 1, No. 3 (2003), pp. 36–47

TIME DIVERSIFICATION

Jack L. Treynor [a]

To maintain constant dollar risk, an investor concerned with his terminal wealth must sell when the stock market rises and buy when it falls. Although an asset with constant dollar risk doesn't exist in nature, it can be approximated with actual investment positions.

Many investors are primarily concerned with their wealth at the end of their careers. Yet most of our theory is concerned with the current year's investment choices. How does each year's investment result affect the investor's terminal wealth? How do the gains and losses from the early years interact with the gains and losses from the later years? In particular, do they add or multiply?

1 A Parable

Suppose you personally had the following experience:

At the beginning of a 50-year investment career, you borrowed \$1.00 and invested it. Fifty years later, you pay off the loan. Assume the riskless rate of return is zero.

Over 50 years, the borrowed dollar appreciated to \$117.39. So the accounting at the end of your career is

Gross wealth	\$117.39
Pay of loan	\$1.00
Net wealth	\$116.39

Now, suppose that instead of borrowing, you received a \$1.00 bequest from your late, lamented Aunt Matilda. Then, you could account for the terminal impact of the bequest as follows:

Net wealth with own dollar	\$117.39
Net wealth with borrowed dollar	\$116.39
Terminal impact of inheritance	\$1.00

If you took the same dollar investment risk with or without the bequest, your terminal wealth differed by the original dollar, appreciated at the riskless rate of zero. Was the dollar worth \$117.39 50 years later? Or merely \$1? If the latter, then the remaining \$116.39 was the reward for taking 50 years of risk.

[a]Treynor Capital Management, Inc., Palos Verdes Estates, California, USA.

As the parable suggests, it is not obvious how their wealth and risk-taking interact to determine the investors' wealth at retirement.

Let

$$
\begin{aligned}
u &= \text{market's rate of return} \\
v &= \text{investor's rate of return} \\
r &= \text{riskless rate} \\
h &= \text{dollars currently invested} \\
w &= \text{initial wealth} \\
\beta &= \text{level of relative (systematic) risk} \\
h\beta &= \text{level of dollar (systematic) risk}
\end{aligned}
$$

If u and v are rates of return, then $u - r$ and $v - r$ are rates of *excess* return—rates of return to risk taking. For a perfectly diversified asset, beta (β) is of course the ratio of its excess return to the market's excess return. In other words

$$\beta = \frac{v - r}{u - r}$$

Transposing, we have the so-called "market model":

$$
\begin{aligned}
v - r &= \beta(u - r) \\
v &= \beta(u - r) + r
\end{aligned}
$$

The dollar gain or loss to an investor who invests an amount h in the risky asset is

$$hv = h\beta(u - r) + hr$$

If he had wealth w, then his dollar investment in the riskless asset was

$$w - h$$

for a riskless gain of

$$r(w - h)$$

and a total dollar gain/loss of

$$h\beta(u - r) + hr + wr - hr = h\beta(u - r) + wr$$

We see that the investor's dollar gain or loss consists of two terms: one that does not depend on his risk and one that does not depend on his wealth.

2 The Buy-and-Hold Investor

Many finance scholars (Ibbotson-Sinquefield; Cornell; Dimson, Marsh and Staunton) believe the risk in the US stock market's rate of return is roughly stationary across time.

At the end of this paper, we offer some evidence. But of course if the risk in rate of return is stationary, then the dollar risk is proportional to the market level.

Now consider a buy-and-hold investor, who invests his/her wealth in the stock market and then lets it ride as the market level fluctuates: he/she will experience constant relative risk. But this means that the *dollar* risk—the risk of his/her dollar gain or loss from the market's excess return—will fluctuate with his/her wealth.

Buy-and-hold investors do not lever. If they did, they would be constantly buying and selling in order to offset the effects of market fluctuations on their desired leverage. But when the market level fluctuates, the beta of a diversified asset does not change. So, for buy-and-hold investors, the only thing that changes is the value of their portfolio. Over a short time period (a year, say) the market model holds: investors get the riskless return on their current wealth, plus a risky excess return equal to their constant beta times their current wealth times the excess return on the market. Restating the model in terms of the investor's wealth at times t and $t-1$ we have

$$W_t - W_{t-1} = h_t\beta_t(u_t - r) + rW_{t-1}$$

$$W_t = h_t\beta_t(u_t - r) + (1 + r)W_{t-1}$$

Under constant relative risk, each period's exposure to stock market risk is proportional to that period's beginning wealth. We then have

$$W_t = W_{t-1}\beta(u_t - r) + (1 + r)W_{t-1}$$

$$W_t = W_{t-1}[\beta(u_t - r) + (1 + r)]$$

Letting

$$q_t = \beta(u_t - r) + (1 + r)$$

we have

$$W_t = W_{t-1q_t}, \quad W_{t-1} = W_{t-2q_{t-1}}$$

$$W_t = q_t q_{t-1} W_{t-2}, \quad W_T = q_T q_{T-1} \cdots q_1 W_0$$

Under buy-and-hold investing, the growth factors for the individual years multiply. So a bad year—a 40% loss, say, in any one year—means a 40% loss in terminal wealth.

When the market level is high investors, being richer, feel more able to bear the higher dollar risk. So, they may feel comfortable focusing on relative risk. But this special case tends to obscure the more general truth that terminal wealth depends on the dollar gains and losses in the individual years of the investor's career.

3 Time Diversification

We had for the general case

$$W_t - W_{t-1} = h_t\beta_t(u_t - r) + rW_{t-1}$$

Gains or losses from past risk-taking affect this year's beginning wealth. But it appreciates at the riskless rate. This year's reward to risk depends only on this year's risk.

Let the dollar gain or loss from risk taking in year t be

$$z_t = h_t\beta_t(u_t - r)$$

Then, the investor's wealth W_T satisfies

$$\begin{aligned} W_t - W_{t-1} &= z_t + rW_{t-1} \\ W_t &= z_t + (1+r)W_{t-1} \\ W_{t-1} &= z_{t-1} + (1+r)W_{t-2} \\ &\vdots \\ W_1 &= z_1 + (1+r)W_0 \end{aligned}$$

The terminal wealth W_T equals

$$z_T + (1+r)z_{T-1} + (1+r)^2 z_{T-2} + \cdots + (1+r)^T W_0$$

Let Z_t be the gain or loss in year t on investing \$1.00 in the stock market. Then, we have

$$z_t = h_t\beta_t Z_t$$

Unless he plans to market time, the investor will want each of the individual years to have the same potential impact on his terminal wealth "portfolio." Optimal balance requires

$$W_T - W_0(1+r)^T = \sum_0^T (1+r)^{T-t} h_t\beta_t Z_t = \sum_0^T Z_t$$

In order to have the same dollar impact on terminal wealth, each year's Z must have the same weight. But, unless the riskless rate of return r is zero, the terminal impact of one year's gain or loss depends on the time lag separating it from the terminal year. In order for each of the Z_t, with presumably equal risks, to have the same potential impact on the risky portion of the investor's terminal wealth (the expression on right-hand side), the current-dollar risk $h_i B_t$ must vary enough over time to offset this effect. So, we have

$$h_i\beta_t = \frac{1}{(1+r)^{T-t}} = (1+r)^{t-T}$$

Note that, if the effective riskless rate is positive, the investor's dollar risk $h_t\beta_t$ should actually increase as he ages.[1]

We have seen that for the buy-and-hold investor there is no such thing as time diversification. But, if investors make whatever trades are necessary to sever next year's bet from last year's outcome, then, their gains and losses from each individual year add (algebraically) rather than multiply. Impacts from the individual years on their terminal wealth are

1. cross sectionally diversified, so that all their risk bearing is fully compensated (under the CAPM);
2. mutually uncorrelated.

Unless investors are rash enough to predict that the prospects for next year are different from the prospects for last year, they should be making roughly the same dollar bet on both years. In order to do so, however, they will need to sell every time the market rises and buy every time it falls. They will need to do a lot of buying and selling.

On the one hand, the potential for time diversification is there, even if the buy-and-hold investor cannot realize it. On the other, the cost of trading back to a constant level of dollar risk every time the stock market rises or falls may be daunting. Is this why hardly anyone has tried time diversification?

4 Risk and Reward

Consider one year's rate of return on the US stock market. It has a certain distribution, with a certain standard deviation and a certain mean. Even if that distribution is indeed roughly stationary across time, we can measure only the actual rates of return for past years. The investors' probability of terminal loss—of arriving at the end of their career with less wealth than they started out with—depends on both the market risk and the market premium, the expected reward for taking this risk. Because its error can be reduced by subdividing the time sample more finely, estimating the standard deviation is not a problem. Dimson and his co-authors of *The Millenium Book*[2] estimate real annual rates of return on the market at 20.3% and 20.1% for the US and UK, respectively.

But sample error is a potential problem for estimates of the mean. Take the authors' 100 year sample: the standard deviation of the sample mean is

$$\frac{0.20}{\sqrt{100}} = \frac{0.20}{10} = 0.02$$

The Central Limit Theorem applies to the dispersion of means of randomly drawn samples. There is roughly one chance in three that when a normally distributed sample mean is 0.06 (6%), the true universe mean is less than 0.04 or more than 0.08. Although they can benefit greatly from reflecting on Dimson's numbers, we think investors have to make their own judgment about the market premium. Accordingly, we include in Table 1 a range of market premiums, as well as a range of possible career lengths.

5 Terminal Dollars

The terminal impact of the dollar gains and losses of particular years depends on the riskless interest rate. Unless investors' riskless rates are zero, a current dollar corresponds to a different number of terminal dollars, depending on their age. But if they are time diversifying, then they want their potential gains and losses at different ages to have the same terminal impact. So it is useful for them to measure their current risk in terms of what it represents for their terminal wealth—to measure their current risk in terminal dollars. Then, they can time diversify by maintaining a fixed number of "terminal dollars" worth of current risk. In Table 1, for example, the expected gains and associated risks are expressed in terms of one dollar of terminal risk.

Table 1 Terminal reward versus terminal risk.
Expected dollar gain over career for a lifetime risk equivalent to one "terminal" dollar.

	Market premium per year			
Career length	0.04	0.05	0.06	0.07
16	0.64	0.80	0.96	1.12
25	1.00	1.25	1.50	1.75
36	1.44	1.80	2.16	2.52
49	1.96	2.45	2.94	3.43
64	2.56	3.20	3.84	4.48
	Standard deviation of terminal wealth			
Career length	0.04	0.05	0.06	0.07
16	0.80	0.80	0.80	0.80
25	1.00	1.00	1.00	1.00
36	1.20	1.20	1.20	1.20
49	1.40	1.40	1.40	1.40
64	1.60	1.60	1.60	1.60
	Expected career gain/standard deviation of terminal risk			
Career length	0.04	0.05	0.06	0.07
16	0.80	1.00	1.20	1.40
25	1.00	1.25	1.50	1.75
36	1.20	1.50	1.80	2.10
49	1.40	1.75	2.10	2.45
64	1.60	2.00	2.40	2.80

The first two panels in Table 1 sum up market premium and market risk across investment careers varying from 16 to 64 years. Then, the third panel computes ratios of terminal reward to terminal risk. This is done for a range of assumptions about the hard-to-measure market premium.

The risk that investors will be worse off at the end of their career for having taken stock market risk depends on this ratio. If terminal risks are normally distributed, for example, that probability is 0.0036—three chances in 1000—for the most favorable case (a 64 year career length and a 7% risk premium).

Dimson estimates the real riskless rate at 1.2% per annum for the century 1900–2000. It is curious that this number is in the range of what many mutual funds charge shareholders. The effective rate for the time-diversifying investor should also allow for trading costs and taxes. But we defer further discussion until we get to inflation.

6 Constant Dollar Risk

Is there such a thing as a financial asset with constant dollar risk? Such an asset would permit the investor who owned it to achieve time diversification without trading.

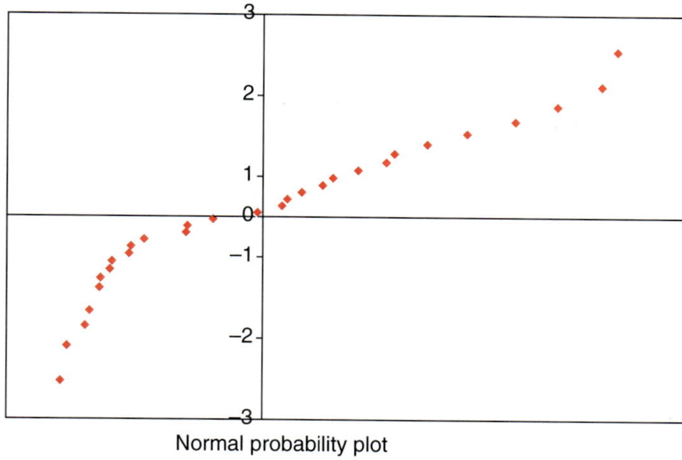

Figure 1 Rate of return on US market 1971–2000.

All commercial risk measurement services focus on *relative* risk—surprise in an asset's value, divided by its beginning value. The only justification for such commercial measures is that the probability distribution of the ratio is stationary (see Figure 1). But, then, dispersion of the asset's dollar risk—surprise in its dollar value—fluctuates with fluctuations in the asset's value.

These comments apply to both individual common stocks and portfolios, including portfolios intended to proxy the value of the whole stock market. Let the stock market level—the value of the market portfolio—be x and the value of an asset with constant dollar risk be y, and let $\mathrm{d}x$ and $\mathrm{d}y$ represent dollar surprise in x and y, respectively. If both assets are completely diversified, then, the market level x determines the value of y. Let the relation between the two values be

$$y = f(x)$$

We ask: What functional dependence of y on x translates the constant relative risk of x into the desired constant dollar risk of y?

When the functional relation between y and x is such that, for all market levels, we have

$$\mathrm{d}y = \frac{\mathrm{d}x}{x}$$

The right-hand side is of course the rate of return on the market. As noted, many finance scholars believe its risk is stationary. The left-hand side and the righthand side being equal, they will necessarily have the same probability distribution. In particular, if the right-hand side—the relative return on the stock market—is stationary across time, the left-hand side will also be stationary. But, whereas the right-hand side is the *relative* change in x—$\mathrm{d}x$ divided by the level x—the left-hand side $\mathrm{d}y$ is the *dollar* change in y. So if, as the market level x fluctuates, its relative risk is truly stationary, then the dollar risk in y is also stationary.

If we take indefinite integrals of both sides, we have

$$y = \ln x + \ln k$$

where $\ln k$ is a constant of integration, or

$$y = \ln kx$$

The asset with constant dollar risk is the asset whose value varies with the logarithm of the market level.

7 Inflation

We do not have the option of investing in the real market level. The values of the market and our log approximation are nominal values. But the risk we want to maintain constant over time—as the price level changes—is the *real* risk. If, as we have argued, the risk in nominal market return is stationary, then the risk of nominal dollar gains and losses in the log portfolio is also stationary. But this means that if, for example, the price level is rising, then the risk of real dollar gains and losses is falling.

Let x be the nominal market level and y be the nominal value of a portfolio that varies with the logarithm of the market level, and let the respective real values be x' and y', where the price level is p. We have

$$x' = \frac{x}{p}, \quad y' = \frac{y}{p}$$

For investment surprises we have

$$\mathrm{d}x' = \frac{\mathrm{d}x}{p}, \quad \mathrm{d}y' = \frac{\mathrm{d}y}{p}$$

The logarithmic portfolio is defined by a relation between nominals

$$\mathrm{d}y = \frac{\mathrm{d}x}{x}$$

Substituting, we have

$$p\,\mathrm{d}y' = \frac{p\,\mathrm{d}x'}{px'} = \frac{\mathrm{d}x'}{x'}$$

We see that, if surprise in the rate of return on the real market level is stationary, surprise in the nominal rate of return will also be stationary.[3] But if surprise in the nominal value of the logarithmic portfolio is stationary, surprise in its real value

$$\mathrm{d}y' = \frac{\mathrm{d}y}{p}$$

will not be. This means that if, for example, the price level is rising over the investors' career, the real risk in their logarithmic portfolio is falling.

Consider, first, the case where the real riskless rate of interest is zero. To offset the effect of inflation, investment positions in recent years in the investor's career should be rescaled relative to early years, with the rescaling from year to year equaling that year's inflation rate.

Then, consider the case where inflation is not a problem but the riskless interest rate is positive rather than zero. Then, investment positions in recent years should be rescaled relative to early years, with the rescaling from year to year being equal to the riskless interest rate.

We see that inflation causes the late nominal gain/loss to have less impact than an early gain/loss and the same is true for the real riskless rate. On the other hand, management fees, trading costs and taxes cause an early gain/loss to have less impact on terminal wealth than a late gain/loss. So, their annual rate of attrition subtracts from the sum of the real rate and the inflation rate—i.e., from the nominal interest rate. If the gain from trading just offsets management fees and the portfolio is not subject to taxes, the terminal impact of a current dollar of nominal gain or less will appreciate at the nominal interest rate.

8 An Approximation

The logarithmic asset is probably not available in today's security markets. But it can readily be approximated using assets that are. Consider the following Taylor series expansion of the logarithmic function, where a is greater than zero:

$$\ln\frac{x}{a} = \left(\frac{x-a}{a}\right) - \frac{1}{2}\left(\frac{x-a}{a}\right)^2 + \frac{1}{3}\left(\frac{x-a}{a}\right)^3 - \cdots$$

Although the accuracy of the approximation increases with the number of terms retained in the series,[4] we retain only the first two. Expanding these terms we have

$$\ln\left(\frac{x}{a}\right) \approx 2\left(\frac{x}{a}\right) - \frac{1}{2}\left(\frac{x}{a}\right)^2 - \frac{3}{2}$$

The investor who seeks time diversification is actually concerned with the corresponding risks. How well does the risk of the right-hand side approximate the risk of the left-hand side? The dollar risk on both sides depends on a product. One factor in the product is the rate of change with respect to the market level x. We have for the respective sides

$$\frac{\mathrm{d}}{\mathrm{d}x}\ln\left(\frac{x}{a}\right) = \frac{1}{a}\left(\frac{1}{x/a}\right) = \frac{1}{x} \approx \frac{1}{a}\left(2 - \frac{x}{a}\right)$$

The other factor in both products is the dollar risk in x. But, if $\mathrm{d}x/x$ is stationary, then, the dollar risk in x is proportional to the (known, non-risky) value of x.

If we invest in the approximation portfolio when x equals a, then, the above rate of change is $1/a$ for both the logarithmic portfolio and the approximation. But the risk in the approximation drifts away from the log portfolio as the market level x moves away from a.

9 The Role of Beta

We have noted that beta is a measure of how much an asset's value changes when the general market level changes—that, specifically, it is the ratio of two rates of excess return. Define x as the market level, y as the (fully diversified) asset's value and level of relative risk by the Greek letter β. Then, we have

$$\frac{\mathrm{d}y/y}{\mathrm{d}x/x} = \beta$$

$$\frac{\mathrm{d}y}{y} = \beta\frac{\mathrm{d}x}{x}$$

Taking the indefinite integral, we have

$$\ln y = \beta \ln x + \ln k$$

where $\ln k$ is a constant of integration. Taking antilogs we have

$$y = kx^{\beta}$$

We see that a diversified asset's value is linked to the market level by a power that equals its beta. Our truncated Taylor series approximation to the logarithmic function of the market level contains two powers of the market level x. Evidently, the terms containing these powers correspond to investment positions in diversified assets with betas of 1 and 2.

10 Accuracy of the Approximation

How bad are the errors in the approximation portfolio? Let

$$a = \text{beginning market level}$$

$$x = \text{market level at the end of the year}$$

$$\mathrm{d}x = \text{change in market level}$$

$$\sigma_{\mathrm{d}x} = \text{standard deviation of change}$$

$$y = \text{value of approximation portfolio}$$

$$\mathrm{d}y = \text{change in value of approximation}$$

$$\sigma_{\mathrm{d}y} = \text{standard deviation of change}$$

As noted, its dollar risk is the product of its rate of change with respect to the market and the dollar risk in the market. The first column in Table 2 displays a range of possible ratios of the ending market level x to the beginning market level a. The second column shows the resulting new market levels. The third column shows the standard deviation of the market's dollar risk for the following year—assuming its relative risk, the standard deviation of its rate of return, is still 20%.

The fourth column shows the rate of change of the approximation portfolio with respect to change in the stock market level. The fifth column is the product of the third

Table 2 Approximation errors.

x/a	x	σ_{dx}	dx/dy	σ_{dy}	% Error
1.30	1.30a	0.26a	0.70/a	0.1820	9.00
1.25	1.25a	0.25a	0.75/a	0.1875	6.25
1.20	1.20a	0.24a	0.80/a	0.1920	4.00
1.15	1.15a	0.23a	0.85/a	0.1955	2.25
1.10	1.10a	0.22a	0.90/a	0.1980	1.00
1.05	1.05a	0.21a	0.95/a	0.1995	0.25
1.00	1.00a	0.20a	1.00/a	0.2000	0.00
0.95	0.95a	0.19a	1.05/a	0.1995	0.25
0.90	0.90a	0.18a	1.10/a	0.1980	1.00
0.85	0.85a	0.17a	1.15/a	0.1955	2.25
0.80	0.80a	0.16a	1.20/a	0.1920	4.00
0.75	0.74a	0.15a	1.25/a	0.1875	6.25
0.70	0.70a	0.14a	1.30/a	0.1820	9.00

and fourth columns. Because the third column measures dollar risk in the market level, and the fourth column measures its rate of change with respect to that level, the fifth column measures dollar risk in the approximation portfolio.

The dollar risk in the ideal, logarithmic portfolio is 20% of the initial market level a, no matter what the subsequent change in market level. But the approximation is imperfect. The fifth column shows how its dollar risk drifts progressively farther from the correct, constant value as the new market level x moves away from the beginning level a. (It may be worth noting, however, that the dollar risk of the approximation portfolio is always less than or equal to the correct value.) The sixth column expresses the errors as percentages of the correct dollar risk.

Table 2 shows that a 20% move up or down in the market level changes the dollar risk in the approximation portfolio by only 4%. To trade back to constant dollar risk every time their portfolio changed 4%, conventional investors would have to trade

$$\left(\frac{0.20}{0.04}\right)^2 = 5^2 = 25$$

that is, 25 times as often. (If the dispersion of random fluctuations over a time interval varies with the square root of its length, the length of the time interval varies with the square of the stipulated dispersion.) Is this why conventional investors do not attempt to time diversify?

11 Rebalancing

We have seen that, when the market has moved up or down one standard deviation, or 20%, the new standard deviation for the approximation portfolio is no longer 20% of the original dollar investment, but merely 18.2%. (Roughly one year in three, the market moves more than 20%.) When the market level x moves away from the "beginning" level a, two things happen:

1. the approximation breaks down as the risky positions' 4 : 1 ratio breaks down;
2. the scale, or magnitude, of net risk moves away from beginning net risk.

There are many combinations of the two risky positions that will satisfy the 4 : 1 condition and, hence, restore the logarithmic character of the portfolio. Also, there are many combinations that will restore the original net risk. But one, and only one, combination of the two positions can satisfy both conditions. If the investor changes the "beginning" market level a in this ratio to the current market level x, the ratio reverts to its original value of 1. But when the values of the risky positions were based on a ratio value of 1, they

1. were in the accurate 4 : 1 ratio; and
2. had the desired level of net dollar risk that the investors wanted to maintain over their lifetime.

What the new value of a does not do is retain the same net investment in the two risky positions they had before we changed the ratio back to 1. This is where the third, constant, "riskless" term in the Taylor series formula comes in: when we are making the trades in the risky assets dictated by the change in the ratio, these trades free up or absorb cash, which then flows to or from the third, riskless, position. (Obviously, changes in the value of the riskless position do not change the portfolio's risk[5] so if, after these trades, the risky positions have the correct risk, so has the portfolio.)

In Table 3, the beginning market level is arbitrarily set at 1000. Then, the long position is

$$2(1000) = 2000$$

and the short position is

$$\tfrac{1}{2}(1000) = 500$$

So, the net value of the two risky positions (the "risky equity") is then

$$2000 - 500 = 1500$$

Each rebalancing returns the risky equity to 1500. But offsetting transfers to or from the riskless asset preserve the investor's total equity.

Table 3 shows how the approximation portfolio would have functioned using actual US stock market data for end-of-year levels from 1977 to 2000. Although, given the limited data, rebalancings could not be triggered by daily market closes, there were 11 rebalancings during this period.

Table 3 devotes three states of calculation (separated by semicolons in the third column) to each year (except 1978). For the current value of a, the first type calculates the ratios x/a and $(x/a)^2$. The second type applies the coefficients in the approximation formula to the respective ratios, and then multiplies all three terms in the formula by 1000. (For example, the initial value of the riskless term becomes -1500.) The third stage calculates the new risky equity, and the change since the last rebalancing.

Rebalancing makes the third stage of calculation more complicated. Since each rebalancing wipes out the difference between the current risky equity and the original

Table 3 Calculations for approximation portfolio 1977–2000 (see text).

Year	US mkt index	
1977	169	
1979	179	$179/169 = 1.0592, 1.0592^2 = 1.1218; 2(1059) - 1/2(1122); 2118 - 561 = 1557; 1557 - 1500 = 57$
1980	210	$210/169 = 1.243, 1.243^2 = 1.544; 2(1243) - 1/2(1544); 2486 - 772 = 1714, 1714 - 1500 = 214$
1981	225	$225/210 = 1.0714, 1.0714^2 = 1.1479; 2(1071) - 1/2(1148); 2142 - 574 = 1568, 1568 + 214 - 1500 = 282$
1982	208	$208/210 = 0.990, 0.990^2 = 0.9810; 2(990) - 1/2(981); 1980 - 491 = 1489, 1489 + 214 - 1500 = 203$
1983	281	$281/210 = 1.3381, 1.3381^2 = 1.7905; 2(1338) - 1/2(1790) = 2676 - 895 = 1781; 1781 + 214 - 1500 = 495$
1984	283	$283/281 = 1.007, 1.007^2 = 1.014; 2(1007) - 1/2(1014); 2014 - 507 = 1507, 1507 + 495 - 1500 = 502$
1985	324	$324/281 = 1.1530, 1.1530^2 = 1.328; 2(1153) - 1/2(1328); 2306 - 665 = 1641, 1641 + 495 - 1500 = 636$
1986	409	$409/281 = 1.456, 1.456^2 = 2.119; 2(1456) - 1/2(2119); 2912 - 1059 = 1853, 1853 + 495 - 1500 = 848$
1987	516	$516/409 = 1.2616, 1.2616^2 = 1.5917; 2(1262) - 1/2(1592); 2524 - 796 = 1727, 1727 + 848 - 1500 = 1075$
1988	478	$478/409 = 1.169, 1.169^2 = 1.366; 2(1169) - 1/2(1366); 2338 - 683 = 1655, 1655 + 848 - 1500 = 1003$
1989	577	$577/409 = 1.411, 1.411^2 = 1.990; 2(1411) - 1/2(1990); 2822 - 995 + 1827, 1827 + 848 - 1500 = 1175$
1990	609	$609/577 = 1.0554, 1.0554^2 = 1.114; 2(1055) - 1/2(1114); 2110 - 557 = 1553, 1553 + 1175 - 1500 = 1228$
1991	695	$695/609 = 1.141, 1.141^2 = 1.302; 2(1141) - 1/2(1302); 2282 - 651 = 1631, 1631 + 1228 - 1500 = 1359$
1992	765	$765/695 = 1.1007, 1.1007^2 = 1.2116; 2(1101) - 1/2(1212); 2202 - 606 = 1596, 1596 + 1359 - 1500 = 1455$
1993	806	$806/695 = 1.160, 1.160^2 = 1.345; 2(1160) - 1/2(1345); 2320 - 672 = 1648, 1648 + 1359 - 1500 = 1455$
1994	841	$841/806 = 1.0434, 1.0434^2 = 1.0887; 2(1043) = 1/2(1088); 2086 - 544 = 1542, 1542 + 1507 - 1500 = 1549$
1995	1000	$1000/841 = 1.189, 1.189^2 = 1.414; 2(1189) - 1/2(1414); 2378 - 707 = 1671, 1671 + 1549 - 1500 = 1720$
1996	1235	$1235/1000 = 1.2350, 1.2350^2 = 1.5252; 2(1235) - 1/2(1525); 2470 - 763 = 1707, 1707 + 1720 - 1500 = 1927$
1997	1593	$1593/1235 = 1.290, 1.290^2 = 1.664; 2(1290) - 1/2(1664); 2580 - 832 = 1748, 1748 + 1927 - 1500 = 2175$
1998	1987	$1987/1593 = 1.2473, 1.2473^2 = 1.5558; 2(1247) - 1/2(1556); 2494 - 778 = 1716, 1716 + 2175 - 1500 = 2391$
1999	2513	$2513/1987 = 1.2647, 1.2647^2 = 1.5995; 2(1265) - 1/2(1600); 2530 - 800 = 1730, 1730 + 2391 - 1500 = 2621$
2000	2728	$2728/2513 = 1.0856, 1.0856^2 = 1.1784; 2(1086) - 1/2(1178); 2172 - 589 = 1583 + 2621 - 1500 = 2704$

investment (in this example, 1500), the third stage also calculates the new value of the riskless asset, reflecting the cash freed up or absorbed in returning the risky positions to their original values.

The value of the approximation portfolio to the investor includes the net value of both his risky positions and the accumulating sum of these (algebraic) additions to the riskless asset. Thus, the three-stage entry for a rebalancing year reflects both the effect of rebalancing, which takes place at the beginning of that year, and the effect on the two risky positions of the subsequent change in market level, between the beginning and the end.[6]

12 The Evidence

The last three decades of the century included several painful market collapses as well as a celebrated bull market. The nominal market level increased 16 times, the real level four. Surely this period is a worthy test of whether

1. the risk in the markets' rate of return is really stationary;
2. the dollar risk in the logarithmic portfolio is really stationary.

In order to test whether risks were stationary, we need to be able to measure *ex ante* risk *ex post*. Actuaries use a special kind of graph paper called "probability paper" to do this. Its vertical axis is conventional, with horizontal lines equally spaced. But its horizontal axis is variously compressed and stretched so that, when drawings from a normal sample are ranked from lowest to highest and then accorded equal probability increments (rather than equal distances) on that axis, they plot as a straight line. Depending on the chosen scale of the conventional vertical axis, the slope of that line reflects the sample's dispersion.

The point, of course, is that if the sample is drawn from a universe with different dispersions—if, across time, the risk is not stationary—then, the sample cannot plot as a straight line.

Were the two risks really stationary over the sample period? Figure 1 displays the data for the market's rate of return. Figure 2 displays the data for the year-to-year change in the dollar value of the logarithmic portfolio.

Did the approximation portfolio really track the logarithmic portfolio? Figure 3 displays the data for the dollar values. Figure 4 displays the data for the year-to-year changes in dollar value of the two portfolios—i.e., for their risks.

13 Implementing the Approximation Portfolio

As the market level goes up, the value of the short position increases, even as the value of the long position increases. Rebalancing entails reducing the long and short positions after the stock market has gone up and increasing the long and short positions after the stock market has gone down.

Brokers who borrow the stock the investor sells short will demand "margin"—valuable assets to protect them in case the investor is unable to cover because the

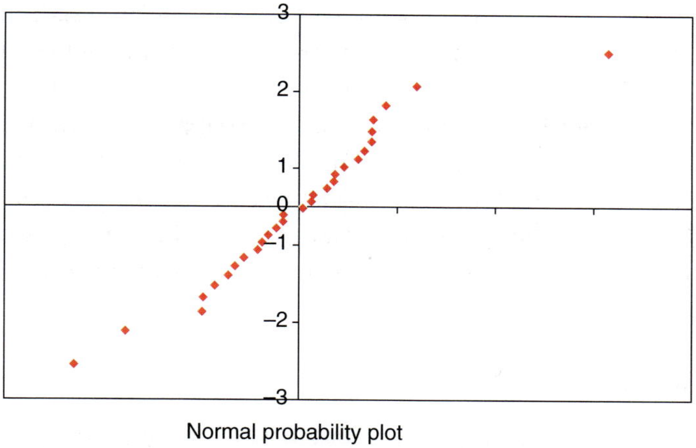

Figure 2 Year to year changes in the dollar value of a portfolio that varies with the logarithm of the US market (1972–2000).

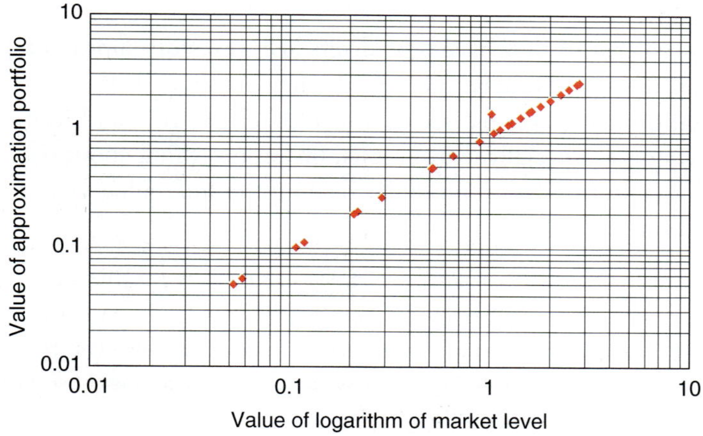

Figure 3 US experience 1980–2000.

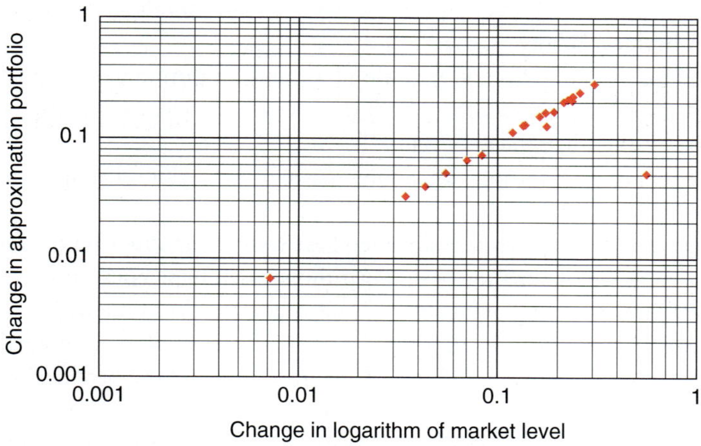

Figure 4 US experience 1972–2000.

market has risen too much. If the investors deposit their long position with the broker, their margin does not start to shrink until the market level has doubled (five standard deviations). It does not run out until the market level has quadrupled ($3 \times 5 = 15$ standard deviations of annual stock market return). But, in the meantime, the investor has rebalanced to less risky positions, over and over.

On the other hand, when the market falls the investors lose margin. But they do not lose all of it until the market level reaches zero. The $4:1$ target ratio assures that the long position will always provide more margin for the short position than even the most timid broker would require.

14 Should Risk Decline with Age?

We have argued that, if their real riskless rate is zero—or just large enough to offset trading and other costs—investors who want to time diversify should take the same dollar risk in the last year of their investment career as they take in the first. Does not this prescription conflict with the intuition that an old investor should take less risk than a young investor?

We have seen that, if they have time diversified, investors approaching the end of their career are likely to be richer than when they began. But, then, the same dollar risk at the end of their career represents a smaller relative risk; and relative risk is the way most investors—especially conventional investors—think about risk.

Is time diversification (constant dollar risk) just an unfamiliar way of expressing a familiar intuition?

Notes

1 Obviously, the investor's savings at various points in his career also contribute to terminal wealth, appreciated forward at the effective riskless rate. Let his savings in year t be Δt. Then, their contribution to terminal wealth is

$$s_0(1+r)^T + s_1(1+r)^{T-1} + \cdots + s_T = \sum s_t(1+r)$$

2 Dimson, E., Marsh, P. and Staunton, M. (2000). *The Millenium Book.* ABN-AMRO and the London Business School.

3 Past inflation has the same effect on the units of measure for the numerator and denominator. Current inflation adds algebraically to both market gains and losses, but affects the mean of these numbers rather than the dispersion.

4 There are other power series approximations—even other Taylor series approximations—to the logarithmic function.

5 When we use year-end data for the market level, we restrict our opportunities for rebalancing back to an accurate approximation of the logarithmic asset. In practical applications, changes in the market level can be followed and responded to almost continuously.
When increasing approximation error forces us to rebalance back to our original investment positions, these positions should be scaled up from those of the previous rebalancing by a factor reflecting appreciation over the interval between rebalancings. (If the price level is inflating very rapidly, rescaling does not have to wait for the next rebalancing. Then, however, the investor incurs additional trading costs.)

[6] Question: if rebalancing restores the original dollar risky positions at rebalancing, why is this not evident in JLT's 22 year example using actual US stock market data? Answer: Whereas rebalancing occurs at the beginning of the year, the worksheet numbers are based on market level at the end.

Keyword: Time diversification

Journal Of Investment Management
Vol. 1, No. 2 (2003), pp. 14–29

A PRACTICAL FRAMEWORK FOR PORTFOLIO CHOICE

Richard O. Michaud[a]

Traditional portfolio optimality criteria often have serious theoretical or practical limitations. A financial planning portfolio choice framework consisting of a resampled efficient portfolio set and multiperiod geometric mean analysis is a practical alternative for many situations of investment interest. While Monte Carlo financial planning is a more flexible framework, geometric mean analysis may be less error prone, theoretically justifiable, and convenient. Controversies that have limited applications of geometric mean analysis are resolvable by improved understanding of distributional properties and rational decision-making issues. The geometric mean is also useful in rationalizing a number of investment paradoxes.

Optimal portfolio choice is the central problem of equity portfolio management, financial planning, and asset allocation. Portfolio optimality in practice is typically defined relative to a Markowitz (1952, 1959) mean–variance (MV) efficient portfolio set. Markowitz or classical efficiency is computationally efficient, theoretically rigorous, and has widespread applicability. For example, Levy and Markowitz (1979) show that MV efficient portfolios are good approximations to portfolios that maximize expected utility for many utility functions and return generating processes of practical interest.[1] While there are many objections to MV efficiency, most alternatives have no less serious limitations.[2]

However, there are two main limitations of classical efficiency as a practical framework for optimal portfolio choice. (1) Classical efficiency is estimation error insensitive and often exhibits poor out-of-sample performance. (2) Some additional criterion is required for portfolio choice from an efficient set. The estimation error limitations of classical efficiency and a proposed solution—the resampled efficient frontier—are detailed in Michaud (1998). The major focus of this report is to showthat the distribution of the multiperiod geometric mean within a financial planning context can be the framework of choice for choosing among a properly defined efficient portfolio set for many applications of interest in investment practice.

A roadmap for the paper is as follows. A brief review of classical versus resampled MV efficiency issues for defining a practical efficient portfolio set is provided. Common optimality criteria, such as the long-term geometric mean, utility function estimation, and probability objectives, are shown to have significant theoretical or practical limitations. A financial planning approach, which describes the multiperiod consequences of single-period investment decisions as a framework for choosing among efficient

[a]New Frontier Advisors, Boston, MA 02110, USA.

portfolios, avoids many of the limitations of conventional and *ad hoc* optimality criteria. The pros and cons of the two main financial planning methods, Monte Carlo simulation and geometric mean analysis, are presented. The geometric mean distribution is also useful for resolving some outstanding financial paradoxes and providing valuable investment information in practice. The special case of asset allocation for defined benefit pension plans is presented. A brief summary of the results is given.

1 Classical Versus Resampled Efficiency

Classical MV efficiency is estimation error insensitive. Jobson and Korkie (1980, 1981) show that biases in optimized portfolio weights may be very large and that the out-of-sample performance of classically optimized portfolios is generally very poor. Simple strategies like equal weighting are often remarkably superior to classical efficiency.[3] In addition, classical efficiency is very unstable and ambiguous; even small changes in inputs can lead to large changes in optimized portfolio weights. Managers typically find the procedure hard to manage and often leading to unintuitive and unmarketable portfolios. The limitations of MV efficiency in practice are essentially the consequence of portfolios that are overly specific to input information. MV efficiency assumes 100% certainty in the optimization inputs, a condition never met in practice. Managers do not have perfect forecast information and find it difficult to use an optimization procedure that takes their forecasts far too literally.

Resampled efficiency uses modern statistical methods to control estimation error.[4] Resampled optimization is essentially a forecast certainty conditional generalization of classical MV portfolio efficiency.[5] Statistically rigorous tests show that resampled efficient portfolios dominate the performance, on average, of associated classical efficient portfolios. In addition, managers find that resampled efficient portfolios are more investment intuitive, easier to manage, more robust relative to changes in the return generating process, and require less trading. Since investors are never 100% certain of their forecasts, there is never a good reason for an investor to use classical over resampled efficiency in practice. Unless otherwise stated, in what follows we assume that the efficient portfolio set is defined in terms of properly forecast certainty conditioned, MV resampled efficient portfolios.[6]

2 Portfolio Optimality Criteria

A number of portfolio optimality criteria have been proposed either based on the MV efficient set or directly. The three most common in finance literature are probably utility function estimation, short- and long-term probability objectives, and the (long-term) geometric mean. All have important theoretical or practical limitations. A brief review of the limitations of utility function and probability objective optimality criteria is provided because the issues are largely well known in the investment community. The misuses of the geometric mean are explored in more depth not only because they are less well known but also because the principles involved apply to a number of *ad hoc* optimality criteria in current investment usage.

2.1 *Utility Functions*

Defining portfolio optimality in terms of the expectation of a utility function is the traditional finance textbook solution. Utility functions may have widely varying risk-bearing characteristics. In this approach, a utility function is chosen and its parameters estimated for a given investor or investment situation. The set of portfolio choices may or may not be confined to portfolios on the efficient frontier. The optimal portfolio is defined as the one with maximum expected utility value.

An expected utility approach is generally not a practical investment solution for optimal portfolio choice. Investors do not know their utility function. Also, utility function estimation is very unstable. It is well known that choosing an appropriate utility function even from a restricted family of utility functions may be very difficult. In cases where a family of utility functions differs only by the value of a single parameter, even small differences of the estimated parameter may lead to very different risk-bearing characteristics (Rubinstein, 1973). Multiple-period utility functions solved with a dynamic programming or continuous-time algorithm only compound the difficulties of utility function estimation as a portfolio choice framework. As a practical matter, investors have a very difficult time explaining something as simple as why they choose one risk level over another or why risk preferences may change over time.

2.2 *Short- and Long-Term Return Probabilities*

The consequences of investment decisions over an investment horizon are often described in terms of the probability of meeting various short- and long-term return objectives. For example, an investor may wish to find a strategy that minimizes the probability of less than zero (geometric mean) return over a 10-year investment horizon. Other multiperiod return objectives include maximizing a positive real return or some other hurdle rate over an investment horizon. Long-term return probabilities may be approximated with the normal or lognormal distribution to the geometric mean or with Monte Carlo methods. The results are often interesting and seductively appealing. However, the tendency to define an optimal strategy based on probability objectives, long- or short-term, has serious limitations. Markowitz (1959, p. 297) notes that return probability objectives may appear to be conservative but are often dangerous and reckless. Return probability objectives are also subject to Merton–Samuelson critiques, discussed below, and cannot be recommended.

2.3 *The Long-Term Geometric Mean Criterion*

The geometric mean or compound return over N periods is defined as

$$G_N(\underline{r}) = \prod (1 + r_i)^{1/N} - 1 \tag{1}$$

where $\underline{r}$ represents the vector of returns $r_1, r_2, \ldots, r_N$ in periods $1, \ldots, N$, and $r_i > -1$. The usual assumptions associated with the geometric mean are that returns are measured independent of cash flows and the return generating process is independent and stationary over the investment horizon. The stationary distribution assumption is not always necessary for deriving analytical results but is convenient for many purposes.

The geometric mean is a summary statistic used in finance to describe the return over multiple equal duration discrete time intervals. Intuitively, the geometric mean statistic describes the growth rate of capital over the N-period investment horizon. It is a widely used measure of historical investment performance that is of interest to fund managers, institutional trustees, financial advisors, and sophisticated investors.

The geometric mean is usually introduced to students with the following example: Suppose an asset with a return of 100% in one period followed by −50% in the second period. The average return over the two periods is 25% but the actual return is zero. This is because a dollar has increased to two at the end of the first period and then decreased to a dollar at the end of the second. The geometric mean formula (1) gives the correct return value, 0%. It is the measure of choice for measuring return over time. This example is pedagogically useful; it is simple, straightforward, and, within its context, correct. However, this example is easily misunderstood.

As the number of periods in the investment horizon grows large, the (almost sure) limit of the geometric mean is the point distribution:

$$G_\infty(\underline{r}) = e^{E(\log(1+r))} - 1 \tag{2}$$

The point distribution limit (2) or long-term geometric mean is also the limit of expected geometric mean return. Formula (2) has been the source of important errors in financial literature.

Properties of the (long-term) geometric mean have fascinated many financial economists and have often been proposed as an optimality criterion.[7] For example, the approximation for the long-term geometric mean, expressed in terms of the mean, μ, and variance, σ^2 of single-period return,

$$G_\infty(\underline{r}) \approx \mu - \frac{\sigma^2}{2} \tag{3}$$

can be used to find the portfolio on the MV efficient frontier that maximizes long-term return.[8] Intuitively, such a portfolio has attractive investment properties. Another optimality criterion motivated by properties of the long-term geometric mean is given in Hakansson (1971b). In this case, the criterion for portfolio optimality is

$$\text{Max}\, E(\log(1+r)) \tag{4}$$

As Hakansson shows, maximization of (4) leads to almost certain maximization of long-term geometric mean return while optimal MV efficient portfolios may lead to almost certain ruin.[9] There are important theoretical and practical objections that have been raised of the Hakansson criterion (4) and its near relative (3). The theoretical objections are discussed in the next section. From a practical point of view, the investment horizon is not infinite. For finite N, the Hakansson optimal portfolio has a variance that is often very risky. Hakansson optimal portfolios may be near, at, or beyond the maximum expected return end of the efficient frontier.[10] For many investors and institutions, the Hakansson proposal is often not a practical investment objective.

2.4 *Merton–Samuelson Critique of the Long-Term Geometric Mean Criterion*

Merton and Samuelson raised serious theoretical objections to the proposals in Hakansson (1971b).[11] While there are a number of technical details, the basic thrust of their objections consists of the inadvisability of financial decision-making motivated by statistical properties of objective functions however intuitive or attractive. Financial decision-making must be based on expected utility maximization axioms. An objective function that is not consistent with appropriate rationality axioms leads to decisions that do not satisfy some basic rationality principle. As importantly, no one utility function is likely to be useful as a general theory of portfolio choice for all rational investors.[12]

While addressed to Hakansson (1971b), the Merton–Samuelson critiques are very general and are applicable to many *ad hoc* optimality criteria in current use in the investment community.[13] It seems self evident that the notion of portfolio optimality and investment decision-making must necessarily rest on rationality principles similar to, if not precisely, those of classical utility.[14] We assume Merton and Samuelson's views throughout our discussions.

3 Properties of the Geometric Mean Distribution

If the number of periods is finite, the geometric mean distribution has a mean and variance and possesses many interesting and useful properties for finance and asset management. The following simple example may provide helpful guidance. Suppose an asset with two equally probable outcomes in each investment period: 100% or −50%. What is the expected geometric mean return for investing in this asset over the investment horizon? In general it is not 0%. A correct answer requires more information.

Suppose we plan to invest in this asset for only one period. The expected return of the investment is 25% not 0%. Suppose you are considering investing in the asset for two or three investment periods. The expected geometric mean return is 12.5% over two periods and 8.26% over three periods. For any finite horizon, the investment has a variance as well as an expected return. It is only at the limit, when the number of investment periods is very large, that the expected growth rate of investing in this asset is 0%.[15]

An improved understanding of the properties of the geometric mean return distribution is necessary to address and resolve outstanding fallacies and to properly apply it in practice.[16] Four properties of the geometric mean distribution with a focus on financial implications are given below. The reader is referred to Michaud (1981) for mathematical and statistical proofs and more technical and rigorous discussion.

3.1 *Horizon Dependence*

The expected geometric mean is generally horizon dependent and monotone decreasing (or nonincreasing) as the number of periods increases.[17] The two-outcome example above illustrates the monotone decreasing character of the expected geometric mean and non-equality to the limit (2) when the number of periods N is finite. It is an amazingly common error, repeated in many journal papers, including finance and statistical texts, that the expected geometric mean is equal to the almost sure limit (2) for finite N. An important corollary is that maximizing $E(\log(1 + r))$ is generally not equivalent to maximizing the expected geometric mean return when N is finite. The lognormal distribution is the exception where the equality and maximization equivalence are correct.

An important consequence of this result is to highlight the often-critical limitations of the lognormal assumption for applications of geometric mean analysis. While it is easy to show that empirical asset return distributions are not normal, if only because most return distributions in finance have limited liability, it is just as easy to show that empirical asset returns are not lognormal, if only because most assets have a non-zero probability of default. Unless empirical returns are exactly lognormal, important properties of the geometric mean are ignored with a lognormal assumption. In general, lognormal distribution approximations of the geometric mean are not recommendable.[18]

A short digression on the related subject of continuously compounded return may be of interest. A return of 20% over a discrete time period is equal to the continuously compounded rate 18.23%. Financial researchers and practitioners often use the average of continuously compounded returns for multiperiod analyses, usually explicitly or implicitly with a lognormal distribution assumption. However, the lognormal distribution assumption is not benign; it implies horizon independence and is not consistent with most empirical returns in finance. The average of continuously compounded returns may be insufficient as a description of multiperiod return and should be used with care.

3.2 *The Geometric Mean Normal Distribution Approximation*

It is well known that the geometric mean is asymptotically lognormally distributed.[19] However, it is also true that it can be approximated asymptotically by a normal distribution.[20] This second result turns out to have very useful applications. Asymptotic normality implies that the mean and variance of the geometric mean can be convenient for describing the geometric mean distribution in many cases of practical interest. The normal distribution can also be convenient for computing geometric mean return probabilities for MV efficient portfolios. A third important application is given in the next section.

3.3 *The Expected Geometric Mean and Median Terminal Wealth*

The medians of terminal wealth and of the geometric mean, G_M, are related according to the formula

$$\text{Median of terminal wealth} = (1 + G_M)^N \tag{5}$$

Because of asymptotic normality, the expected geometric mean is asymptotically equal to the median and, consequently, the expected geometric mean is a consistent and convenient estimate of median terminal wealth via (5). Since the multiperiod terminal wealth distribution is typically highly right-skewed, the median of terminal wealth, rather than the mean, represents the more practical investment criterion for many institutional asset managers, trustees of financial institutions, and sophisticated investors.[21] As a consequence, the expected geometric mean is a useful and convenient tool for understanding the multiperiod consequences of single-period investment decisions on the median of terminal wealth.

3.4 The MV of Geometric Mean Return

A number of formulas are available for describing the N-period mean and variance of the geometric mean in terms of the single-period mean and variance of return.[22] Such formulas do not typically depend on the characteristics of a particular return distribution and range from simple and less accurate to more complex and more accurate.[23] The simplest but pedagogically most useful formulas, given in terms of the portfolio single-period mean μ and variance of return ρ^2 are:

$$E(G_N(\underline{r})) = \mu - \frac{(1 - 1/N)\sigma^2}{2} \tag{6a}$$

$$V(G_N(\underline{r})) = \frac{(1 + (1 - 1/N)\sigma^2/2)\sigma^2}{N} \tag{6b}$$

Formulas (6a) and (6b) provide a useful road map for understanding the multiperiod consequences of single-period efficient investment decisions. Note that (6a) shows explicitly the horizon dependent character of expected geometric mean return.

4 Financial Planning and Portfolio Choice

Financial planning methods are widely used for cash flow planning and portfolio choice in institutional consulting practice. Monte Carlo simulation and geometric mean methods are commonly associated with financial planning studies. Both methods describe the short- and long-term investment risk and return and distribution of financial consequences of investing in single-period efficient portfolios. An appropriate risk level is chosen based on visualization and assessment of the risk and return tradeoffs in financial terms for various investment horizons. Applications include defined benefit pension plan funding status and required contributions, endowment fund spending policy and fund status, investor retirement income, and college tuition trust funds. Such studies range from simply examining multiperiod return distributions and objectives to large-scale projects that include specialist consultants.[24] In this context, a low risk investment may often be risky relative to a higher risk alternative for meeting a specific financial goal. Financial planning methods have often been useful in identifying strategies or funding decisions that are likely to lead to insolvency or significant financial distress.[25]

Figure 1 displays a standard framework for a financial planning study. The risk and return of a candidate efficient portfolio is given, capital for investment and inflation assumptions input, the length of the investment horizon and draw down period defined, and results displayed in various ways as appropriate.

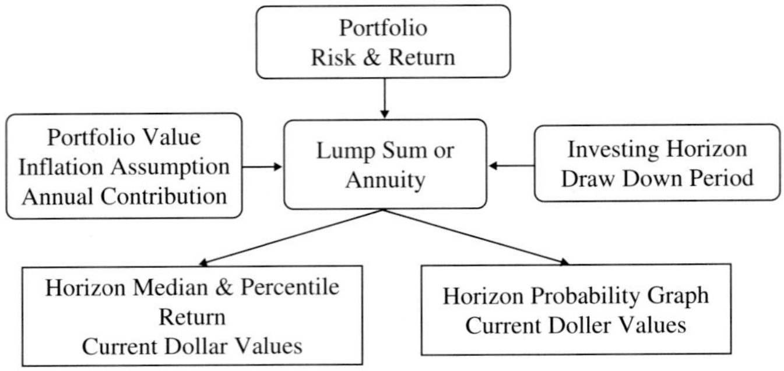

Figure 1 Financial planning framework.

4.1 Monte Carlo Financial Planning

Monte Carlo simulation methods are widely used for cash flow financial planning and what-if exercises. Monte Carlo methods are characterized by flexibility; virtually any cash flow computable outcome, including accounting variables and actuarial procedures, can be analyzed. Various legal and tax events are readily modeled in a Monte Carlo framework.

4.2 Geometric Mean Financial Planning

The geometric mean distribution is also a flexible financial planning tool. Straightforward applications include planning for future college tuition, endowment and foundation asset allocation and spending rules, and 401 K pension plan retirement planning (Figure 2).[26] The special case of defined benefit pension plans is treated in a later section. Variations include allowing for contributions and/or withdrawals during the investment period that may be constant or vary in value, defined either as actual cash values or as percent of fund value in each time period, in nominal or current dollars. The draw down period can be defined either in nominal or current

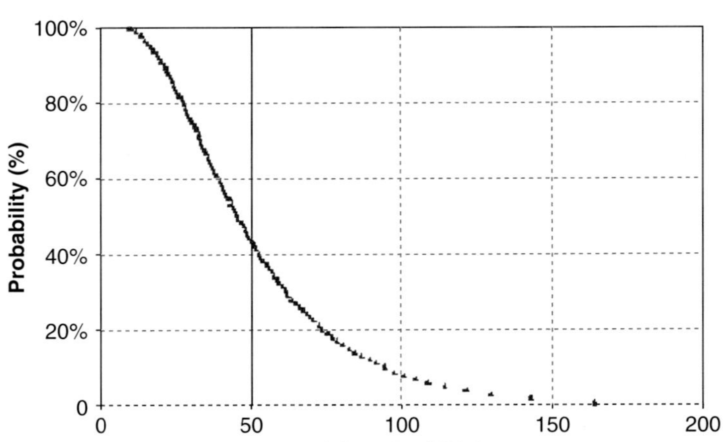

Figure 2 Twenty-year annuity distribution.

dollars as annuities, fund values, or spending levels. Varying cash flow schedules in the contribution and draw down periods can be useful in addressing multiple objective situations.[27]

Note that the Merton–Samuelson objections to the geometric mean as an optimality criterion are not operative in a financial planning context. As in Monte Carlo simulation, the geometric mean is simply used as a computation engine to estimate the multiperiod consequences of single-period efficient investment decisions. Properties of the geometric mean also provide the mathematical foundation of the Monte Carlo simulation financial planning process, an important issue, which we discuss further below.

4.3 Monte Carlo Versus Geometric Mean Financial Planning

The advantage of Monte Carlo simulation financial planning is its extreme flexibility. Monte Carlo simulation can include return distribution assumptions and decision rules that vary by period or are contingent on previous results or forecasts of future events. However, path dependency is prone to unrealistic or unreliable assumptions. In addition, Monte Carlo financial planning without an analytical framework is a trial and error process for finding satisfactory portfolios. Monte Carlo methods are also necessarily distribution specific, often the lognormal distribution.[28]

Geometric mean analysis is an analytical framework that is easier to understand, computationally efficient, always convergent, statistically rigorous, and less error prone. It also provides an analytical framework for Monte Carlo studies. An analyst armed with geometric mean formulas will be able to approximate the conclusions of many Monte Carlo studies.

For many financial planning situations, geometric mean analysis is the method of choice. A knowledgeable advisor with suitable geometric mean analysis software may be able to assess an appropriate risk level for an investor from an efficient set in a regular office visit. However, in cases involving reliably forecastable path-dependent conditions, or for what-if planning exercises, supplementing geometric mean analysis with Monte Carlo methods may be required.[29]

5 Geometric Mean Applications to Asset Management

Geometric mean properties have useful applications for asset management in situations where investment risk in each period is relatively constant over the investment horizon. This assumption is often satisfied for institutional equity strategies and many asset allocation applications and financial planning situations.

5.1 The Critical Point and Maximum Growth Rates

Assume that single-period portfolio efficiency is monotone increasing in expected return as a function of portfolio risk.[30] Formula (6a) teaches that N-period expected geometric mean return might not be a monotone increasing function of (single-period) efficient portfolio risk.[31] In other words, there may exist an interior "critical point"

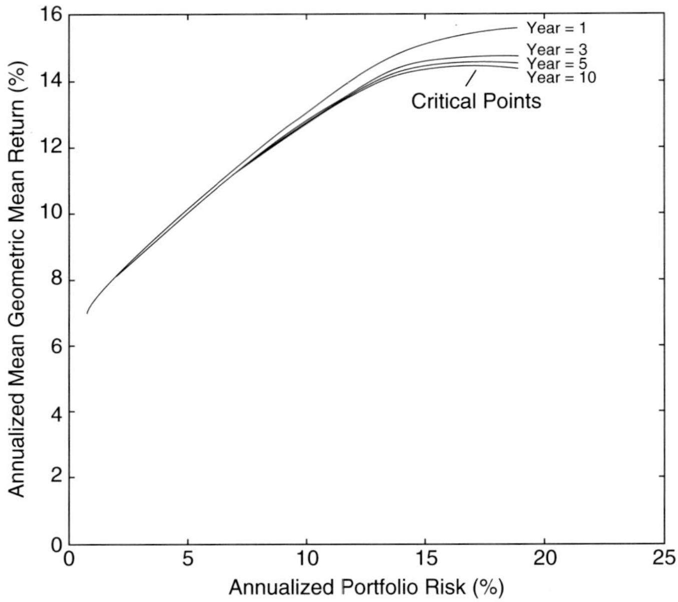

Figure 3 Efficient frontier expected geometric mean return versus portfolio risk for 1-, 3-, 5-, 10-year horizons.

on the single-period efficient frontier that has the highest expected geometric mean return.[32] This critical point can be found analytically under certain conditions or computationally using a search algorithm.[33] Institutional asset managers may often want to avoid efficient portfolios if they imply less expected geometric mean return and median wealth as well as more risk relative to others.[34]

Figure 3 provides an example of the expected geometric mean as a function of single-period portfolio risk associated with a single-period MV efficient frontier. There are four curves. The top curve is the MV efficient frontier. The three curves below the efficient frontier display the expected geometric mean as a function of single-period portfolio risk for three investment horizons: 3, 5, and 10 years.[35] Note that the expected geometric mean curves show that a critical point exists ranging roughly from 17% to 19% portfolio risk.

An interior efficient frontier critical point may not exist (Michaud, 1981). The non-existence of an interior point often means that the maximum expected geometric mean return portfolio is at the upper end point of the efficient frontier and all single-period efficient portfolios can be described as multiperiod MV geometric mean efficient.[36] When an interior critical point exists, it is generally horizon dependent, with limit the efficient portfolio with expected geometric mean return equal to the almost sure limit (2). The geometric mean formulas and critical point analysis can also be used to estimate an upper bound for efficient portfolio growth rates in capital markets under the assumptions.[37] Investors are well advised to know the multiperiod limitations of risk prior to investment, particularly when leveraged strategies are being used.

6 Resolving Financial Paradoxes with Geometric Mean Analysis

A good model for investment behavior typically provides unexpected insight in totally different contexts. In this regard, the geometric mean distribution is often useful in rationalizing investment behavior and resolving paradoxes of financial management. Three examples are given below, which have interest in their own right and demonstrate the power and investment usefulness of geometric mean analysis.

6.1 CAPM and the Limits of High Beta Portfolios

The security market line of the capital asset pricing model implies that expected return is linearly related to systematic risk as measured by β. Taken literally, the implication is that managers should take as much β risk as they can bear. In practice, many managers do not take much more than market risk ($\beta \approx 1$) and even high-risk active portfolios seldom have a β larger than 3. Are asset managers not acting in their own and their client's best interests?

Michaud (1981) derives formulas for the critical point for β under the security market line assumption. The critical β for a market with expected annual return of 10%, risk free rate of 5%, and standard deviation of 20% for an investment horizon of 5 years is approximately 1.85. Longer horizons or larger market standard deviations lead to a smaller critical β. On the other hand, relatively recent capital market history in the US has exhibited historically low volatility and has been associated with increased popularity of leveraged hedge fund strategies. Lower market volatility, when persistent, rationalizes the use of higher leveraged strategies. In these and other situations, investment practice often mirrors the rational implications of geometric mean results.

6.2 Taxes and the Benefits of Diversified Funds

Consider providing investment advice to an investor who owns a one stock portfolio that has performed well over a recent period. Typical financial advice is to sell the stock and buy a diversified fund. This is because the one stock portfolio has a great deal of undiversified risk. According to investment theory, diversifiable risk is not associated with long-term return and should be largely avoided.

From the investor's point of view, the advice may often not be congenial. If the stock has a larger β than the diversified fund, financial theory implies higher expected return. Also, selling the stock will certainly result in substantial capital gains taxes and loss of portfolio value. So how can the diversified fund recommendation be rationalized? This situation is a problem encountered by financial advisors many times in their career.

The benefits of the diversified fund are not generally justifiable from single-period investment theory but often are from MV geometric mean analysis. In this context, geometric mean analysis may lead to the computation of a "crossover" point where the diversified fund is expected to outperform, and is consequently more investment attractive than, the undiversified portfolio beyond some period in the investment horizon. In many cases, the crossover point can be surprisingly short and of serious practical consideration.

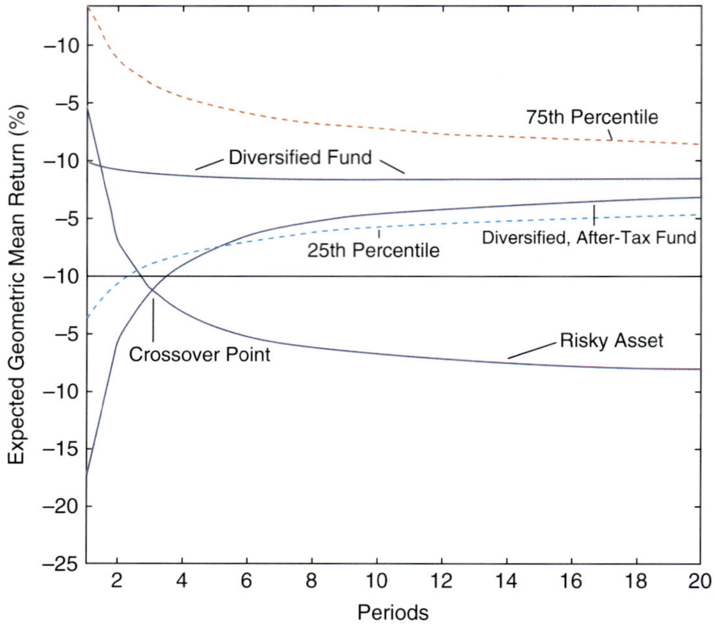

Figure 4 Crossover return analysis risky asset, diversified, diversified after-tax.

Assume that the investor's one stock portfolio has a $\beta = 2$ and a market correlation of 0.5. Assume a diversified market portfolio with expected annual return of 10% and standard deviation of 20% and a risk free rate of 5%. Assume a return generating process consistent with the security market line of CAPM and that capital gains taxes reduce capital value by 25%. Figure 4 displays the expected geometric mean return as a function of annual investment periods over a 20-period investment horizon for the undiversified, diversified, and diversified after-tax portfolios. In the first period, the top curve or undiversified fund has significantly higher expected return than either the middle curve (diversified fund) or bottom curve (diversified fund after-taxes). However, the exhibit shows that, over time, the expected geometric means of the diversified funds cross over and outperform the undiversified fund. This is true even when the initial loss of capital due to taxes is factored into the analysis. The diversified funds are likely to outperform the undiversified fund well within four years even considering taxes.

This example dramatically shows the power of diversification over time. It should also be noted that the example is far from extreme. Many high-performing one stock portfolios encountered in financial planning and investment consulting have β significantly in excess of 2. On the other hand, a less volatile market environment than that assumed may have significantly improved the performance of the undiversified fund.[38] While the results depend on the assumptions, and a crossover point need not exist, investment in diversified funds is often well rationalized by multiperiod geometric mean analysis in many cases of practical interest.[39]

6.3 Asset Allocation Strategies that Lead to Ruin[40]

Suppose an investor invests 50% of assets in risky securities in each time period. Either the return matches the investment or it is lost. Both events are equally likely. This is a fair investment game similar to an asset mix investment policy of equal allocation to risky stocks and riskless bonds with rebalancing. In this case, investment policy leads to ruin with probability one. This is because the likely outcome of every two periods results in 75% of original assets. However, the investment is always fair in the sense that the expected value of your wealth at the end of each period is always what you began with. For two periods the expected geometric mean return is negative and declines to the almost sure long-term limit of -13.4%, which is found using (2).

This example vividly demonstrates the difference between the expected and median terminal wealth of an investment strategy. It shows that the expected geometric mean return implications of an investment decision are often of significant interest.

7 The Special Case of Defined Benefit Pension Plan Asset Allocation

Monte Carlo asset–liability simulation methods are prevalent in investment-planning practice for defined benefit pension funds. This is due to the perception that the funding of actuarially estimated liabilities and the management of actuarially estimated plan contributions is the appropriate purpose of invested assets. In this context, geometric mean analysis appears to have limited portfolio choice value. However, the traditional actuarial valuation process typically ignores the dynamic character of the economics of pension funding risk.[41] These same issues make Monte Carlo asset–liability simulation studies for defined benefit pension plans often irrelevant or misleading.

7.1 Economic Nature of Defined Benefit Pension Plans

Defining an appropriate and useful investment policy begins by understanding the true economic nature of a pension plan. A pension plan is deferred compensation. It is part of the total wage and fringe benefit package associated with employee compensation. Far from being a corporate liability or drag on firm profitability, it is a US government sponsored asset for promoting corporate competitiveness. This is because pension contributions are tax-advantaged. If the firm is to remain competitive for human capital and total employee compensation remains the same, pension plan termination leads to greater, not less, corporate expense. Corporations should prefer employee compensation in the form of plan contributions than direct compensation.

While actuarial methods and assumptions are designed to manage the cost of the pension plan to the corporation, there are many economic forces that are at work. If total employee compensation is competitive relative to other firms, a more than normal percent of payroll plan contributions may only mean that the firm has decided to tilt total compensation towards deferred rather than current. If total compensation is high relative to competing firms, this may be part of a conscious firm policy of attracting human capital. Alternatively, there are many things the firm may want to do besides change their asset allocation in order to manage plan contributions. For example, the benefit formula, employee workforce, or level of current compensation can be reduced, all of which has direct implications for required contributions.

An appropriate asset allocation comes from an understanding of the business risks of the firm and its ability to grow and compete for human capital over time and has little, if anything, to do with actuarial valuation.[42] A contemporary example of the dangers associated with asset allocations derived from a conventional understanding of pension liabilities is given in the next section.

7.2 A Cautionary Tale for Pension Fund Asset Allocation

As an example, the economic and market climate in the year 2001 has much to teach in terms of true economic pension liability risks and appropriate asset allocation. The year saw a dramatic decline in interest rates leading to an increase in the present value of actuarially estimated pension liabilities. At the same time equity values fell significantly leading to a serious decline in the funding status of many US pension plans. Were large allocations to equities a terrible mistake? Should pension plans redirect their assets to fixed income instruments to reduce their funding risk in the future?

During this same period, due in part to declining equity values and associated economic conditions, many corporations downsized their workforce, froze salaries, reduced or eliminated bonuses, and shelved many internal projects. All these factors impact workforce census, expected benefits, and pension liabilities. Because the actuarial valuation process uses many non-economic long-term smoothing assumptions, liability valuation is typically little influenced by changes in expected benefits or the business risks of the firm.[43] An updated actuarial valuation with few smoothing assumptions, which more closely approximates financial reality, is likely to find that many US corporations had very diminished pension liabilities in this period and may be far less underfunded. Financial reality will eventually emerge from the actuarial valuation process in the form of much reduced pension liability, all other things being the same. This is because promised benefits have to be paid whatever the assumptions used to estimate them. An asset allocation based on actuarial valuation methods may often have serious negative investment consequences on plan funding when markets and economic productivity rebound and the value of non-fixed income assets become more attractive.

7.3 Economic Liabilities and Asset–Liability Asset Allocation

It is beyond the scope of this report to describe the economic risk characteristics of a defined benefit pension plan or other institutional or personal liabilities and how they may be modeled.[44] Asset–liability asset allocation problems require an understanding of changes in economic factors and capital market rates and their relationship to the economic nature of liabilities or use of invested assets.[45] Actuarial methods often have limited and even dangerous decision-making asset allocation value.

The recommended alternative is to define the resampled efficient set in a benchmark framework relative to an economic model of liability risk.[46] MV geometric mean analysis and Monte Carlo simulation may then be used to derive the multiperiod financial planning implications of efficient portfolios.

8 Conclusion

Geometric mean analysis is far more robust and applicable to a far wider range of portfolio choice applications than is widely perceived. It can rationalize much investor behavior while providing very useful information for investors and financial advisors for improving the value of invested assets. It can avoid overly risky and leveraged investments and strategies by providing investors with a realistic view of long-term capital growth rates. It is also analytically and computationally very convenient. Used properly, MV geometric mean analysis is often fundamentally important for investment consulting, financial planning, and asset management. However, the appropriate definition of the resampled efficient portfolio set remains paramount in the investment value of any financial planning procedure.

Appendix A

A.1 Additional Critical Point Issues

Formula (3) is a very standard approximation to the expected geometric mean. It has a number of practical limitations that are shared with many other approximations in widespread use. When N is finite, the horizon dependence property illustrated in (6a) shows that the portfolio that maximizes formula (3) might not represent well the critical point portfolio. Another issue is that neither (3) nor (6a) may be sufficiently accurate approximations of $E(G_N(\underline{r}))$ and the critical point when N is large. A more accurate formula from Michaud (1981, Appendix) of the long-term geometric mean return in terms of the single-period mean and variance of return, is

$$G_\infty(\underline{r}) = (1+\mu)\exp\left\{-\left[\frac{\sigma^2}{(2(1+\mu)^2)}\right]\right\} - 1 \tag{A.1}$$

Acknowledgment

I am indebted to Robert Michaud for many helpful comments. All remaining errors are my responsibility.

Notes

[1] Currently, there are serious controversies on the appropriate framework for rational decision-making under uncertainty for finance. The characteristics of investor gains and loss behavior have raised valid objections concerning the limitations of Von Neumann–Morgenstern (1953) utility axioms and alternative frameworks based on psychological principles proposed. This issue is well beyond the scope of this report. Recent research, for example Luce (2000), shows that an expanded set of utility axioms may serve as a basis for characterizing rational decision-making that addresses the gains and loss behavior objections. Luce

shows that his axioms are consistent with recent psychological empirical data and competing non-axiomatic frameworks are not.

2 Michaud (1998, Ch. 3) provides a review of the major proposed alternatives to classical efficiency and notes that classical efficiency is far more robust than is widely appreciated.

3 This result is a simple way to rationalize why many investors do not use classical optimization in their investment decisions.

4 Resampled efficiency, as described in Michaud (1998, Chs. 6 and 7), was co-invented by Richard Michaud and Robert Michaud and is a US patented procedure, #6,003,018, December 1999, patent pending worldwide. New Frontier Advisors, LLC, has exclusive licensing rights worldwide.

5 The number of returns used to estimate simulated optimization inputs, a free parameter in the resampled efficiency process, is used to condition the optimization according to an investor's assumed level of forecast certainty. This parameter is calibrated from one to ten to facilitate the user experience. Roughly, at level one the optimized portfolios are similar to the benchmark or equal weighting; at level ten the portfolios are similar to a classical optimization. Various additional research updates of resampled efficient optimization are available at www.newfrontieradvisors.com/publications.

6 Incorporating forecast certainty as part of the definition of practical portfolio optimality is a rational, even necessary, consideration. In terms of enhanced utility axioms, Bourbaki (1948), commenting on Godel (1931), explains that rationality axioms do not characterize but follow from and codify scientific intuition. There is currently a widespread misperception in finance concerning the role of rational utility axioms and rule-based systems in scientific thought. A review of these and related issues is given in Michaud (2001). As in the case of gains and loss behavior, rule-based utility systems that do not accommodate characteristics of rational thought should be considered incomplete and reflect the need for extensions or revisions as in Luce (2000). Resampled efficiency's inclusion of forecast certainty in defining portfolio optimality is simply another case where extensions or alternative formulations of utility axioms and an enhanced notion of rational decision-making in finance are necessary.

7 An incomplete list is: Breiman (1960), Kelly (1956), Latane (1959), Markowitz (1959, Ch. 6), Hakansson (1971a,b), Thorp (1974).

8 Markowitz (1959, Ch. 6).

9 This result will be further illustrated in Section 6.3.

10 Hakansson (1971a) shows that the max $E(\log(1 + r))$ portfolio may not be on the single-period classical efficient frontier.

11 Merton and Samuelson (1974) and Samuelson and Merton (1974).

12 It should be noted, as in Hakansson (1974), that the objections raised by Merton and Samuelson can be avoided by removing the statistical motivation to the argument in Hakansson (1971b). In fact, log utility is an objective function in very good expected utility axiom standing. However, without the statistical argument, log utility is simply one of many possibly interesting investment objectives.

13 A different class of *ad hoc* methods for identifying optimal portfolios has to do with questionnaires that investors are asked to answer that purport to measure risk preferences and result in a recommended "model" portfolio from a predefined set. Such methods typically have no theoretical justification and may provide little, if any, reliable or useful information for investors.

14 Von Neumann and Morgenstern (1953).

15 In this case 0% is also the almost sure limit of the geometric mean.

16 A surprisingly widespread simple asset allocation error is to use geometric instead of arithmetic mean inputs in a classical optimization to moderate the effect of large return and risk assets and make the solutions more acceptable to investors. Stein methods, discussed in Michaud (1998, Ch. 8) are often the appropriate methods for shrinking outlier data for the purpose of improving forecastability.

17 A statistic may or may not be dependent on the number of observations in a sample. Examples include sample size independence of the sample mean and sample size dependence of the sample variance.

18 Unless otherwise noted, our results in the following are non-parametric and do not depend on the lognormal return distribution assumption.

19 Applying the log function to each side of the equality (1) and invoking the central limit theorem implies that the N-period geometric mean distribution is asymptotically lognormal.

20 The fact that a distribution can asymptotically be well approximated by two different distributions is not unique in probability theory. The binomial distribution can be approximated asymptotically by both the normal and Poisson distribution under certain conditions. Intuitively, a lognormal characterization of the asymptotic geometric mean return distribution may seem more natural because of the skewness normally associated with multiperiod returns. However, the Nth root function reduces much of the skewness effect when N is reasonably large.

21 The relationship between N-period geometric mean return and terminal wealth is given by: $W_N(\underline{r}) = (1 + G_N(\underline{r}))N = \prod(1 + r_i)$. Applying the log function to each side of the equality and invoking the central limit theorem leads to the conclusion that N-period terminal wealth is asymptotically lognormal.

22 For example, Young and Trent (1969).

23 Michaud (1981) provides caveats on the applicability and approximation accuracy of these and other formulas.

24 One early comprehensive Monte Carlo study of pension fund investment policy that included an examination of the volatility of pension liabilities under workforce census changes, corporate policy, and market rate assumptions is given in Michaud (1976).

25 The author first encountered this effect in 1974 when conducting a Monte Carlo simulation study of proposed spending and risk policies for the Harvard College Endowment Fund. Under some proposals that were subsequently rejected, the simulations showed that the fund may have run out of money within roughly twelve years. Multiperiod insolvency cases were also encountered in Monte Carlo studies for individuals that proposed to spend capital at unsustainable rates.

26 For example: A prospective retiree has \$500,000 to invest for retirement. There are ten years until retirement. The fund has an expected return of 10% and a 20% standard deviation. The goal is to purchase a retirement annuity that will provide \$50,000 annual income in constant dollar terms. A life expectancy of 20 years in retirement and a 3% inflation rate is assumed. What is the likelihood of the \$50 K annuity and median annuity value at retirement? Using simple annuity formulas, a geometric mean analysis shows that there is a 43% chance of reaching the \$50,000 annuity objective for a 20-year period in retirement with a median value of \$45,000. The 20-year distribution of annuity values and probabilities are displayed in Figure 2. A less risky strategy of 7% portfolio return and 10% standard deviation leads to a 17% probability of meeting the \$50,000 annuity objective with a median annuity value of \$38,000.

27 The assumption that allows geometric mean analysis to address these and other long-term investment planning issues and multiple objectives is that the consequence of cash flows leaves the underlying return generating process unchanged. Adjustment for the impact of intermediate cash flows is implemented using multiple geometric mean investment horizon assumptions.

28 Limitations of the lognormal assumption were described in Section 3.1.

29 Many tax and legal situations are extremely complicated. Often the only available solutions for cash flow planning are heuristics that have evolved from experience and insight. In such cases, Monte Carlo methods may be the only recourse. Also the impact of trading decisions and costs over time may only be resolvable with Monte Carlo methods. In these and other cases, geometric mean analysis followed by detailed Monte Carlo simulation, assuming economic feasibility, is the recommended procedure.

30 Unlike classical efficiency, the resampled efficient frontier may curve downward from some point and may not be monotone increasing in expected return as a function of portfolio risk. The investment implications include limitations of high-risk assets not well represented by classical efficiency.

31 Markowitz (1959, Ch. 6) noted this possibility from his simulations relative to the geometric mean limit formula (3).

32 While efficient frontiers in practice often satisfy a budget constraint and non-negative portfolio weights, neither resampled efficiency nor geometric mean critical point analysis is limited to such frontiers. In particular, a critical point can be computed for unbounded leverage efficient frontiers as in Hakansson (1971a) and can be very revealing.

33 Michaud (1981) provides analytical solutions for the critical point in terms of portfolio β.

34 It should be emphasized that the critical point is a total, not residual, risk–return geometric mean concept.

35 The efficient frontier is based on annualized historical monthly return Ibbotson Associates (Chicago, Il) index data for six asset classes—T-Bills, intermediate government bonds, long-term corporate bonds, large capitalization US equity, small capitalization US equity, international equity—from January 1981 to December 1993. See Appendix A for additional critical point issues.

36 The exceptional case is given in Hakansson (1971a) where the critical point is at the origin.

37 This result is given in Michaud (1981).

38 An all or nothing trading strategy is not the only way to implement a multiperiod diversification program. Roughly, the same principles apply to diversifying a fixed amount of capital over multiple periods in order to manage trading and other costs.

39 The tax effect could have been dealt with in a number of ways. It is unlikely that many investors would convert 100% of a one stock portfolio into a diversified fund in the first period. However, the tax effect is something of an illusion. Unless taxes can be avoided in some way altogether, the one stock portfolio is likely to be subject to tax at some point in the investment horizon and the comparison may be even more favorable for diversified funds than illustrated.

40 From Block (1969).

41 For example, Michaud (1979) notes the irrelevance of the widely used actuarial interest rate in defined benefit plans as an investment objective for asset allocation.

42 See Michaud (1998, Ch. 10) for further discussion of these issues.

43 The standard rationale for smoothing assumptions is that required contributions should not be affected greatly by relatively ephemeral volatility in capital markets. However, this

argument has the critical flaw that the firm's business risks do not exist in isolation to capital market volatility or changes in the domestic and global economy.

44 An important issue, ignored here, is the impact of the 50% nondeductible reversion tax now assessed on excess assets from a terminated US defined benefit pension plan. These taxes alter the economics of pension plan liability risk. See Ippolito (2002) for further discussion.

45 These and related issues are discussed further in Michaud (1998, Ch. 10).

46 See Michaud (1998, Ch. 10).

References

Block, F. (1969). "Elements of Portfolio Construction." *Financial Analysts Journal* May/June.

Bourbaki (1948). "L'architecture des mathematiques." In: Le Lionais, F. (ed.) *Les Grands Courants de la Pensee Mathematique.* Paris. English translation: *American Mathematical Monthly* 57, 1950.

Breiman, L. (1960). "Investment Policies for Expanding Businesses Optimal in a Long Run Sense." *Naval Research Logistics Quarterly.*

Godel, K. (1931). "Uber formal unentscheidbare Satze der Principia Mathematica und verwandter Systeme I." *Monatsh. Math. Phys.* **38**, 173–198.

Hakansson, N. (1971a). "Capital Growth and the Mean–Variance Approach to Portfolio Selection." *Journal of Financial and Quantitative Analysis* **6**(1), 517–557.

Hakansson, N. (1971b). "Multi-Period Mean–Variance Analysis: Toward a General Theory of Portfolio Choice." *Journal of Finance* **26**(4), 857–884.

Hakansson, N. (1974). "Fallacy of the Log-Normal Approximation to Optimal Portfolio Decision-Making Over Many Periods: Comment." *Journal of Financial Economics* March.

Ippolito, R. (2002). "Replicating Default Risk in a Defined-Benefit Plan." *Financial Analysts Journal* September/October.

Jobson, D. and Korkie, B. (1980). "Estimation for Markowitz Efficient Portfolios." *Journal of the American Statistical Association* September.

Jobson, D. and Korkie, B. (1981). "Putting Markowitz Theory to Work." *Journal of Portfolio Management* 7(4), 70–74.

Kelly, J. (1956). "A New Interpretation of Information Rate." *Bell System Technical Journal.*

Latane, H. (1959). "Criteria for Choice Among Risky Ventures." *Journal of Political Economy* April.

Levy, H. and Markowitz, H. (1979). "Approximating Expected Utility by a Function of the Mean and Variance." *American Economic Review* **69**, 308–317.

Luce, R.D. (2000). *Utility of Gains and Losses: Measurement-Theoretical and Experimental Approaches.* Mahway, New Jersey: Lawrence Erlbaum Assocs.

Markowitz, H. (1952). "Portfolio Selection." *Journal of Finance* March.

Markowitz, H. (1959). *Portfolio Selection: Efficient Diversification of Investments.* New York: Wiley.

Merton, R.C. and Samuelson, P. (1974). "Fallacy of the Log-Normal Approximation to Optimal Portfolio Decision-Making over Many Periods." *Journal of Financial Economics* March.

Michaud, R. (1976). "Pension Fund Investment Policy." Presentation to: The Institute for Quantitative Research in Finance, Spring Seminar.

Michaud, R. (1979). "The Actuarial Interest Rate as an Investment Objective." Quantitative Investment Strategies: Bache Halsey Stuart Shields, New York, September.

Michaud, R. (1981). "Risk Policy and Long-Term Investment." *Journal of Financial and Quantitative Analysis* June.

Michaud, R. (1998). *Efficient Asset Management: A Practical Guide to Stock Portfolio Optimization and Asset Allocation.* New York: Oxford University Press, 2001. First published by Harvard Business School Press.

Michaud, R. (2001). "The Behavioral Finance Hoax." Presentation to: Scottish Institute for Research in Finance, Edinburgh, Scotland, September.

Rubinstein, M. (1973). "Comparative Statics Analysis of Risk Premiums." *Journal of Business* **46**(4), 605–615.

Von Neumann, J. and Morgenstern, O. (1953). *Theory of Games and Economic Behavior*, 3rd edn. Princeton, NJ: Princeton University Press.

Samuelson, P. and Merton, R.C. (1974). "Generalized Mean Variance Tradeoffs for Best Perturbation Corrections to Approximate Portfolio Decisions." *Journal of Finance* March.

Thorp, E. (1974). "Portfolio Choice and the Kelly Criterion." Reprinted in Bicksler, J.C. and Samuelson, P. (ed.) *Investment Portfolio Decision Making*. Lexington, MA: Lexington Books.

Young, W.E. and Trent, R.H. (1969). "Geometric Mean Approximation of Individual Security and Portfolio Performance." *Journal of Financial and Quantitative Analysis* June.

Journal Of Investment Management
Vol. 3, No. 1 (2005), pp. 29–44

A MARKOV CHAIN MONTE CARLO METHOD FOR DERIVATIVE PRICING AND RISK ASSESSMENT

Sanjiv R. Das[a] *and Alistair Sinclair*[b]

Derivative security pricing and risk measurement relies increasingly on lattice representations of stochastic processes, which are a discrete approximation of the movement of the underlying securities. Pricing is undertaken by summation of node values on the lattice. When the lattice is large (which is the case when high accuracy is required), exhaustive enumeration of the nodes becomes prohibitively costly. Instead, Monte Carlo simulation is used to estimate the lattice value by sampling appropriately from the nodes. Most sampling methods become extremely error-prone in situations where the node values vary widely. This paper presents a Markov chain Monte Carlo scheme, adapted from Sinclair and Jerrum (Information and Computation 82 (1989)), that is able to overcome this problem, provided some partial (possibly very inaccurate) information about the lattice sum is available. This partial information is used to direct the sampling, in similar fashion to traditional importance sampling methods. The key difference is that the algorithm allows backtracking on the lattice, which acts in a "self-correcting" manner to minimize the bias in the importance sampling.

1 Overview

This paper explores a novel algorithm for the pricing of derivative securities. There are now hundreds of different types of derivative securities, each with their own peculiar characteristics. Yet, no single approach works for every type of contract, and, indeed, the literature in finance is replete with a vast number of different pricing models.

The goal in this paper is to propose a novel pricing model that is tailored to some derivatives of more recent interest, for which dominant models do not as yet exist. The algorithm is based on a Markov chain Monte Carlo approach, developed in a different context by Sinclair and Jerrum (1989). While the use of Monte Carlo methods is well established for pricing derivatives, our approach differs in several respects: it uses backtracking to prevent the accumulation of errors in importance sampling; it has rigorously provable error bounds; and it is, in principle, applicable to derivative pricing on any nonrecombining lattice. In addition to describing the algorithm, we also present some initial experimental results that illustrate its application to a simple barrier option pricing problem.

Financial securities are called "derivatives" if their value is derived from some other primary underlying security or economic variable. The "underlying" could very well

[a]Santa Clara University, Leavey School of Business, 500 El Camino Real, Santa Clara, CA 95053-0388, USA (corresponding author).

[b]University of California, Berkeley, CA, USA.

be a derivative too, and it is not uncommon to see derivatives on derivatives. Options and futures are well known and very common forms of derivatives. To set notation, a "call" option C_0 on a stock S_0 (where the subscript zero indicates "initial price" at time 0) is a contract in which the buyer of the option receives at the maturity of the contract (i.e., at time T) the difference between the stock price S_T and a preset "strike" price K, *if* this amount is positive. Thus, the payoff at maturity is

$$C_T = \max(0, S_T - K) \tag{1}$$

(A "put" option P_0 is the converse contract and pays off when $K > S_T$.) For the privilege of always receiving a non-negative payoff, the option buyer must pay an upfront premium to the option writer. The objective of any algorithm for the pricing of options is to determine as precisely as possible what the fair premium C_0 (or P_0 for puts) should be.

Therefore, the pricing of options requires assumptions about the stochastic process that governs the underlying security (a stock, for example), and a computation of the fair value of the option under strict economic assumptions that ensure that no arbitrages (i.e., "free lunches") are permitted. The price of a call option is given by

$$C_0 = E_0^*[e^{-rT} \max(0, S_T - K)] \tag{2}$$

where r is the market's risk-free rate of interest, and the expectation $E^*(\,\cdot\,)$ is taken over the possible final stock prices S_T, and sometimes over the paths of r as well. The probability measure under which E^* operates is known as the "risk-neutral" measure, and is derived from no-arbitrage principles. No discussion of this aspect of option pricing is offered here, and the reader is referred to the seminal work of Harrison and Kreps (1979) for a complete exposition. If the probability density of S_T under the risk-neutral measure is denoted $f(S_T)$, then the pricing model involves an integral as follows:

$$C_0 = \int_K^{\infty} e^{-rT}(S_T - K) f(S_T)\, dS_T \tag{3}$$

In a few limited cases, such as when S_T is log-normal, this integral yields a closed form solution. [See, e.g., Merton (1990, Chapter 3) for background on continuous-time modeling of security prices.] Most often, however, numerical integration is required, leading to a search for fast, accurate numerical algorithms.

These techniques usually consist of building a layered "lattice" depicting the evolution of the security price in time, and performing the required computations on it. If we use a lattice approach, the continuous-time, continuous-space model is transformed into a discrete-time, discrete-space one, leading to approximation error. This error can be mitigated by choosing a denser lattice representation for the stochastic process. The trade-off comes from the corresponding increase in computational effort of traversing a denser lattice.

A "lattice" is the generic term for any graph we build for the pricing of financial securities, and is a layered directed graph in which the nodes at each level represent the possible values of the underlying security in a given period. The entire life of the option spans time period T. The time step between levels $t-1$ and t is denoted $h(t)$, so that $\sum_t h(t) = T$. We shall denote the number of levels by d; thus, when $h(t) = h$ is the same for all t, we have $d = T/h$. Edges in the lattice are permitted only between nodes at successive levels; an edge from node i at level $t-1$ to node j at level t is labeled with the probability, $p_{ij}(t)$, of the corresponding change in the security price (from $S_i(t-1)$ to $S_j(t)$). We always have $\sum_j p_{ij}(t) = 1$ for all i and t.

We always assume that each node (except the single node at level 0) has in-degree 1, so that the lattice is a *tree*.[1] The starting security price S_0 comprises the single "root" (node at level 0) of the lattice, and the last level, or "leaves" of the lattice, correspond to all the possible final outcomes of the stock price. Figure 1 illustrates an example of such a lattice, which happens to be a balanced binary tree (i.e., each node has exactly two children). The transition probabilities p_{ij} are omitted.

Given the graphical representation of the stochastic process on the lattice, we can price the derivative security by computing the expected, discounted value of the payoffs at maturity under the risk-neutral measure. The lattice solution is a discretized version of Eq. (3):

$$C_0 = \sum_{l=1}^{L} \mathrm{e}^{-rT} \max(0, S_l(d) - K) \times \Pr(l) \tag{4}$$

where l indexes the leaves, L is the total number of leaves, and $\Pr(l)$ is the probability of reaching leaf l. Hence, each leaf value is given by $v_l = \mathrm{e}^{-rT} \max(0, S_l(d) - K) \times \Pr(l)$, which consists of three components: (i) the discounting factor e^{-rT}; (ii) the terminal payoff $\max(0, S_l(d) - K)$;[2] and (iii) the probability of the leaf $\Pr(l)$. The probability $\Pr(l)$ of a leaf l is just the product of probabilities of all the edges on the path to the leaf, i.e., $\Pr(l) = \prod_t p_{ij}(t)$, where the product is over all edges (i, j) on the path from the root to l.

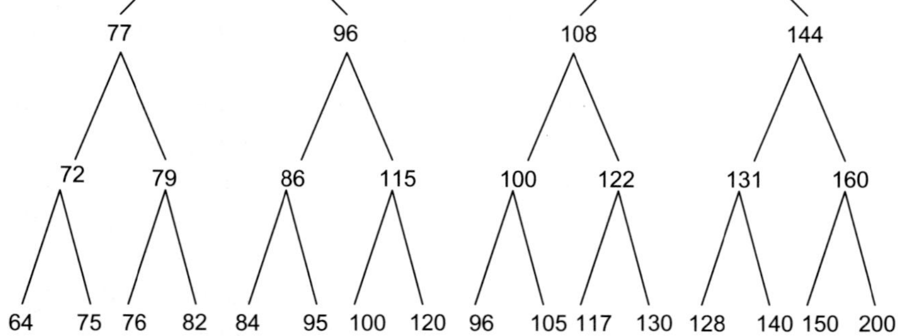

Figure 1 Examples of a stock price tree (lattice).

The derivative security's value on the lattice can easily be computed by dynamic programming. We first compute the payoff $C_l(d) = \max(0, S_l(d) - K)$ at each leaf of the tree. To obtain the value at a node at level $t-1$, we weight each "child" node j of i at level t by the probability $p_{ij}(t)$ of the edge from i to j. Thus, dynamic programming computes the value of node i as follows:

$$C_i(t-1) = \mathrm{e}^{-rh(t)}\left[\sum_j p_{ij}(t)C_j(t)\right], \quad \forall\, i, t \tag{5}$$

This eventually results in the desired value C_0.

The running time of dynamic programming is proportional to the size of the tree (i.e., the total number of nodes). In a typical (nonrecombining) tree of depth d, this will be *exponential* in the depth d. In other words, the size of the tree undergoes a "combinatorial explosion" as the depth increases. For example, in a *binary tree*, where each node is connected to two nodes at the next level (see, e.g., Figure 1), the size (and hence the running time) is proportional to 2^d. This is prohibitively large for values of d much above 20 or so. But in most cases of interest a discrete approximation with only about 20 time periods is not sufficient for a good approximation to the continuous time process. Our algorithm, sketched in the next section, is designed to overcome the effects of this combinatorial explosion. The algorithm will have a running time only *polynomial* in d, the depth of the tree.

2 Basic Ideas

A standard approach toward mitigating the above combinatorial explosion in the lattice is to use *Monte Carlo simulation.* This involves repeatedly sampling leaves of the lattice by simulating the branching probabilities $p_{ij}(t)$ of the underlying stock. When a leaf is sampled, its discounted payoff $\mathrm{e}^{-rT}\max(0, S_l(d) - K)$ is computed. The sample average of many leaves (i.e., Σ/N, where N is the number of leaves sampled and Σ is the sum of their discounted payoffs) is taken as the estimate of the desired value C_0. The problem with this approach is that, although the estimator is unbiased, it may have very high variance; specifically, its variance will be σ^2/N, where σ^2 is the variance of the payoffs (under the distribution induced by the underlying stock). This problem is particularly acute in situations where the payoff is highly skewed, i.e., large payoffs are associated with low probability leaves. In this situation σ^2 is very large, so the number of samples, N, has to be very large also in order to ensure a good statistical estimate.

The naive Monte Carlo approach can be improved using the idea of "importance sampling," which attempts to sample leaves with probabilities closer to their actural values, rather than to their probabilities according to the stochastic process governing the underlying stock. Suppose that we have available some information about the total contribution to the sum in (4) of all the leaves l in any given subtree; in other words, for each node i at level t, we have an estimate $\tilde{V}_i(t)$ of the quantity $\tilde{V}_i(t) = \sum_{l \in T_i} v_l$, which is the sum of the values of all the leaves l in the subtree T_i rooted at i. If in our Monte Carlo simulation we branch according to these subtree values,[3] rather than the probabilities $p_{ij}(t)$ associated with the underlying stock, then we would expect the variance to decrease. Indeed, if our estimates $\tilde{V}_i(t)$ were exact, we would sample each leaf with probability *exactly* proportional to its value, which would give us an estimator with zero variance![4]

Now, of course, in practice we will have only rough estimates $\tilde{V}_i(t)$. But if we use these approximate values to guide our brancing over many levels of the tree (large d), then the errors in the approximations may tend to accumulate so that the leaf sampling probabilities are again very far from being proportional to their values, resulting again in large variance. Indeed, over d levels it is possible to accumulate an error that is exponenetial in d, so that exponentially many samples will be needed to get a good estimate.

We overcome this obstacle by adapting an algorithm of Sinclair and Jerrum (1989), which was first introduced in the context of "approximate counting" in combinatorics. The algorithm is based on the idea of importance sampling as described above, but it uses *backtracking* as a means of "self-correcting" the estimates that drive the branching down the tree. Thus, the algorithm moves down the tree with probabilities proportional to the estimates $\tilde{V}_i(t)$ as above, but at each step it also has probability of moving *back* to the previous level. This backtracking probability will also be proportional to the corresponding estimate $\tilde{V}_i(t-1)$ at the previous level, so that if, for example, that estimate was actually an overestimate (and thus this branch was taken with too high probability), it will make backtracking more likely, thus mitigating the effect of the inflated probability. The resulting process is a Markov chain (a weighted random walk) on the tree, which converges to a stationary distribution in which the probability of each leaf is exactly proportional to its value.

Simulation of the Markov chain gives us a way of sampling leaves with the desired probabilities. However, since a leaf can be reached by many different sample paths, we can no longer get away with the very simple estimator described above for importance sampling. Instead, we apply a recursive estimation technique that uses leaf samples from successively smaller subtrees to obtain a statistical estimate of the value of the whole tree. The details of the algorithm are spelled out in the next section.

As indicated earlier, this kind of importance sampling approach is most useful in situations where the tree is highly skewed, i.e., where high payoffs correspond to low path probabilities $\Pr(l)$ for the leaf. In these situations naive Monte Carlo methods will lead to estimators with high error, since they will explore regions of the tree that are high in probability, instead of regions that are high in value. Such "needle in a haystack" problems occur frequently in finance. In the case of credit options, for example, this is quite severe. A credit option pays off a large sum when a firm defaults during period $[0, T]$, a low probability event, and pays nothing when the company is solvent at T, a high probability event in the case of most firms. Another example of this phenomenon is that of barrier options, where the option payoff may depend on the stock price remaining within narrow regions of the state space. We shall give an example of such an application, together with experimental results for our algorithm, in Section 4.

Finally, we mention that there are several alternative approaches commonly taken to improve the efficiency of a naive Monte Carlo estimator, such as antithetic variate techniques, control variate methods, non-random sampling, Sobol space approaches, etc. A good recent reference for all these methods as applied in finance is Glasserman (2003).

3 The Algorithm

The Markov Chain Monte Carlo (MCMC) method is an approach that has proven to be very successful in combinatorics, statistical physics, statistical inference in probability models, computing volumes and integration, and combinatorial optimization. See Jerrum and Sinclair (1996) for a survey of these applications, and of some of the tools available for analyzing the rate of convergence (and hence the experimental error).

3.1 Set-Up

For simplicity we consider only *(full) binary* trees, in which each node has out-degree exactly two. There is nothing special about binary trees, and everything we say can be generalized to arbitrary trees (with suitable minor modifications). In a binary tree of depth d, the total number of nodes is $2^{d+1} - 1$ and the number of leaves is 2^d.

3.2 Overall Structure

The algorithm consists of two components: a "random sampling" component and a "recursive estimation" component. The goal of the random sampling component is to sample each leaf in a given subtree with probability proportional to its value $v_l \equiv e^{-rT} \max(S_l(d) - K, 0) \Pr(l)$. The recursive estimation component uses these random samples in successively smaller subtrees in order to obtain an estimate of $C_0 = \sum_l v_l$, the aggregated value of all the leaves.

3.3 Recursive Estimation

We first describe the recursive estimation component, which is fairly standard. The idea here is the following. Suppose we sample leaves with probabilities proportional to their values. In a sample of N leaves, let N_1, N_2, respectively, denote the number of leaves in the two subtrees whose roots are the children of the root. Assume w.l.o.g. that $N_1 \geq N_2$.[5] Let V_1 denote the sum of leaf values in the first subtree. Then the quantity

$$\tilde{V}_0 = V_1 \times \frac{N_1 + N_2}{N_1} \tag{6}$$

is clearly a good estimator of V_0, the aggregated value of all leaves in the entire tree.

Now we can apply the above idea recursively on the first subtree to obtain an estimate $\tilde{V}_1$ of V_1, and so on down the tree. At each level we use random sampling to obtain an unbiased estimate $\tilde{R}_t = N_1(t)/(N_1(t) + N_2(t))$ of the proportion of leaves

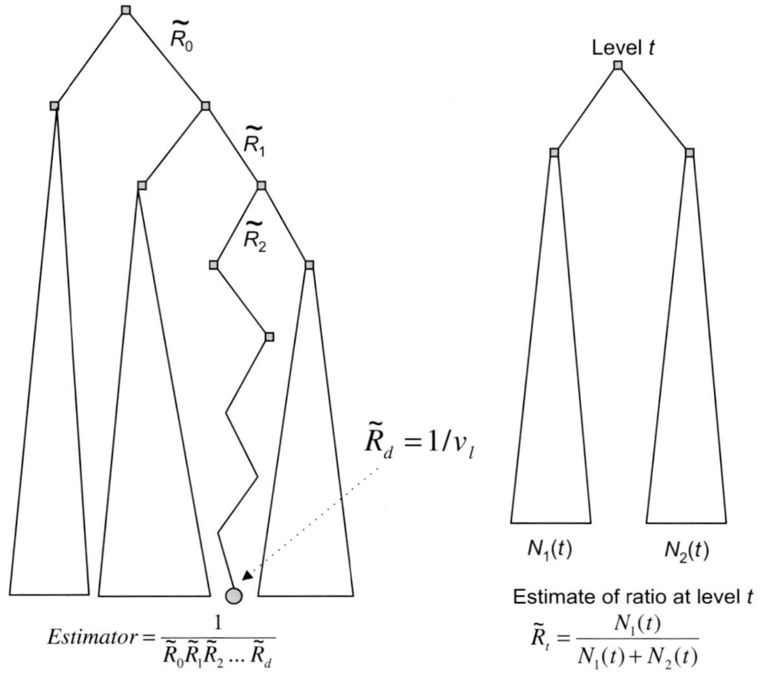

Figure 2 The recursive estimation procedure.

sampled in one of the two subtrees at this level. Our final estimate for $C_0 = V_0$ is then

$$\tilde{C}_0 = \prod_{t=0}^{d} \frac{1}{\tilde{R}_t} \tag{7}$$

At the bottom level d, the "tree" consists of the single leaf node l and the estimate $\tilde{R}_d$ (which is in fact exact) is just $1/v_l$, where v_l is the value of this leaf (Figure 2).

The efficiency of the above scheme depends on the number of samples, N, we need to take at each level to ensure that (7) is a good estimate with high probability. This in turn depends on the variance of the estimator. As we shall argue in Appendix A, it suffices to take $N = O(d/\epsilon^2)$ to obtain an estimate that is within a factor $(1 \pm \epsilon)$ of C_0 with high probability.

3.4 Random Sampling

The random sampling is achieved via a novel use of MCMC. This proceeds by simulating a weighted random walk (a Markov chain) on the lattice (binary tree), viewed as an *undirected* graph; i.e., backtracking to previous levels is allowed. From any given node x, transitions are permitted to the "parent" y of x, and to the two "children" z_1, z_2 of x. The transition probabilities are determined as follows. For any node x in the tree, let V_x denote the aggregated weight of all leaves in the subtree T_x, rooted at x, i.e., $V_x = \sum_{l \in T_x} v_l$. Also, let $\tilde{V}_x$ be an estimate of V_x obtained from some other source

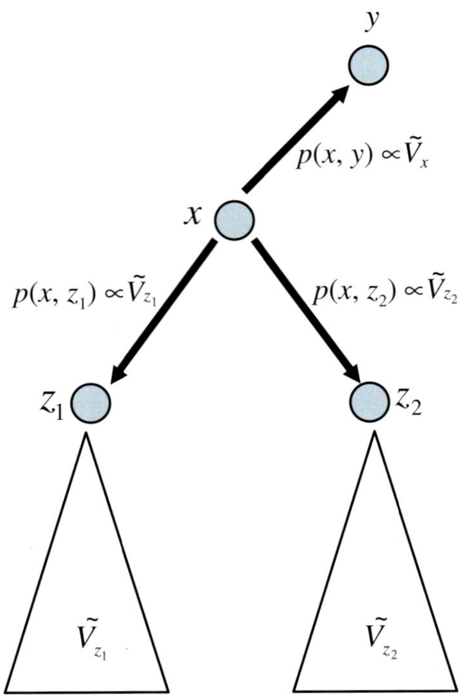

Figure 3 The Markov chain.

(see below). Then the transition probabilities from x are (Figure 3):

$$\begin{aligned} p(x,y) &= \frac{\tilde{V}_x}{\tilde{V}_x + \tilde{V}_{z_1} + \tilde{V}_{z_2}} \\ p(x,z_1) &= \frac{\tilde{V}_{z_1}}{\tilde{V}_x + \tilde{V}_{z_1} + \tilde{V}_{z_2}} \\ p(x,z_2) &= \frac{\tilde{V}_{z_2}}{\tilde{V}_x + \tilde{V}_{z_1} + \tilde{V}_{z_2}} \end{aligned} \tag{8}$$

Notice that the estimate $\tilde{V}_x$ determines *both* the probability of branching *down* to x from its parent y, *and* the probability of branching *back up* to y from x. Thus, if $\tilde{V}_x$ is an overestimate, then both of these probabilities will tend to become inflated. It is this feature that makes the algorithm "self-correcting."

The transition probabilities at the root and the leaves are special cases. At the root (which has to parent), we branch only to the two children with probabilities $\tilde{V}_{z_1}/(\tilde{V}_{z_1} + \tilde{V}_{z_2})$ and $\tilde{V}_{z_2}/(\tilde{V}_{z_1} + \tilde{V}_{z_2})$ respectively. At the leaves (which have no children), we backtrack to the parent with probability $\frac{1}{2}$, and remain in place (a "self-loop") with probability $\frac{1}{2}$.[6]

We now discuss the estimates $\tilde{V}_x$. These can be obtained in any way, e.g., by solving some approximation to the stochastic process under investigation that has a closed form solution, or by using a crude upper or lower bound on the value of a subtree. We assume only that, for all nodes x, $\tilde{V}_x$ approximates the true value V_x within ratio β, i.e.,

$$\frac{1}{\beta} V_x \leq \tilde{V}_x \leq \beta V_x \quad \forall\, x$$

for some $\beta \geq 1$. Moreover, when x is a leaf l, we assume that $\tilde{V}_x = v_l$ is exact (which we may do w.l.o.g. since we can compute the exact value of any given leaf as explained earlier).

Given all the above ingredients, we argue in Appendix A that the Markov chain has the following properties:

1. The Markov chain is *ergodic*, i.e., starting at any state (node) it converges to some fixed *stationary distribution* π over the nodes, independent of the starting state. Moreover, for any leaf l the probability π_l is proportional to the leaf value v_l, and the total probability $\sum_l \pi_l$ of all the leaves is at least $1/(\beta d + 1)$.
2. The "mixing time" of the Markov chain, i.e., the number of simulation steps required to ensure that the distribution of the simulated chain is close to the stationary distribution π, starting at the root, is $O(\beta^2 d^2 \log(\beta^2 d))$, where d is the depth of the subtree on which the Markov chain resides.

To obtain a sample leaf from any given subtree, we proceed as follows: simulate the Markov chain on that subtree, starting from its root, for τ steps, where τ is at least the mixing time for that subtree. If the final node is a leaf, output that leaf; if not, restart the simulation from the root. Property (1) above ensure that leaves will be sampled with probability proportional to v_l, as required.[7] It also ensures that the simulation will output a leaf with probability at least $1/(\beta d + 1)$. Thus, the total (expected) time to sample a leaf is $O(\beta d \tau)$. By Property (2) above, this is at most $O(\beta^3 d^3 \log(\beta^2 d))$, which is polynomial in d.

3.5 *Overall Running Time*

Putting the above two ingredients together, we see that the total running time is the number of samples times the time per sample, which is $O(\beta^3 d^4 \epsilon^{-2} \log(\beta^2 d))$. This is a polynomial function of d, and for large d compares favorably with the exponential time $O(2^d)$ required by dynamic programming.

We note also the dependence of the running time on β, the error in our approximations for the subtree values. This produces a factor of essentially $O(\beta^3)$, which again is not catastrophic. Note also that the algorithm can be viewed as taking as input β-approximations to these values (one might think in terms of $\beta \approx 2$ or $\beta \approx 10$) and outputting much better approximations (within ratio $1 + \epsilon$ for small ϵ). In particular, we get a much better approximation to the value $V_0 = C_0$, which is the sum of the values of all the leaves in the tree. This, of course, is the desired price of the security.

4 An Application: Barrier Options

In this section, we present an illustrative application of the algorithm to the pricing of barrier options. In the next section, we will point out other possible applications of the approach.

A barrier option may be a call, put, or digital option; here, we restrict our attention to double-barrier knockout digitals. This is an option that pays off a large sum M if the stock price remains within a pre-specified range (bounded by two "barriers") for the entire period of the option. The initial stock price is denoted S_0, and the barriers are denoted S_{high} and S_{low}, respectively. The risk-neutral evolution of the stock price over discrete periods of time h is the following: in each period, the stock price either moves up by a factor U or down by a factor D. Thus, at time $t + h$, the stock takes values in the set $S(t + h) = US(t) \cup DS(t)$. The lattice is therefore a full binary tree of depth d (where T is the total time period and $d = T/h$). The payoff is M at all leaves whose path from the root does not cross either of the two barriers; i.e., all immediate stock prices along the path remain within the range $[S_{\text{low}}, S_{\text{high}}]$. At all other leaves the payoff is zero. To keep matters simple, the risk-free interest rate is assumed to be zero. As shown in Cox *et al.* (1979), the no-arbitrage principle dictates that the probability of an up-move in the stock price is equal to $p = (1 - D)/(U - D)$; a down-move occurs with probability $1 - p$.

For the purposes of experimentation, assume that $U = 1/D$, which means in fact that the lattice is recombining. We do this because it provides us with a closed-form solution for the stock price (summation of leaf values) in every subtree, which we can use both as a means for testing our algorithm and as a source for the approximate information required by the algorithm (see below). However, we stress that the algorithm itself is oblivious to this recombining property, and is working over the full binary tree of depth d.

As is apparent, this is a particularly hard problem when the range between the barriers is relatively narrow, since then the probability of a payoff is low. Naive simulation of the stock price will be very wasteful because the simulation will almost always generate paths of value zero. By contrast, our MCMC algorithm will sample leaves with probabilities proportional to their values, and thus concentrate the samples in the desired central portion of the tree.

Because we have analytical solution for this problem, we are able to evaluate exactly the quantity V_x (the sum of leaf values in the subtree rooted at x) at any node x of the tree. In particular, by evaluating this at the root we get the desired value $V_0 = C_0$ of the option, so we can judge how well our algorithm is doing. Moreover, we can use the exact values V_x to generate the *approximate* values $\tilde{V}_x$ needed by the algorithm by simply perturbing V_x by some specified factor β. This allows us to experiment with varying degrees of approximation β. Note in particular that, whatever the value of β, if $V_x = 0$ then $\tilde{V}_x = 0$. Therefore, the algorithm will never cross the barriers during simulation.

For comparison, we also compare our MCMC approach with a standard Importance Sampling (IS) algorithm that makes use of exactly the same approximate value $\tilde{V}_x$ (see below for a detailed specification). This is a fair and appropriate comparison (unlike with naive simulation, which has access to no additional information). When there is no error in our estimates $\tilde{V}_x$, (i.e., $\beta = 1$), we would expect IS to be perfectly accurate. However, as β increases, so that the estimates become less accurate, we would expect IS to accumulate significant errors over the tree, and eventually to be outperformed by the MCMC algorithm.

As an illustration, we fix the depth (number of periods) of the tree to be $d = 40$. The initial stock price is set to be $S_0 = 100$, and the payoff $M = 100{,}000$. The interest rate is zero. The stock volatility is $\sigma = 30\%$ per year, and the maturity of the option is taken to be $T = 1$ year. Since there are $d = 40$ periods, the time interval is $h = T/d = 0.025$. The up move in the stock price is $U = e^{\sigma\sqrt{h}}$, and the down move is $D = e^{\sigma\sqrt{h}}$. The lower and upper barriers are set to be $S_{\text{low}} = 93.158$ and $S_{\text{high}} = 107.400$. The probability of an up move is 0.4881 and that of a down move is 0.5112. Note that this problem has a very narrow range, with at most two consecutive rises or falls possible if the stock is to remain within the barriers. The probability of a nonzero payoff at maturity is on the order of one in a million. Hence, this is a canonical "needle in a haystack" problem.

We ran the following two types of simulations:

1. *The MCMC approach.* Here, we implement the algorithm described in the preceding section for the binary tree above of fixed depth $d = 40$, with various different approximation ratios β. We obtain the approximate values $\tilde{V}_x$ as follows. Using the closed form for the sum of leaf values in any subtree, we compute V_x exactly. Then, we multiply V_x by either β or β^{-1}, the choice being made by a fair coin toss, independently for each x. Thus, all of our estimates will be off by a factor of exactly β, and are equally likely to be under- or over-estimates.

   We fix number or leaf samples taken per level to 10,000 (recall that this number depends only on the depth d, and not on β). The number of Markov chain steps for each simulation depends on the approximation ratio β as well as on the depth d of the current subtree; following our analysis in the previous subsection, we take it to be $C\beta^2 d^2 \log(\beta^2 d)$, where C is a constant. We first arbitrarily set $C = 1$ for this experiment. Finding that it provided accurate estimates, we established the minimum run time for the importance sampler, which we exceeded in our experiments so as to bias the comparison in favor of importance sampling. Subsequently, to bias the results against MCMC, we reduced C to one-tenth, i.e., $C = 0.1$.

   By simulating the Markov chain on appropriate subtrees, and taking the resulting leaf samples, we compute a sequence of ratios $\tilde{R}_t$, one for each level. The final output is the product of the reciprocals of these ratios, as described in the previous section.
2. *Importance Sampling.* This is essentially equivalent to the MCMC approach but without backtracking. From a node x in the tree, IS branches down to one of the two children z_1, z_2 of x with probabilities $\tilde{V}_{z_1}/(\tilde{V}_{z_1} + \tilde{V}_{z_2})$ and $\tilde{V}_{z_2}/(\tilde{V}_{z_1} + \tilde{V}_{z_2})$, respectively. Eventually, it will reach a leaf l, with necessarily non-zero payoff M.[8]

During branching, IS keeps track of both the true probability of the leaf, $\Pr(l)$, and the probability p with which the leaf was actually reached (i.e., the product of the branching probabilities along the path taken). The value output by IS is then $M\Pr(l)/p$, i.e., the leaf value adjusted for the importance sampling.

For a fair comparison, we ran IS for at least as long as the MCMC approach with $C = 1$, i.e., we allowed IS to take repeated independent samples as described above until it had used a similar running time MCMC.[9] The final output of IS was then the mean of all these samples.

In order to compare the performance of the algorithms, we ran each algorithm five times. We recorded the following data: (i) the mean value of five runs, (ii) the standard deviation of these values, (iii) the run time of the algorithm, and (iv) the maximum and minimum of run values. All experiments were run on a Windows PC on an Intel 3.2 GHz processor with 1 MB of RAM. Programs are written in Java (ver. 1.4) and run on a Windows XP platform. No attempt was made to optimize the code.

The results are presented in Table 1. We ran our experiment with $\beta = \{1, 2, 3\}$ for the IS, and did not raise β further, as the IS became very inaccurate (see top panel of Table 1). We then generated results for the MCMC (with $C = 0.1$) and

Table 1 Comparison of run times and estimator accuracy for the IS and MCMC algorithms. Run times are in milliseconds.

Importance sampling

	$\beta = 1$		$\beta = 2$		$\beta = 3$	
Run no.	Est. value	CPU time	Est. value	CPU time	Est. value	CPU time
1	0.0929	13066426	0.1955	43218362	0.0492	57756313
2	0.0941	13244863	0.0810	43333972	0.0527	57653343
3	0.0929	13098622	0.0812	43208828	0.0265	57035578
4	0.0929	13019433	0.1607	43182917	0.0250	57448016
5	0.0943	13096241	0.1067	43111802	0.0275	57781609
Mean	0.0934	13105117	01250	43211176	0.0362	57534972
St. dev.	0.0007		0.0511		0.0121	

MCMC sampling

	$\beta = 1$		$\beta = 2$		$\beta = 3$		$\beta = 5$	
Run no.	Est. value	CPU time	Est. value	CPU time	Est. value	CPU time	Est. value	CPU time
1	0.0924	356140	0.0961	1448094	0.0975	3843578	0.1016	16331234
2	0.0916	355516	0.0960	1442141	0.0890	3847797	0.0977	14941203
3	0.0991	361313	0.0843	1493046	0.0978	3894750	0.0955	14442125
4	0.0883	354671	0.0942	1443282	0.0937	4074860	0.0966	14422719
5	01008	355454	0.0894	1445750	0.0966	4196750	0.0909	14568000
Mean	0.0945	356618	0.0920	1454463	0.0949	3971547	0.0965	14938856
St. dev.	0.0047		0.0046		0.0033		0.0034	

True mean value = 0.0943

$\beta = \{1, 2, 3, 5\}$, and found that this gave acceptable accuracy, at much smaller run times.

When $\beta = 1$, the estimates $\tilde{V}_x$ are exactly equal to their correct values V_x, and the IS algorithm provides an exact result with zero variance (apart from minor rounding errors), as it should. As we inject errors into the estimates by increasing β, the performance of IS degrades significantly, even though it has time to over-sample the leaves.

As expected, the MCMC algorithm does not perform as well as importance sampling when $\beta = 1$ (the standard error is seven times that of importance sampling), as it always suffers from some statistical error. However, as β increases its performance does not degrade. This demonstrates the ability of the MCMC algorithm to correct for substantial errors in the approximate values supplied for the subtrees.[10] While these experiments are very limited, we believe that they provide a proof of concept for the potential usefulness of the MCMC approach in derivative pricing.

5 Discussion

We stress again that the illustrative application to barrier options presented in the previous section is a very simple one, intended purely as a proof of concept. Indeed, given that an analytic solution is available in this case, there is really no need for simulation at all; moreover, the lattices is in reality recombining so exhaustive enumeration would in fact be quite feasible here. However, note that our implementation made no use of the recombining property, and it used the analytic solution only in order to generate approximations $\tilde{V}_x$ (which are deliberately perturbed versions of the exact values). Our aim is to illustrate how the MCMC approach is able to correct errors in the information supplied to it. We note also that the running time of the simulations is fairly large. While this is in part due to the fact that we made no attempt to optimize the code, it is also an inherent feature of the method: being computationally intensive, it is most likely to be useful in situations where the combinatorial explosion of the size of the lattice defeats all other methods.

We note also that our assumption that the lattice is a binary tree is inessential, and large (non-uniform) branching can easily be incorporated. In particular, even with a binary tree, one might investigate a possible speed-up of the algorithm by jumping down (and up) by two or more levels at a time. (Thus, we would classify our leaf samples according to which of the *four* subtrees two levels below they belong to. We would then choose the "heaviest" of these subtrees and recursively estimate its weight.) It would be interesting to investigate the tradeoff between the reduction in the number of levels of the tree and the larger number of samples needed at each level to control the variance of the overall estimate.

The MCMC technique requires approximations $\tilde{V}_x$ for the value of the tree under any given node x, and, hence, the natural question arises as to how to come up with such approximations in more realistic examples. One possibility is to use a simplification of the actual stochastic process on the underlying stock, for which a known closed-form solution exists. Say, for instance, we are pricing stock options assuming an equity process with stochastic volatility. The value of a subtree under a given node may then be approximated using the well-known Black and Scholes (1973) pricing equation, which assumes instead that the volatility of the equity process is constant. A second possibility is to approximate subtree values using a much sparser tree for the same stochastic process. Thus, if the depth of the actual tree is $d = 40$, say, we might obtain approximate values using a tree of depth only 10 (which is small enough to be rapidly evaluated by exhaustive enumeration). Other strategies are also possible. Note also that subtrees whose total value is known to be very small can safely be eliminated. We stress that, whatever method is used to obtain the approximation $\tilde{V}_x$, the MCMC algorithm is in principle able to correct any error in these approximations. Of course, the larger the error β in the approximations, the larger the simulation time we need to allow for each sample.

There are many settings in which Monte Carlo simulation is required in pricing financial securities. Path-dependent options are common examples, where even if the stock process can be embedded on a recombining lattice, if the payoff is path-dependent, the pricing scheme needs to be implemented on a nonrecombining tree, making exhaustive enumeration impractical. For instance, though there are recombining lattice algorithms for pricing options in the GARCH(1,1) case (see Ritchken and Trevor, 1999), the GARCH(p, q) model requires Monte Carlo methods. Likewise, stochastic volatility models pose the same difficulties. Models with recombining lattice versions for this pricing problem are few and far between, and rely on restrictive choices of stochastic processes for volatility. Closed-form solutions are also known only in a few cases (as in Heston, 1993). In particular, our MCMC approach could be useful for the pricing of volatility arbitrage strategies, and smile trading, which have highly skewed payoffs. The MCMC approach may also be useful in providing error correction in some cases where importance sampling is currently used. A classic problem where IS may be enhanced with MCMC is in the area of Value-at-Risk estimation. The most popular class of term structure models, i.e., the Libor Market Models (LMMs), now rely heavily on simulation, and our approach may be adapted to this realm as well.

Appendix A: Properties of the Algorithm

In this appendix, we provide a brief sketch of the arguments leading to the stated properties. This is based on the work of Sinclair and Jerrum (1989).

A.1 Discussion of Variance

In Section 3, we claimed that only $O(d/\varepsilon^2)$ leaf samples per level are required to obtain an estimate that is within a factor $(1 \pm \varepsilon)$ of the tree sum C_0 with high probability. Recall from (7) that our overall estimator is

$$\tilde{C}_0 = \prod_t \frac{1}{\tilde{R}_t}$$

For convenience, we will work with the reciprocal estimator

$$\tilde{Z}_0 = \prod_t \tilde{R}_t$$

The efficiency of the estimator is governed by the quantity

$$\gamma(\tilde{Z}_0) = \frac{\mathrm{Var}(\tilde{Z}_0)}{\mathrm{E}(\tilde{Z}_0)^2}$$

By a standard application of Chebyshev's inequality, the probability that the estimator deviates by more than a $(1 \pm \varepsilon)$ factor from its mean is at most $\gamma(\tilde{Z}_0)/\varepsilon^2$. The same holds for the original estimator $\tilde{C}_0$. Thus, it suffices to analyze $\gamma(\tilde{Z}_0)$.

Now he have

$$\begin{aligned}
\mathrm{Var}(\tilde{Z}_0) &= \mathrm{Var}\left(\prod_t \tilde{R}_t\right) = \mathrm{E}\left(\prod_t \tilde{R}_t^2\right) - \mathrm{E}\left(\prod_t \tilde{R}_t\right)^2 \\
&= \prod_t \mathrm{E}(\tilde{R}_t^2) - \prod_t \mathrm{E}(\tilde{R}_t)^2 = \prod_t [\mathrm{Var}(\tilde{R}_t) + \mathrm{E}(\tilde{R}_t)^2] - \prod_t \mathrm{E}(\tilde{R}_t)^2 \\
&= \prod_t \left[\left(\frac{\mathrm{Var}(\tilde{R}_t)}{\mathrm{E}(\tilde{R}_t)^2} + 1\right)\mathrm{E}(\tilde{R}_t)^2\right] - \prod_t \mathrm{E}(\tilde{R}_t)^2 \\
&= \left[\prod_t (\gamma(\tilde{R}_t) + 1) - 1\right] \prod_t \mathrm{E}(\tilde{R}_t)^2
\end{aligned}$$

and hence

$$\gamma(\tilde{Z}_0) = \prod_t (\gamma(\tilde{R}_t) + 1) - 1 \tag{A.1}$$

Now each $\tilde{R}_t$ is an unbiased estimator of the proportion $p(t)$ of leaf value lying in one of the two subtrees at level t. It is obtained as the sum of N Bernoulli trials, each with "success" probability $p(t)$. Thus, its mean is $p(t)$ and its variance is $(1/N)p(t)(1-p(t))$, and hence $\gamma(\tilde{R}_t) = (1/N)(1 - p(t))/(p(t))$. Recall that we always choose the subtree with the larger number of samples; this means that, with high probability, $p(t) \geq \frac{1}{4}$ (and we shall neglect the small probability of this not being the case). Thus, $\gamma(\tilde{R}_t) \leq 3/N$. Plugging this into (A.1) we get

$$\gamma(\tilde{Z}_0) \leq \prod_t \left(1 + \frac{3}{N}\right) - 1 = \left(1 + \frac{3}{N}\right)^d - 1 \leq \mathrm{e}^{3d/N} - 1$$

Taking $N = 3kd$ we get $\gamma(\tilde{Z}_0) \leq \mathrm{e}^{1/k} - 1 \approx 1/k$. Thus, we see that a sample size of $N = O(d/\varepsilon^2)$ at each level suffices, as claimed.

A.2 Discussion of Property (1)

We note first that the Markov chain is *irreducible* (i.e., any state can be reached from any other state) and *aperiodic* (because of the self-loops on the leaves). By the standard theory of Markov chains, this implies it is ergodic.

To compute the stationary distribution π, we associate with each (undirected) edge $\{x,y\}$ of the tree a *weight* equal to $\tilde{V}_x$, the estimate of the aggregated value V_x of the subtree rooted at the *lower* end x of the edge. For any node x, we define the degree $d(x)$ of x to be the sum of the weights of the edges incident at x. Thus, if x has parent y and children z_1, z_2, then

$$d(x) = \tilde{V}_x + \tilde{V}_{z_1} + \tilde{V}_{z_2}$$

Now from the definition (8), we see that our Markov chain makes transitions from x with probabilities $\tilde{V}_x/d(x)$, $\tilde{V}_{z_1}/d(x)$, $\tilde{V}_{z_2}/d(x)$, which are proportional to the edge weights. The same is true for the special case of leaves l, if we view the self-loop as an edge with weight v_l and set $d(l) = 2v_l$. Hence, our Markov chain is a standard random walk on the *edge-weighted* tree, which implies that its distribution is proportional to the node degrees; i.e., $\pi(x) = d(x)/D$ where $D = \sum_x d(x)$ is a normalizing constant. This immediately shows that, for any leaf l, $\pi(l) = 2v_l/D$, as we claimed.

Now consider any node x. Note that

$$d(x) = \tilde{V}_x + \tilde{V}_{z_1} + \tilde{V}_{z_2} \le \beta(V_x + V_{z_1} + V_{z_2}) = 2\beta V_x \tag{A.2}$$

In the first step here we have used the fact that each $\tilde{V}.$ is a β-approximation to $V.$; in the second step we have used the fact that $V_x = V_{z_1} + V_{z_2}$ (because both of these expressions is equal to the aggregated value of all leaves in the subtree rooted at x). If we now sum (A.2) over all nodes x at any given level t of the tree (other than the leaves), we get

$$\sum_{x \text{ at level } t} d(x) \le 2\beta \sum_{x \text{ at level } t} V_x = 2\beta C_0 \tag{A.3}$$

(Clearly the sum of V_x over all nodes x at any level is the total leaf sum C_0.) On the other hand, if we carry out the same sum at the leaf level, we get

$$\sum_{\text{leaves } l} d(l) = \sum_l 2v_l = 2C_0 \tag{A.4}$$

Putting together (A.3) and (A.4) we see that

$$D = \sum_x d(x) \le 2\beta d C_0 + 2C_0 = 2C_0(\beta d + 1) \tag{A.5}$$

Using (A.4) again, we get that the total probability of the leaves is

$$\sum_l \pi(l) = \frac{1}{D}\sum_l d(l) \ge \frac{2C_0}{2C_0(\beta d + 1)} = \frac{1}{\beta d + 1}$$

as we claimed. This concludes the verification of Property (1).

A.3 Discussion of Property (2)

The "mixing time" of an ergodic Markov chain (X_t) with stationary distribution π is defined as the time until the distribution of X_t is within total variation distance[11] δ

of π, starting from some given state X_0, i.e.,

$$\tau_{X_0}(\delta) = \min\{t: \|X_t - \pi\| \leq \delta\}$$

Standard techniques for the analysis of mixing times, specialized to our random walk on an edge-weighted rooted tree of depth d, tell us that

$$\tau_{X_0}(\delta) \leq d \log(\pi(X_0)^{-1} + \log(\delta^{-1})) \left(\min_x \frac{p(x,y)\pi(x)}{\pi(T_x)} \right)^{-1} \tag{A.6}$$

where $p(x,y)$ is the probability of backtracking from x to its parent y, and $\pi(T_x)$ denotes the total stationary probability of all nodes in the subtree T_x rooted at x. The intuitive explanation for the minimization in (A.6) is that expresses the minimum "escape probability" from any subtree, normalized by the "weight" of that subtree: if this quantity is large then the random walk cannot get trapped in any subtree for too long (relative to the weight of the subtree), and hence the mixing time is not too large. The factor $\log(\pi(X_0)^{-1})$ captures the effect of the initial state X_0, and the factor d arises from the diameter of the tree. The term $\log(\delta^{-1})$ is the price we have to pay for increasing accuracy (i.e., decreasing deviation from the stationary distribution); for simplicity, we shall assume that this term can be absorbed into the term $\log(\pi(X_0)^{-1})$ in our application and will therefore neglect it for the remainder of this discussion. Equation (A.6) is a special case of a general "multicommodity flow" technique for bounding mixing times; a full derivation can be found, e.g., in Sinclair (1992).

To bound the right-hand side in (A.6) for our Markov chain, consider any node x and its subtree T_x. By definition of the transition probabilities $p(x,y)$ we have

$$p(x,y)\pi(x) = \frac{\tilde{V}_x}{d(x)} \times \frac{d(x)}{D} = \frac{\tilde{V}_x}{D}$$

Also, by similar reasoning to the derivation of (A.5), we have

$$\pi(T_x) = \frac{1}{D} \sum_{z \in T_x} d(z) \leq \frac{2V_x}{D}(\beta d + 1)$$

Hence, the minimum in (A.6) is given by

$$\min_x \frac{p(x,y)\pi(x)}{\pi(T_x)} \geq \frac{\tilde{V}_x}{D} \times \frac{D}{2V_x(\beta d + 1)} \geq \frac{1}{4\beta^2 d}$$

where we have used the fact that $\tilde{V}_x / V_x \geq 1/\beta$ (and $\beta d + 1 \leq 2\beta d$). Also, since we always start our simulation from the root, we have, again by similar reasoning,

$$\pi(X_0) \geq \frac{d(\text{root})}{D} \geq \frac{1}{\beta} \times \frac{1}{\beta d + 1} \geq \frac{1}{2\beta^2 d}$$

Plugging all this into Eq. (A.6) we get the following bound on the mixing time:

$$\tau_{\text{root}}(\delta) \leq d \log(2\beta^2 d) \times 4\beta^2 d = O(\beta^2 d^2 \log(\beta^2 d))$$

This concludes the justification of Property (2).

Notes

[1] Note that we do not consider so-called "recombining lattices," where the in-degree is greater than 1. Recombining lattices typically do not suffer from the combinatorial explosion of the number of nodes (see below), so the need for faster algorithms is not so acute here.

[2] In more complex options, the terminal payoff may not be a function only of the terminal price $S_l(d)$, but may depend on the *path* leading to leaf l.

[3] That is, from node i at level $t-1$, branch to node j at level t with probability proportional to $\tilde{V}_j(t)$. In this strategy, when we reach a leaf the value of our estimator is not the discounted payoff at the leaf as before, but rather this value times the ratio $\Pr(l)/p$, where p is the product of the branching probabilities we actually took to reach the leaf.

[4] In fact, if these estimates were exact then we would have nothing to do because the estimate at the root, $\tilde{V}_0$, would be equal to $V_0 \equiv C_0$, which is what we are trying to compute!

[5] If not, then simply interchange the labels 1 and 2. The purpose of choosing the subtree with larger value is to minimize the variance; the estimator would still make sense if we used the smaller subtree in place of the larger one but the variance would be higher.

[6] This seemingly arbitrary detail is actually important for the algorithm as specified here: if we did not have this self-loop probability then the Markov chain would be *periodic*, i.e., it would always be at odd levels of the tree at odd time steps and even levels at even time steps, and hence would not converge to a stationary distribution.

[7] Strictly speaking, there will be a small error here because the distribution of the chain will not be exactly π, but very close to it. We can absorb this error into the other sources of statistical error in the algorithm.

[8] Like the MCMC algorithm, IS will also never cross the barriers because it is using the same values $\tilde{V}_x$.

[9] In fact, since the running time of MCMC was quite large, IS had time to over-sample all its leaves, thus dispensing with any statistical error. However, IS is still left with the systematic error resulting from the skewed distribution from which it samples leaves.

[10] We also ran the importance sampler much longer, basing the run times on the MCMC algorithm run times with $C = 1$.

[11] For two probability distributions μ_1, μ_2 over a finite set Ω, the total variation distance $||\mu_1 - \mu_2||$ is defined as $(1/2)\sum_{x\in\Omega} |\mu_1(x) - \mu_2(x)|$.

References

Black, F. and Scholes, M. (1973). "The Pricing of Options and Corporate Liabilities." *Journal of Political Economy* **81**, 637–654.

Cox, J., Ross, S. and Rubinstein, M. (1979). "Option Pricing: A Simplified Approach." *Journal of Financial Economics* 7, 229–264.

Glasserman, P. (2003). *Monte Carlo Methods in Financial Enginering.* New York: Springer-Verlag.

Harrison, J. and Kreps, D. (1979). "Martingales and Arbitrage in Multiperiod Securities Markets." *Journal of Economic Theory* **20**, 381–408.

Heston, S.L. (1993). "A Closed-Form Solution for Options with Stochastic Volatility with Applications to Bond and Currency Options." *Review of Financial Studies* **6**(2), 327–343.

Jerrum, M. and Sinclair, A. (1996). "The Markov Chain Monte Carlo Method: An Approach to Approximate Counting and Integration." In: Hochbaum, D.S. (ed.) *Approximation Algorithms for NP-hard Problems.* Boston: PWS Publishing, pp. 482–520.

Merton, R.C. (1990). *Continuous-Time Finance.* New York: Blackwell.

Ritchken, P. and Trevon, R. (1999). "Pricing Options Under Generalized GARCH and Stochastic Volatility Processes." *Journal of Finance* **54**, 377–402.
Sinclair, A. and Jerrum, M. (1989). "Approximate Counting, Uniform Generation and Rapidly Mixing Markov Chains." *Information and Computation* **82**, 93–133.
Sinclair, A. (1992). "Improved Bounds for Mixing Rates of Markov Chains and Multicommodity Flow." *Combinatorics, Probility and Computing* **1**, 351–370.

Keywords: Markov chain Monte Carlo; derivative pricing; risk assessment; importance sampling

Journal Of Investment Management
Vol. 2, No. 3 (2004), pp. 20–34

ACTIVE RISK AND INFORMATION RATIO

Edward Qian[a] *and Ronald Hua*[b]

One of the underlying assumptions of the Fundamental Law of Active Management is that the active risk of an active investment strategy equates estimated tracking error by a risk model. We show there is an additional source of active risk that is unique to each strategy. This strategy risk is caused by variability of the strategy's information coefficient over time. This implies that true active risk is often different from, and in many cases, significantly higher than the estimated tracking error given by a risk model. We show that a more consistent *estimation of information ratio is the ratio of average information coefficient to the standard deviation of information coefficient. We further demonstrate how the interaction between information coefficient and investment opportunity, in terms of cross-sectional dispersion of actual returns, influences the IR. We then provide supporting empirical evidence and offer possible explanations to illustrate the practicality of our findings when applied to active portfolio management.*

1 Introduction

Information ratio (IR), the ratio of average excess return to active risk, is an important performance measure for active investment management. One result regarding *ex ante* IR is Grinold's (1989) Fundamental Law of Active Management, which states that the expected IR is the expected information coefficient (IC) times the square root of breadth. IC refers to the cross-sectional correlation coefficient between forecasts of excess returns and actual returns. For equity portfolios—the focus of the present paper, the breadth is the number of stocks within a select universe. In mathematical terms, the relationship is

$$\mathrm{IR} = \overline{\mathrm{IC}}\sqrt{N} \tag{1}$$

Throughout the paper, the bar denotes the expected value.

Equation (1), while providing insight to active management, is based on several simplified assumptions. Various studies re-examine this result when different assumptions are used. For instance, one of the assumptions is that active portfolio is a pure long–short portfolio free of long-only constraint. Grinold and Kuhn (2000) examine how IR deviates from Eq. (1) under the long-only and other portfolio constraints using simulation techniques. Recently, Clarke *et al.* (2002) developed a framework for measuring such deviations by including a "transfer coefficient" on the right-hand side of Eq. (1). In addition to the long-only constraint, they also study the impact of

[a]PanAgora Asset Management, 260 Franklin street, Boston, MA 02110, USA. E-mail: eqian@panagora.com (corresponding author).

[b]Putnam Investments, One Post Office Square, Boston, MA 02109, USA.

constraints in terms of turnover as well as factors such as size and style. Both studies conclude that portfolio constraints generally tend to lower *ex ante* IR, as given in Eq. (1).

Equation (1) hinges on another simplified assumption regarding active risk of investment strategies. Namely, it assumes that the active risk of an investment strategy is identical to the tracking error estimate by a risk model. Our research shows that *ex post* active risk often significantly exceeds the target tracking error by risk models, even after appropriately controlling risk exposures specified by a risk model. In this paper, we will unveil an additional source of active risk that accounts for this discrepancy. This new source of risk stems from the variability of IC, i.e., the correlation between forecasts and actual returns. Hence, it is unique to each investment strategy and we shall refer to it as strategy risk. Mathematically, it is the standard deviation of IC, i.e., std(IC).

The previous research mentioned above, while acknowledging the average IC of different strategies, assumes that all strategies have the same active risk if they have the same target tracking error. This simplified assumption is not adequate in characterizing different investment strategies. As we will show below, the true active risk is a combination of the risk-model risk and the strategy risk. Although there are other alternative measurements of active risk, we consider standard deviation of excess return or tracking error in the present paper. We use active risk and tracking error interchangeably.

It is no surprise that the variability of IC plays a role in determining the active risk. Just imagine two investment strategies, both taking the same risk-model tracking error σ_{model} over time. The first strategy is blessed with perfect foresight and it generates constant excess return every single period. In other words, it has a constant positive IC for all periods such that std(IC) is zero. Such a risk-free strategy, admittedly hard to find, has constant excess return, and thus, no active risk whatsoever. However, the risk model is not aware of the prowess of the strategy and dutifully predicts the same tracking error all the time. In this case, the risk model undoubtedly overestimates the active risk. In contrast, the second strategy is extremely volatile with large swings in its excess return, i.e. its IC varies between -1 and $+1$ with a large std(IC). As a result, its active risk might be much larger than the risk model estimate. Thus, the two strategies with identical risk-model tracking error have very different active risk in actuality.

In practice, the difference between active investment strategies is not that extreme. However, our experience shows that risk-model tracking error given by most commercially available risk models routinely and seriously underestimates the *ex post* active risk.[1] This underestimation could have serious practical consequences. For example, an enhanced index product with low risk-model tracking error but high standard deviation of IC could be far more risky, because the true active risk is larger.

Our results will enable portfolio managers to obtain more accurate estimates of active risk of their active strategies, and as a result, better estimates of IR. Furthermore, they can be used jointly with the results of Grinold and Kuhn (2000) and Clarke *et al.* (2002) by portfolio managers to provide realistic IR estimates.

2 Notations and Main Results

To facilitate our analysis, we introduce the following notations and terminologies.

- *Risk-model tracking error, denoted as* σ_{model}: It is the tracking error or the standard deviation of excess returns estimated by a generic risk model such as BARRA, and it is also referred to as *risk-model risk* or *target tracking error.*
- *Strategic risk, denoted as* std(IC): It is the standard deviation of IC of an investment strategy over time. It is unique to each active investment strategy, conveying strategy-specific risk profile.
- *Active risk, denoted as* σ: It is the active risk or tracking error of an investment strategy measured by the standard deviation of excess returns over time.

Our main result regarding the active risk is the following: the active risk is a product of the strategy risk, the square root of breadth, and the risk-model tracking error:

$$\sigma = \text{std(IC)}\sqrt{N}\sigma_{\text{model}} \tag{2}$$

This result has several clear implications. First, the active risk is *not* the same for different investment strategies due to varying levels of strategy risks. Second, only rarely does the active risk equal the risk-model tracking error. It happens only when strategy risk, std(IC), is exactly equal to the reciprocal of the square root of N. This is true in an ideal situation, in which the standard deviation of IC is proportional to the sampling error of a correlation coefficient, which is the reciprocal of the square root of N. In reality, however, as our empirical results will show, the standard deviation of IC bears little relationship to this theoretical sampling error, and is significantly different for different strategies.

We note that our paper is not a critique of any risk model because our focus is not the same as studying the measurement error of risk models over a single rebalancing period. In those studies (e.g. Hartmann *et al.*, 2002), one analyzes the performance of risk models over a single, relatively short period, during which the examined portfolios are bought and held. The approach is to compare predicted tracking errors of a risk model to the realized tracking errors using either daily or weekly excess returns for many simulated portfolios. Hartman *et al.* (2002) attribute the difference between the estimated risk and the *ex post* tracking error to several items: estimation error in covariances in a risk model, time varying nature of covariances, serial auto-correlations of excess returns, and the drift of portfolio weights over a given period. Depending on how these factors play out in a given period, a risk model can overestimate as well as underestimate with seemingly equal probability *ex post* tracking errors of simulated portfolios. There is no clear evidence of bias one way or the other.

In contrast, we study the active risk of an investment strategy over multiple rebalancing periods, during which the active portfolio is traded periodically based on the forecasts of that investment strategy. While it is useful to consider the single-period active risk of a buy-and-hold portfolio, it is arguably more practical to analyze the active risk over multiple rebalancing periods. Our analysis reveals a clear underestimation bias of risk-model risk even if the risk model is adequate. This is because using a risk model alone is not enough to accurately estimate the true active risk. Only through consideration of strategy risk can an unbiased estimate of active risk be obtained.

Because of more realistic estimate of active risk, our estimate of IR is different from that of Eq. (1). We shall show that IR of an investment strategy is

$$\mathrm{IR} = \frac{\overline{\mathrm{IC}}}{\mathrm{std(IC)}} \tag{3}$$

Equation (3) is very intuitive. Since IR measures the ratio of average excess return to the standard deviation of excess return, if IC were the sole determinant of excess return, then IR would be the ratio of average IC to the standard deviation of IC. In most of the cases we have studied, IR is lower than that of Eq. (1) because the true active risk tends to be higher than the risk-model tracking error.

3 Cross-Sectional IC and Single-Period Excess Return

To derive the IR of an active investment strategy over multiple periods, we start by calculating a single-period excess return, which is the summed product of active weights and subsequent realized actual returns. We use active mean–variance optimization to derive the active weights under the following framework. First, we model security risk by a generic multi-factor fundamental risk model, such as the BARRA risk model. Second, the optimal active weights are selected by mean–variance optimization while neutralizing portfolio exposures to all risk factors, in addition to being dollar neutral. We have done so for two reasons. First, the alpha factors we shall study in the empirical section below are employed by quantitative managers mostly to exploit stock specific returns. The second reason is more technical. Imposing binding constraints on all risk factors allows us to derive an analytical solution for the optimal portfolio weights without knowing the historical covariance matrices of risk factor returns. While it is certainly possible to extend our analysis to strategies that also take factor bets, the research is out of the scope of this article. While we reasonably expect that different factor-related strategies would have their own component of strategy risk, practitioners should use caution when applying our results directly to those strategies.

Under these conditions, Appendix A gives the exact solution for the active weights $w_{i,t}$ for security i and time t. The excess return for the period is the summed product of the active weights $w_{i,t}$ and the subsequent actual return $r_{i,t}$. To reflect dollar and factor neutral constraints, we recast the summed product expression by adjusting both the forecasts and the actual returns to obtain

$$\alpha_t = \lambda_t^{-1} \sum_{i=1}^{N} R_{i,t} F_{i,t} \tag{4}$$

where λ is a risk-aversion parameter used in the optimization, R is the risk-adjusted actual return, and F is the risk-adjusted forecast. They are the "raw" return or forecast adjusted for dollar and factor neutrality, and then normalized by security specific risk (Appendix A).

So far, our derivation of Eq. (4), in Appendix A, has been standard. Similar analyses can be found in Grinold (1989) and Clarke *et al.* (2002). From this point on, our analysis uses a different approach. In previous work (Grinold, 1994; Clarke *et al.*, 2002), one makes an assumption about the expected returns of individual securities, such as "Alpha is Volatility Times IC Times Score" (Grinold, 1994). The validity of such a normative approach, which has its origin in risk modeling, is questionable in reality. We shall adapt a descriptive approach with no assumptions regarding individual securities.[2] We write Eq. (4) as the covariance between the risk-adjusted returns and forecasts, which in turn can be rewritten as a product of IC and their dispersions.[3] We have

$$\begin{aligned} \alpha_t &= \lambda_t^{-1}(N-1)[\text{cov}(\mathbf{R}_t, \mathbf{F}_t) + \text{avg}(\mathbf{R}_t)\,\text{avg}(\mathbf{F}_t)] \\ &= \lambda_t^{-1}(N-1)\,\text{IC}_t\,\text{dis}(\mathbf{R}_t)\,\text{dis}(\mathbf{F}_t) \end{aligned} \tag{5}$$

We use $\mathbf{R}_t$ and $\mathbf{F}_t$ to denote the cross-sectional collections of the risk-adjusted returns and forecasts, and $\text{IC}_t = \text{corr}(\mathbf{R}_t, \mathbf{F}_t)$. The average term in Eq. (5) vanishes because we have made $\text{avg}(\mathbf{R}_t) = 0$ (see Appendix A). Equation (5) states that the single-period excess return is proportional to the IC of that period and the dispersions of the risk-adjusted returns and forecasts for that period. The intuition is clear: the excess return is a function of IC, which measures the forecast's cross-sectional ranking ability, the dispersion of the forecasts, which reflects the perceived cross-sectional opportunity, and the dispersion of the actual returns, which represents the actual cross-sectional opportunity.

The risk-model risk, on the other hand, depends only on the dispersion of the forecasts through the optimal active weights. They are related by (see Appendix A)

$$\sigma_{\text{model}} \approx \lambda_t^{-1}\sqrt{N-1}\,\text{dis}(\mathbf{F}_t) \tag{6}$$

In other words, the risk-model risk is the dispersion of the risk-adjusted forecasts (which varies from period to period) times the square root of $N-1$ divided by the risk-aversion parameter. Equations (5) and (6) show that, while the excess return depends on IC and both dispersions, the risk-model risk is only a function of the forecast dispersion. In other words, the risk-model risk is independent of IC since the risk model has no knowledge of the information content of the forecasts.

We shall maintain a constant level of risk-model tracking error[4] by varying the risk aversion parameter accordingly. Combining Eqs. (5) and (6) produces the relationship

$$\alpha_t \approx \text{IC}_t\sqrt{N}\sigma_{\text{model}}\,\text{dis}(\mathbf{R}_t) \tag{7}$$

We have replaced $N-1$ with N, which is justified when N is large enough. The excess return of an active strategy in a single period is IC times the square root of breadth times the risk-model tracking error times the dispersion of the risk-adjusted returns. Among the four terms in Eq. (7), the dispersion of the risk-adjusted returns is new and thus deserves some discussion. In theory, if the risk model truly describes the return of every single security, then each risk-adjusted return $R_{i,t}$ is close to a standard normal random variable. The base case estimation for the dispersion of a large number of such random variables is unity.[5] Later, we shall see that this is approximately true for certain risk models. This dispersion represents the degree of opportunity in the market. For a given level of IC and risk-model risk, a greater opportunity leads to a higher excess return.

4 Information Ratio

We derive IR of an investment strategy over multiple periods. Equation (7) is close to a mathematical identity. While it is always true *ex post*, we now use it in *ex ante* by considering its expectation and standard deviation, i.e., the expected excess return and the expected active risk. Among the four terms affecting the excess return, we assume that the number of stocks does not change over time and the risk-model tracking error remains constant. For the two remaining terms that do change over time, IC is associated with greater variability than the dispersion of the risk-adjusted returns. Therefore, as a first approximation we treat the latter also as a constant.

4.1 The Simple Case

Assuming $\text{dis}(\mathbf{R}_t)$ is constant and equal to its mean, the expected excess return is

$$\bar{\alpha}_t = \overline{\text{IC}}_t \sqrt{N} \sigma_{\text{model}} \overline{\text{dis}(\mathbf{R}_t)} \tag{8}$$

The expected excess return is, therefore, the average IC (skill) times the square root of N (breadth) times the risk-model tracking error (risk budget) times the dispersion of actual returns (opportunity).

The expected active risk is

$$\sigma = \text{std}(\text{IC}) \sqrt{N} \sigma_{\text{model}} \overline{\text{dis}(\mathbf{R}_t)} \tag{9}$$

The standard deviation of IC measures the consistency of forecast quality over time. Therefore, the active risk is the standard deviation of IC (strategy risk) times the square root of N (breadth) times the risk-model tracking error (risk budget) times the dispersion of actual returns (opportunity).

The ratio of Eqs. (8) to (9) produces Eq. (3); i.e., IR is the ratio of the average IC to the standard deviation of IC, or IR of IC. We also note that when the mean dispersion is unity, Eq. (9) reduces to Eq. (2).

4.2 A Better Estimation of IR

In reality, the variability in the dispersion of the risk-adjusted return $\text{dis}(\mathbf{R}_t)$ is small but, nonetheless, non-zero. What happens to IR if we include this variability? The following insight from Eq. (7) helps us to understand how the interaction between the IC and the dispersion affects the excess return. To produce a high positive excess return for a single period, we need high and positive IC as well as high dispersion. Conversely, when IC is negative, we would like a low dispersion so that the negative excess return would be small in magnitude. This argument implies that, over the long run, the performance will benefit from a positive correlation between IC and the dispersion. On the other hand, a negative correlation will hurt the average excess return.

Appendix B shows that the expected excess return including this correlation effect is

$$\bar{\alpha}_t = \sqrt{N}\sigma_{\text{model}}\{\overline{\text{IC}_t}\ \overline{\text{dis}(\mathbf{R}_t)} + \rho[\text{IC}_t, \text{dis}(\mathbf{R}_t)]\ \text{std}(\text{IC}_t)\ \text{std}[\text{dis}(\mathbf{R}_t)\}] \quad (10)$$

The additional term consists of the correlation between IC and the dispersion, and the standard deviations of IC and the dispersion. According to Appendix B, the active risk is little affected by the correlation because the coefficient of variation of $\text{dis}(\mathbf{R}_t)$ is much smaller than that of IC and one. Combining Eqs. (9) and (10) produces the new IR estimate

$$\text{IR} = \frac{\overline{\text{IC}_t}}{\text{std}(\text{IC}_t)} + \rho[\text{IC}_t, \text{dis}(\mathbf{R}_t)]\frac{\text{std}[\text{dis}(\mathbf{R}_t)]}{\text{dis}(\mathbf{R}_t)} \quad (11)$$

The second term captures the correlation effect on IR. It has two factors. The first is the correlation between IC and the dispersion over time and the second term is the coefficient of variation of the dispersion. As we mentioned earlier, the coefficient of variation of the dispersion is usually small. Therefore, the effect of the second term is typically small unless the correlation between IC and the dispersion becomes very high, either positive or negative. For most practical purposes, Eq. (3), i.e., the first term in Eq. (11), approximates IR well enough. Nonetheless, Eq. (11) is an improvement.

5 Empirical Examinations

To demonstrate that Eq. (9) is a more *consistent* estimator of *ex ante* active risk, we study empirical results of 60 qantitative equity strategies. To ensure practical relevance, these strategies are based on a set of quantitative factors commonly used by active managers. The set encompasses a wide range of well-known market anomalies, and thus provides a good representation of different categories of quantitative strategies deployed by active managers.

We first briefly describe the data. Then, we apply the analysis to the Russell 3000 indices to demonstrate our theoretical result. To assess the statistical significance of the differences in the strategy risk, we provide a closer examination of two valuation factors—gross profit to enterprise value and forward earnings yield. We introduce a strategy-specific scaling constant κ and use it in conjunction with a risk model to provide a *consistent* forecast of *ex post* active risk. Lastly, we suggest different ways to forecast strategy risk and ascertain the efficacy of such predictions.

5.1 The Data

The quarterly data used in our analysis span 1987 to 2003, with 67 quarters in total. The alpha factors come from a proprietary database and they include seven different categories: price momentum, earnings momentum, earnings surprise, valuation, accruals, financial leverage, and operating efficiency. The values for beta, systematic risk factors, industry risk factors, and stock specific risk come from the BARRA US E3 equity risk model. To ensure factor accuracy and to prevent undue influence from outliers, we first exclude stocks that have factor values exceeding five standard deviations on each side. Next, we bring factor values between three and five standard deviations to the three standard deviation values. The actual number of stocks that are tested against the Russell 3000 index is, therefore, fewer than 3000. In addition, the number of stocks fluctuates from quarter to quarter due to data availability as well as the reconstitution activities of Russell indices. However, the fluctuation is insignificant as to alter the analysis.

In terms of portfolio construction, we form optimal long–short portfolios on a quarterly basis. Subsequently, cross-sectional analyses of alpha and IC and dispersion of the risk-adjusted returns are computed on a quarterly basis. We set the constant risk-model tracking error at 2.5% per quarter. Additionally, to control risk exposures appropriately, we neutralize active exposures to all BARRA risk factors (market beta, 13 systematic risk factors, and 55 industry risk factors) when rebalancing portfolios each quarter. Hence, the risk-model risk is 100% stock specific according to the risk model. The results below are collected on a quarterly basis and are annualized for the purposes of this paper. For example, the annualized target tracking error would be 5%, provided there is no serial auto-correlation in alpha.

5.2 The Russell 3000 Universe

Figure 1 shows the histogram of *ex post* active risk of the 60 strategies. Although the risk-model tracking error is targeted at 5% for all strategies, the *ex post* active risks differ widely with substantial upward bias, indicating the risk model's propensity to underestimate active risk. The average active risk is 7.7% and the standard deviation is 1.7%. The highest active risk turns out to be 13.1% while the lowest is just 5.0%. In other words, almost all strategies experienced *ex post* risk higher than the risk-model tracking error.

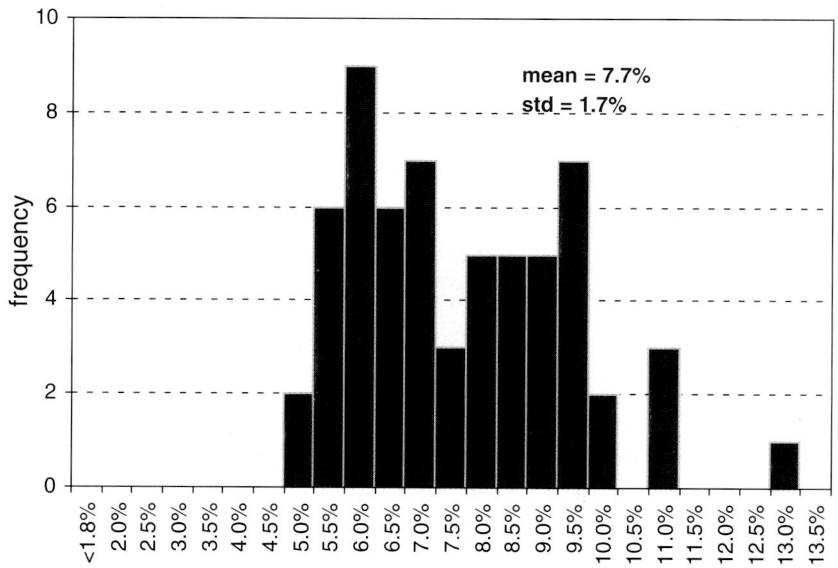

Figure 1 Histogram of the *ex post* active risk of equity strategies.

To gauge the risk model's estimation bias in relative terms, we rearrange Eq. (9) to derive a scaling constant κ that approximates the ratio of true active risk to the risk-model risk, in terms of the standard deviation of IC for each factor and the average number of stocks over time:

$$\kappa = \text{std}(\text{IC})\sqrt{N} \approx \frac{\sigma}{\sigma_{\text{model}}} \tag{12}$$

We have neglected the dispersion of returns, $\overline{\text{dis}(\mathbf{R}_t)}$, because it turns out to be very close to unity with a value at 1.01 and a standard deviation of 0.15. By this measure, the BARRA E3 model shows remarkable internal consistency. Figure 2 shows the histogram of the scaling constant κ for all 60 strategies. Note that for a majority of strategies the model underestimates the *ex post* active risk by 50% or more. Figure 2 resembles Figure 1 quite closely except that the x-axis is rescaled by the risk-model tracking error of 5%. A scatter plot of the active risk and κ (Figure 3) confirms the observation. Additionally, Table 1 reports the estimated coefficients of the regression using the scaling constant κ to explain *ex post* active risk. The R-squared of this regression is 98%, indicating that Eq. (9) is a highly accurate approximation of the *ex post* active risk despite the assumption that $\text{dis}(\mathbf{R}_t)$ is constant over time. More importantly, it seems possible that practitioners can use the scaling constant κ to adjust risk-model tracking error to achieve a *consistent* forecast of active risk. We demonstrate this adjustment below.

5.3 Information Content of Strategy Risk: An Example

The strategy risks of these quantitative strategies vary greatly. Naturally, one wonders about the statistical significance of their differences. These differences are important in terms of forecasting portfolio active risk that incorporates strategy risk. In other words,

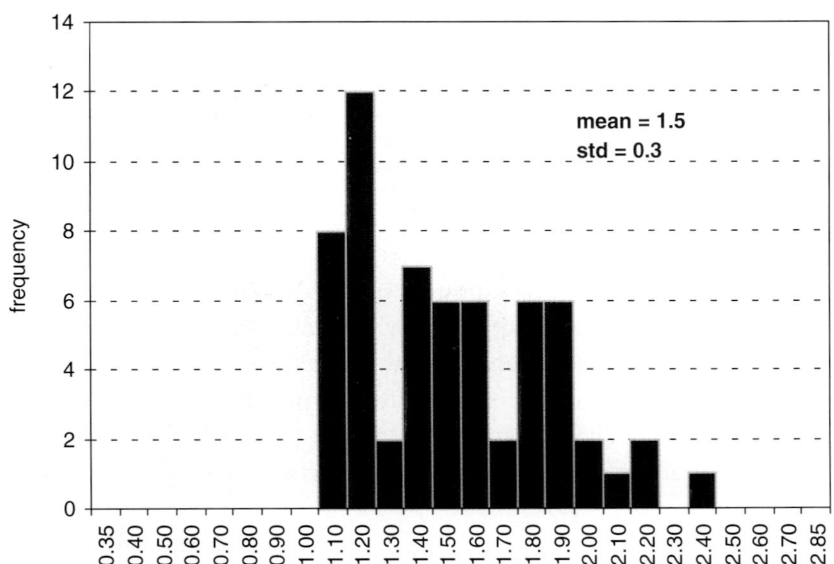

Figure 2 Histogram of the scaling constant κ of equity strategies.

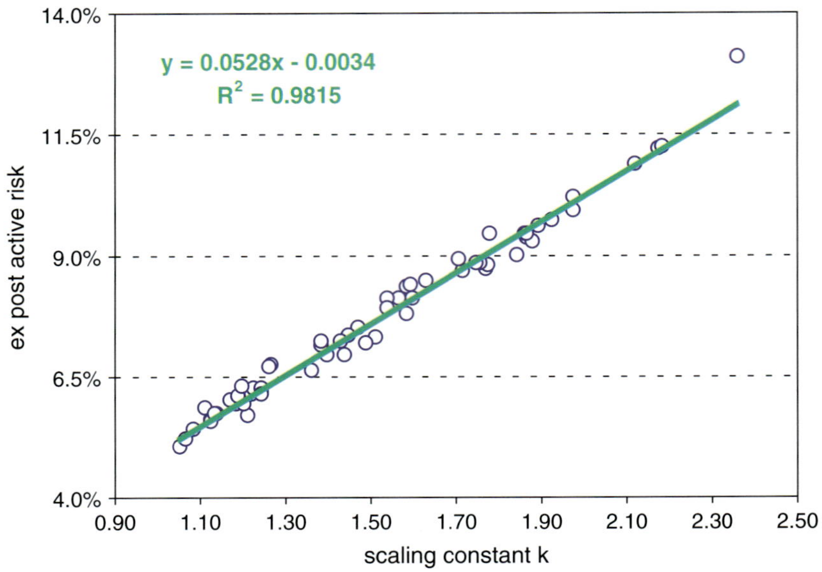

Figure 3 Scatter plot of *ex post* active risk and scaling constant.

Table 1 Summary statistics of coefficient estimates.

	Coefficients	Standard error	*t*-Stat	*P*-value	Lower 95%	Upper 95%
Intercept	−0.0034	0.0015	−2.3260	0.0235	−0.0063	−0.0005
Scaling constant κ	0.0528	0.0009	55.9084	0.0000	0.0509	0.0547

Table 2 Summary statistics of valuation factors.

	Average Alpha	STD of Alpha	IR of Alpha	Average IC	STD of IC	IR of IC	Average dis(*R*)	Average *N*
GP2EV	6.2%	6.9%	0.90	2.4%	2.7%	0.91	1.01	2738
E2P	3.3%	8.7%	0.38	1.4%	3.4%	0.41	1.00	2487

after appropriately controlling risk exposures specified by the BARRA E3 model in our case, does the standard deviation of ICs provide additional insight regarding the risk profile of an equity strategy? The answer to this question is "yes" in many cases. Here we select two valuation factors—gross profit to enterprise value (GP2EV) and forward earnings yield based on IBES FY1 consensus forecast (E2P)—for a closer examination. We test the statistical significance of the difference between the two strategy risks using the *F*-test.

Table 2 shows the summary statistics of these two factors. For GP2EV, the standard deviation of IC equals 2.7%; it is 3.4% for E2P. The *ex post* tracking errors are 6.9% and 8.7%, respectively. Since both standard deviations are estimated over 67 quarters, the degree of freedom equals 66. The variance ratio of the two factors is $(3.4 \times 3.4)/(2.7 \times 2.7) = 1.58$ and α equals 0.032. Thus, in this example, there is enough evidence to reject the null hypothesis that these two factors, from the same valuation category, have the same strategy risk at a 5% confidence level. Our results indicate that the strategy risks of factors selected from different categories, more often than not, are statistically different.

5.4 Consistent Estimator of Active Risk

Can practitioners use strategy risk in conjunction with a risk model to compute a more *consistent* active risk forecast? As a first attempt to answer this question, we divide the testing period into two halves: in-sample period (1986–1994) and out-of-sample period (1995–2003). In the in-sample period, we estimate κ according to Eq. (12) for each of the 60 equity strategies. Then, in the out-of-sample period, we adjust the risk-model tracking error by $1/\kappa$, using strategy-specific κ to compensate the risk model's bias in estimating active risk. The *adjusted* risk-model tracking error is

$$\sigma^*_{\text{model}} = \frac{\sigma_{\text{model}}}{\kappa} \tag{13}$$

Figure 4 shows the distribution of *ex post* active risks in the out-of-sample period when we set the target tracking error at $5\%/\kappa$ (the *adjusted* risk-model tracking error), and for comparison, Figure 5 shows active risk of portfolios targeting the same tracking error at 5% (the original risk-model tracking error). We would like to emphasize again that the *adjusted* risk-model tracking error σ^*_{model} is unique to each equity strategy depending on its κ estimates, while the risk-model tracking error σ_{model} is the same for all strategies. From these two histograms, it is obvious that σ^*_{model} is a more *consistent*

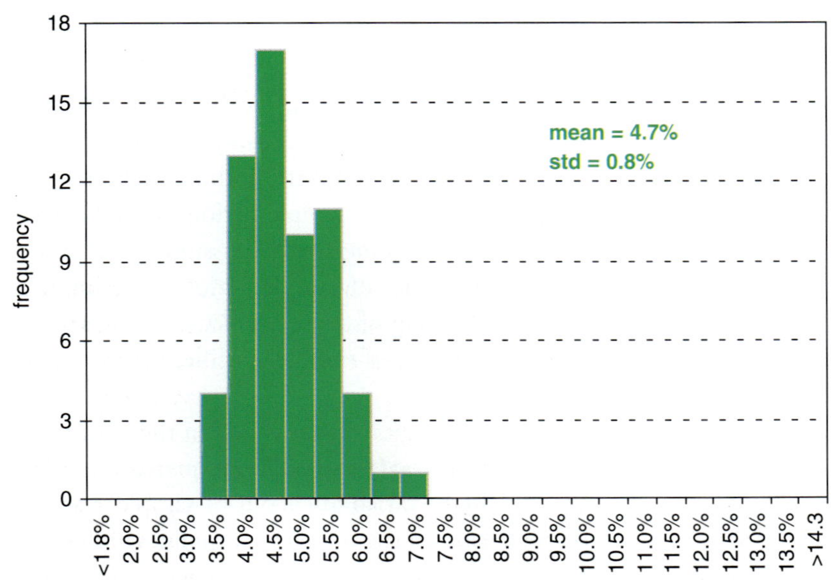

Figure 4 Histogram of the *ex post* active risks using adjusted model TE (1995–2003).

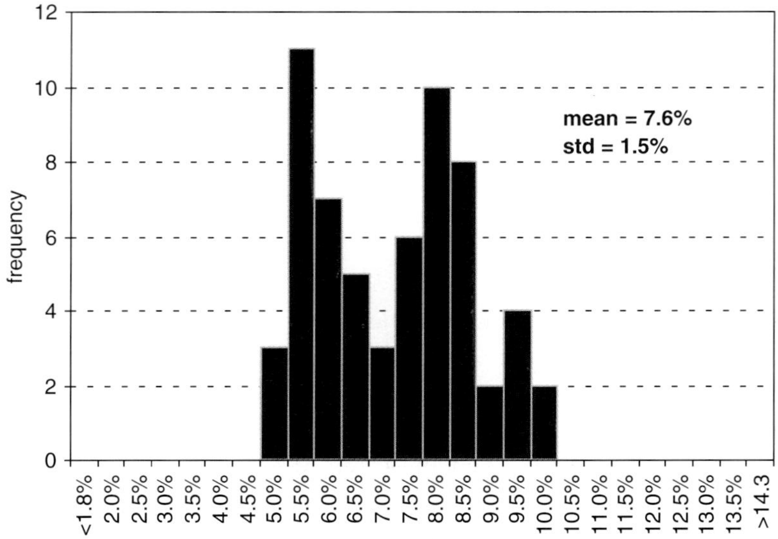

Figure 5 Histogram of the *ex post* active risks using 5% Model TE (1995–2003).

estimator of active risk. First, the average *ex post* active risk is 4.7% when using σ^*_{model}, and 7.6% when using σ_{model}. Thus, the expected *ex post* active risk is much closer to our target of 5% with no bias when using the *adjusted* risk-model tracking error. Second, the *adjusted* risk-model tracking error also provides a tighter, more bell-shaped distribution of *ex post* active risks. The standard deviation of *ex post* active risk is 0.76% when using σ^*_{model}, and 1.45% when using σ_{model}. It is apparent that in this shorter period, the risk model experienced a similar problem of underestimating the true active risks of many strategies.

5.5 Persistence of Strategy Risk

Naturally, one must be able to forecast the strategy risk, std(IC), with *reasonable* accuracy in order to provide a consistent forecast of active risk using Eq. (9). The application of the scaling constant κ above constitutes a simplistic form of forecasting strategy risk—using the strategy risk estimated in the in-sample period as the forecast of the out-of-sample period. Our simplistic forecasting method assumes that strategy risk persists from the in-sample period to the out-of-sample period. One implication of this methodology is that the relative ranking of strategy risks stays the same in both periods. We employ the in-sample and out-of-sample specification to show this is indeed the case.

Figure 6 shows the scatter plot of strategy risks measured in the in-sample period (x-axis) versus that in the out-of-sample period (y-axis). The R-squared of the regression, using in-sample strategy risks to explain the variability of out-of-sample strategy risks, is 52%. Table 3 shows the summary statistics of the coefficient estimates of this regression. The null hypothesis, that in-sample strategy risks have no explanation power of the variability of the out-of-sample strategy risks, is rejected at a 1% confidence level.

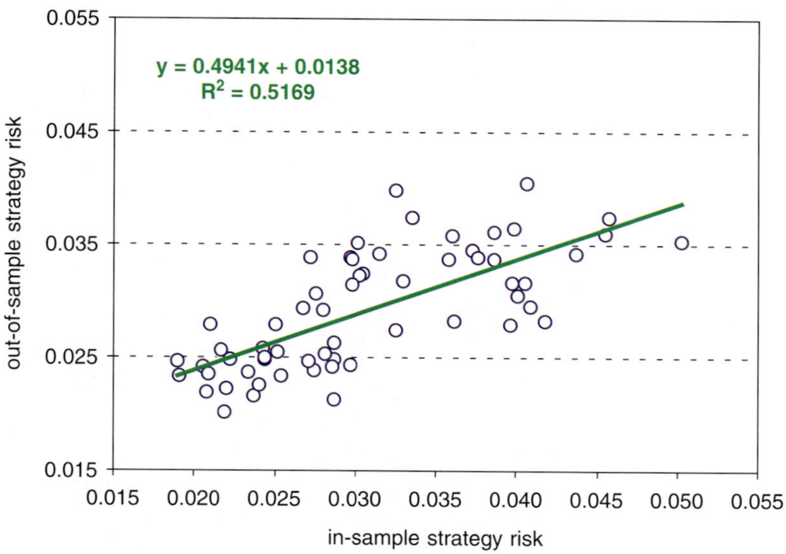

Figure 6 Scatter plot of in-sample strategy risk versus out-of-sample strategy risk.

Table 3 Summary statistics of coefficient estimates.

	Coefficients	Standard error	*t* Stat	*P*-value	Lower 95%	Upper 95%
Intercept	0.0138	0.0020	7.0245	0.0000	0.0099	0.0178
In-sample strategy risk	0.4941	0.0622	7.9449	0.0000	0.3697	0.6186

Hence, it is plausible that, using this simplistic forecast method in conjunction with Eq. (9), active managers can improve their ability to assess portfolio active risk.

6 Conclusion

Among active equity managers, it is commonly known that *ex post* active risk often exceeds the target tracking error specified by a risk model. We attribute this deviation to an additional source of active risk—the strategy risk. Measured as the standard deviation of IC, strategy risk is unique to each investment strategy conveying a strategy-specific risk profile. Furthermore, through analytical derivations, we show that a *consistent* estimator of active risk must incorporate strategy risk in conjunction with the risk-model tracking error. Consequently, we provide a practical extension to the Fundamental Law of Active Management: *ex ante* IR equal to the ratio of average IC to the standard deviation of IC. Additionally, we also demonstrate that IR depends not only on the strength of IC, but also on the correlation between IC and the dispersion of the risk-adjusted returns over time.

Empirical evidence shows that risk models systematically underestimate *ex post* active risk. It is reasonable to expect this, because, by definition, the risk-model risk only accounts for tracking error caused by risk factors and specific risks specified by a risk model. However, all active strategies are exposed to alpha factors, which must have explanatory power for cross-sectional returns beyond the power provided by the risk model. This cross-sectional correlation between the alpha factor and the actual returns introduces additional risk not embedded in the risk model. Equation (9) provides a way to capture both the risk-model risk and the strategy risk associated with alpha factors.

This fact alone does not imply the deficiency of a risk model, because the job of a risk model is to capture the majority of cross-sectional dispersion in security returns embedded in commonly specified risk factors. While it is plausible that a given risk model might be improved with additional risk factors, it is unrealistic to expect a risk model to include all possible fundamental factors in all possible variations, as is often the case when active equity managers search for alpha factors. Combining the risk-model risk and the strategy risk represents a reasonable and realistic solution to the issue.

Our empirical survey of commonly used quantitative equity strategies confirms our analytical results. The difference in strategy risk is often statistically significant. We also illustrate how to use strategy risk to recalibrate the risk-model tracking error so that the *ex ante* active risk reaches a target level. While more sophisticated methods to forecast strategy risk await further research, such a simple modification has already proven far superior to just using the risk-model risk alone.

In addition to these benefits, our analysis also enables practitioners to estimate the *ex ante* excess return and active risk more accurately, without the daunting task of optimized back tests. This is especially true for market neutral equity hedge fund strategies with fewer portfolio constraints because our risk-constrained optimization closely resembles those strategies. For long-only active strategies, or other kinds of strategies with more constraints, our estimation could be combined with those of Grinold and Kahn (2000) and Clarke *et al.* (2002) to provide a more realistic IR estimate. Finally, for active equity managers, our analytical framework can be applied in a number of ways to provide a rigorous risk specification of equity investment strategies in terms of diversification benefit across strategies and most importantly better portfolio IR. For example, Sorensen *et al.* (2003) illustrate a way to combine multiple alpha sources more efficiently in an unconditional framework to achieve the highest portfolio IR. Alternatively, we can also apply the analysis in a conditional framework to take advantage of certain market conditions through tactical rotations of active investment strategies. These rotation tactics can be grounded on careful examination of how the strategy excess return and the strategy risk respond to different macro-environment, market segments (style or sector), and seasonal influences.

Appendix A: Optimal Active Weights and Excess Return

This appendix provides mathematical details of the results in Section 1 regarding the optimal active weights and the excess return.

The active weights is the solution of the following optimization problem: Maximize

$$\mathbf{f}_t' \cdot \mathbf{w}_t - \frac{1}{2}\lambda_t \cdot (\mathbf{w}_t' \cdot \mathbf{V}_t \cdot \mathbf{w}_t) \tag{A.1}$$

subject to

$$\begin{aligned} \mathbf{w}_t' \cdot \mathbf{i} &= 0 \\ \mathbf{w}_t' \cdot \mathbf{B}_t &= 0 \end{aligned} \tag{A.2}$$

The subscript t denotes the period. For clarity, we omit it from our notation hereafter. In Eqs. (A.1) and (A.2), $\mathbf{f} = (f_1, f_2, \ldots, f_N)'$ is the vector of alpha factors or forecasts of excess returns over an index at time t; $\mathbf{w} = (w_1, w_2, \ldots, w_N)'$ the vector of active weights against the index; $\mathbf{B} = (\boldsymbol{\beta}_1, \boldsymbol{\beta}_2, \ldots, \boldsymbol{\beta}_M)'$ the matrix of risk factors with each $\boldsymbol{\beta}_i$ a vector of risk factor; $\mathbf{i} = (1, 1, \ldots, 1)'$ the vector of ones; λ the risk-aversion parameter; and $\mathbf{V}$ the covariance matrix. The number of risk factors is M.

The covariance matrix $\mathbf{V}$ in a multi-factor risk model takes a special form:

$$\mathbf{V} = \mathbf{B} \cdot \Sigma_{\mathbf{B}} \cdot \mathbf{B}' + \mathbf{S} \tag{A.3}$$

where $\Sigma_{\mathbf{B}}$ is the covariance matrix of risk factors, and $\mathbf{S} = \mathrm{diag}(\sigma_1^2, \sigma_2^2, \ldots, \sigma_N^2)$ is the diagonal matrix of stock-specific risks. Equation (A.3) assumes zero correlation between stock-specific risks. Because we require that the active weights are factor neutral, and there is no systematic risk in the active weights whatsoever, we can reduce the objective function (A.1) to the following, provided that we keep all the constraints

$$\mathbf{f}' \cdot \mathbf{w} - \frac{1}{2}\lambda \cdot (\mathbf{w}' \cdot \mathbf{S} \cdot \mathbf{w}) \tag{A.4}$$

We can now solve the optimization of (A.4) with the constraints (A.2) analytically using the method of Langrangian multipliers. We switch from matrix notation to using summations. The new objective function including $M + 1$ Langrangian multipliers (1 for the dollar neutral constraint and M for M risk factors) is

$$\sum_{i=1}^{N} f_i w_i - \frac{1}{2}\lambda \sum_{i=1}^{N} w_i^2 \sigma_i^2 - l_1 \sum_{i=1}^{N} w_i - l_2 \sum_{i=1}^{N} w_i \beta_{1i} - \cdots - l_{M+1} \sum_{i=1}^{N} w_i \beta_{Mi} \tag{A.5}$$

Taking the partial derivative with respect to w_i and equating it to zero gives

$$w_i = \lambda^{-1} \frac{f_i - l_1 - l_2 \beta_{1i} - \cdots - l_{M+1} \beta_{Mi}}{\sigma_i^2} \tag{A.6}$$

The values of Langrangian multipliers are determined by the constraints through a system of linear equations.

Given the active weights, the portfolio excess return is the summed product of the active weights and the actual excess returns

$$\alpha = \sum_{i=1}^{N} w_i r_i = \lambda^{-1} \sum_{i=1}^{N} \frac{f_i - l_1 - l_2 \beta_{1i} - \cdots - l_{M+1} \beta_{Mi}}{\sigma_i^2} r_i \tag{A.7}$$

To arrive at Eq. (4) with the risk-adjusted forecast and the risk-adjusted return, we replace the return r_i by $r_i - k_1 - k_2 \beta_{1i} - \cdots - k_{M+1} \beta_{M1i}$, where $(k_2, \ldots, k_{M+1})$ are the returns to M risk factors. This does not change the equation due to the constraints placed on the active weights. We choose the value of k_1 to make the risk-adjusted return mean zero. Defining

$$F_i = \frac{f_i - l_1 - l_2\beta_{1i} - \cdots - l_{M+1}\beta_{Mi}}{\sigma_i}$$
$$R_i = \frac{r_i - k_1 - k_2\beta_{1i} - \cdots - k_{M+1}\beta_{M1i}}{\sigma_i} \tag{A.8}$$

Eq. (A.7) becomes Eq. (4).

We next calculate the residual variance or equivalently the risk-model tracking error as the sum of active weights squared times the specific variance. The active portfolio has no market risk within the risk model because the active weights are neutral to all risk factors. We have

$$\sigma_{\text{model}}^2 = \sum_{i=1}^{N} w_i^2 \sigma_i^2 = \lambda^{-2} \sum_{i=1}^{N} F_i^2 \tag{A.9}$$

The residual variance is, therefore, the sum of the risk-adjusted forecasts squared. Therefore,

$$\sigma_{\text{model}} = \lambda_t^{-1} \sqrt{\sum_{i=1}^{N} F_{i,t}^2} = \lambda_t^{-1}\sqrt{N-1}\sqrt{[\text{dis}(\mathbf{F}_t)]^2 + [\text{avg}(\mathbf{F}_t)]^2}$$
$$\approx \lambda_t^{-1}\sqrt{N-1}\,\text{dis}(\mathbf{F}_t) \tag{A.10}$$

We have assumed that $\text{avg}(\mathbf{F}_t) \approx 0$ and this approximation is quite accurate in practice.

Appendix B: The Information Ratio

This appendix presents the exact results regarding the expected excess return and active risk. To obtain the expected excess return and active risk based on Eq. (7) we must find the expected value and variance of a product of two random variables. We use x and y to denotes IC and the dispersion of the risk-adjusted returns.

Elementary statistical calculation tells us that

$$E(xy) = \bar{x}\bar{y} + \rho\sigma_x\sigma_y \tag{B.1}$$

The barred variables are averages and σ denotes the standard deviation, and ρ is the correlation. Identifying IC as the variable x and the dispersion of the risk-adjusted returns as the variable y, we obtain the expected excess return as in Eq. (10).

We can also obtain the variance of x times y as

$$\text{Var}(xy) = \sigma_x^2\sigma_y^2 + \rho^2\sigma_x^2\sigma_y^2 + \bar{x}^2\sigma_y^2 + \bar{y}^2\sigma_x^2 \tag{B.2}$$

When $\sigma_y/\bar{y} \ll 1$ and $\sigma_y/\bar{y} \ll \sigma_x/\bar{x}$, i.e., the coefficient of variation for the dispersion of the risk-adjusted returns is much less than 1 and much less than the coefficient of variation for IC, the variance can be approximated by

$$\text{Var}(xy) = \bar{y}^2\sigma_x^2 \tag{B.3}$$

This approximation justifies using Eq. (9) for the active risk.

Notes

[1] This problem has also been recognized by other practitioners. For example, Freeman (2002) notes that "if a manager is optimizing the long-short portfolio, he or she better assume that the tracking error forecast (of a risk model) will be at least 50% too low."

[2] Grinold (1994) proposed this alpha formula mainly for translating cross-sectional z scores into alpha inputs for an optimizer. While such a prescription holds true for a linear time series forecast model, it is not theoretically valid with cross-sectional z scores. We demonstrate in the paper, that such a prescription is not necessary in deriving IR. Furthermore, while it is necessary to use a risk model for individual securities in the mean-variance optimization to form the optimal portfolio, it is not necessary and perhaps overreaching to assume returns of individual securities follow the prescription of the risk model. Instead of such a normative approach, we take a descriptive one, making no explicit assumptions about the expected return of each security.

[3] Later in the paper, we will use the time series standard deviation as well. To avoid confusion we shall use dispersion when describing cross-sectional standard deviation and standard deviation when describing time series standard deviation.

[4] It is difficult to maintain a constant level of risk-model tracking error for all time. One often targets it within a narrow range to accommodate portfolio drift and changing risk model estimates.

[5] The variance of N such independent variables is a scaled chi-square distribution if their mean is zero. It can be proven that when N is large, the dispersion is close to unity, using the approximation of a chi-square distribution (Keeping, 1995).

References

Clarke, R., de Silva, H. and Thorley, S. (2002). "Portfolio Constraints and the Fundamental Law of Active Management." *Financial Analyst's Journal* **58**(5), 48–66.

Freeman, J.D. (2002). "Portfolio Construction and Risk Management: Long–Short/Market-Neutral Portfolios." In: *AIMR Conference Proceeding: Hedge Fund Management.* pp. 41–46.

Grinold, R.C. (1989). "The Fundamental Law of Active Management." *Journal of Portfolio Management* **15**(3), 30–37.

Grinold, R.C. (1994). "Alpha is Volatility Times IC Times Score." *Journal of Portfolio Management* **20**(4), 9–16.

Grinold, R.C. and Kahn, R.N. (2000). "The Efficiency Gains of Long–Short Investing." *Financial Analyst's Journal* **56**(6), 40–53.

Hartmann, S., Wesselius, P., Steel, D. and Aldred, N. (2002). "Laying the Foundations: Exploring the Pitfalls of Portfolio Construction and Optimization." Working Paper, ABN AMRO.

Keeping, E.S. (1995). *Introduction to Statistical Inference.* New York: Dover, p. 87.

Sorensen, E.H., Qian, E., Hua, R. and Schoen, R. (2004). "Multiple Alpha Sources and Active Management." *Journal of Portfolio Management* **30**(2), 39–45.

Keywords: Portfolio management; portfolio optimization; active risk

Journal Of Investment Management
Vol. 3, No. 1 (2005), pp. 99–109

THE YEAR-END PRICE OF RISK IN A MARKET FOR LIQUIDITY

Mark D. Griffiths[a] *and Drew B. Winters*[b]

Musto (1997, Journal of Finance 52*(4), 1861–1882) identifies a year-end effect in commercial paper (CP) and suggests that the price of risk may increase at the year-end. Griffiths and Winters (2003, Journal of Business, forthcoming) show that the timing of the year-end effect in CP is consistent with a preferred habitat for liquidity. However, Griffiths and Winters use data from only one risk class, so we extend their analysis by using spreads between different risk classes to determine if the price of risk does increase at the year-end. Using daily spreads between two risk classes of 7 day, 15 day, and 30 day non-financial CP, we find that the spread does increase at this time. However, the timing of the spread increases and decreases aligns with expectations consistent with a preferred habitat for liquidity at the year-end. This suggests that when liquidity is tight at the year-end, money market investors increase the price of risk.*

1 Introduction

Kidwell *et al.* (1997) describe the money markets as markets for liquidity. That is, investors with temporary cash surpluses store their liquidity by investing in money market securities and borrowers with temporary cash shortages borrow liquidity by issuing money market securities. Hence, money market investors require short-term debt securities that have: (1) maturities that match the anticipated length of time until the surplus cash is needed, (2) low default risk, and (3) high marketability. The securities in the $3 trillion US money markets include: Treasury bills, negotiable CDs, bankers' acceptances, repurchase agreements (repos), Fed funds, and commercial paper (CP).

Musto (1997) identifies a year-end effect in the CP market where the rates increase dramatically when the instrument matures in the new calendar year. Musto suggests that either the price of risk, or the quantity of risk, increases at the end-of-the-year and suggests that the cause is risk-shifting window dressing by money market mutual fund managers.[1] This risk-shifting window dressing hypothesis argues that fund managers shift away from the riskier investments in their portfolio so that, at the year-end disclosure date, the portfolio reported will under-represent the typical risk level of the portfolio. This exodus drives down the price and, thus, increases the yield on CP making it an increasingly expensive source of funds (for borrowers) as the disclosure date approaches.

[a]Jack R. Anderson Professor of Finance, Richard T. Farmer School of Business, Miami University, Oxford, OH 45014, USA. Tel.: 602-978-7612; e-mail: griffitm@t-bird.edu (corresponding author).

[b]Texas Tech University, Federal Reserve Bank of St. Louis.

Griffiths and Winters (2003) revisit the year-end effect in 1 month CP and provide strong evidence that the identified rate effect is not consistent with risk-shifting window dressing. To support risk-shifting window dressing, the rate pressure must continue across the year-end because the portfolio disclosure date is the last trading day of the year and, Griffiths and Winters show that the year-end rate pressure begins to abate prior to that last trading day. They contend that the year-end rate pattern is consistent with a year-end preferred habitat for liquidity.[2]

A preferred habitat for liquidity implies that money market investors have specific investment horizons when they enter the market and choose to invest in securities that match their required horizon. One possible reason for specific investment horizons is that many periodic cash flows occur at the turn-of-a-month, so that the temporary cash surpluses are invested such that they mature before the turn-of-the-month when the cash is needed. Ogden (1987) notes that many regular cash flows occur near the end-of-the-year, but not necessarily on the last day of the year. This implies that a year-end preference for liquidity would create rate increases when the maturity of money market securities spans the investors' year-end cash flow dates followed by rate decreases as the year-end cash obligations dates pass. The rate decrease from the abatement of liquidity preference pressure can occur before the last trading day of the year.

This is also consistent with Garbade's (1999, p. 182) comments on the pricing of Treasury bills with special value that are "attributable to maturities that immediately precede dates when many corporate treasurers need cash to make payments. In addition to quarter-end bills, these include 'month-end' bills maturing at the end of a calendar month . . . and 'tax' bills maturing immediately before important Federal corporate income tax dates . . ."

Griffiths and Winters (2003) extend their analysis to include 1 month money markets in: negotiable CDs, bankers' acceptances, euro-dollar deposits, and T-bills, and find that a year-end preference for liquidity generalizes across these markets. Their analysis uses daily rates from one risk class of borrower in each market, which allowed them to determine that the timing of the year-end rate pattern in the money markets is consistent with a preference for liquidity and not with risk-shifting window dressing. However, their data from one risk class prevents them from analyzing whether the price of risk increases at the year-end and, if the price of risk does increase at the year-end, what is an appropriate explanation for the increase.

We collect daily rates on 7-day, 15-day, and 30-day non-financial CP from 7/1/97 through 6/30/02 for the commercial paper risk categories identified by the Board of Governors as AA and A2/P2. We find year-end patterns for each maturity across both risk classes consistent with the year-end pattern identified by Griffiths and Winters (2003). In addition, we find a year-end pattern in the spread between the AA rates and the A2/P2 rates that aligns with regularities in the rates suggesting that there is an increased price for risk at the year-end but, that the timing of the price increase coincides with year-end liquidity preferences but not with risk-shifting window dressing. In particular, we find that the two different classes of CP both become more expensive for the borrower when the maturity dates of the instruments first begin to cross into the next calendar year. The CP then cheapens just prior to the year-end.

2 Data and Methods

2.1 Data

The Board of Governors of the Federal Reserve System reports daily interest rates on a wide variety of short-term and long-term debt instruments. Beginning in July 1997, the Board began reporting daily interest rates on financial and non-financial CP in initial maturities of 7, 15, 30, 60, and 90 days.[3] They also began reporting 30 day A2/P2 non-financial CP rates in July 1997 and expanded their reporting of A2/P2 rates to include other CP maturities in January 1998. We collect all the non-financial 7, 15, and 30 day rates available from 7/1/97 through 6/30/02.[4] The data reflect the pricing on new issues of CP with same day settlement in immediately available funds.

The Board of Governors reports the definition of AA non-financial commercial paper as short-term credit with at least one "1" or "1+" rating but no ratings other than "1." It reports the definition of A2/P2 non-financial CP as short-term credit with at least one "2" rating but no ratings other than "2."[5] A Moody's rating of "1" suggests a superior ability to repay senior short-term debt, while a Moody's rating of "2" indicates a strong ability to repay senior short-term debt. Thus, CP that is rated "2" is not junk bond quality debt. It is high quality debt that is likely to meet its obligations, but it is not the highest quality debt, and the rating agencies are able to differentiate its borrower's ability to service debt from borrowers in the highest rating category.

Including an examination of daily volume at the year-end could enhance our analysis. However, data on daily volume are not available. The Board of Governors of the Federal Reserve systems provides only monthly outstandings and quarterly volume for various classes of CP.

2.2 Methods

We start with the regression model Griffiths and Winters (2003) used to analyze rate and spread changes at the year-end. However, we only include year-end pressure points in our model since we are focusing on the year-end and because Griffiths and Winters did not find significant turn-of-the-month effects in the months not at the turn-of-the-year. We add to our explanatory variables the first lag of the dependent variable to control for trends in the dependent variable. Our model is as follows:

$$\Delta X_t = \alpha_0 + \alpha_1(\Delta X_{t-1}) + \beta_1\text{BCross} + \beta_2\text{ACross} + \beta_3\text{BYearend} + \beta_4\text{AYearend} + \gamma(\Delta\text{TB}_t) + \varepsilon_t \quad (1)$$

where ΔX_t is the daily change in rates or spreads specified as $X_t - X_{t-1}$, BCross a 0/1 dummy variable that equals 1 on the two trading days before the maturity of the instrument begins to span the year-end and 0 otherwise, ACross a 0/1 dummy variable that equals 1 on the trading day that the maturity of the instrument begins to span the year-end and the following day and 0 otherwise, BYearend a 0/1 dummy variable that equals 1 on the last two trading days of a year and 0 otherwise, AYearend a 0/1 dummy variable that equals 1 on the first two trading days of a new year and 0 otherwise, and ΔTB_t the daily change in 3 month T-bill yields specified as $TB_t - TB_{t-1}$ and is included in the model to control for changes in the general level of short-term interest rates.[6]

We estimate Eq. (1) using OLS with White's (1980) adjustment for heteroscedasticity.

3 Analysis

3.1 Descriptive Analysis

The feature that differentiates risk-shifting window dressing from a preferred habitat for liquidity is the timing of the year-end rate (spread) decrease that returns rates (spreads) to "normal" levels. For risk-shifting window dressing, the decrease must occur after the year-end, while for a preferred habitat for liquidity the decrease may occur before the year-end.[7] In addition, since rates (spreads) are returning to "normal" levels at the year-end, we must see that, prior to the year-end, during the period when the maturity of the instrument spans the year-end, rates (spreads) are "abnormally" high. We will demonstrate the presence of this year-end regularity in our data with a series of plots. The X-axis in each plot is trading days relative to the year-end. In each plot, the X-axis has a 0, which is not a trading day but instead marks the break point between the years. Trading day −1 is the last trading of the year while trading day 1 is the first trading day of the new year.

We begin with Figure 1 which plots daily average rates around the year-end for 7, 15, and 30 day AA non-financial CP. In Figure 1, trading day −4 is the first trading day when new 7 day CP matures in the new year and day −10 is the first day that new 15 day CP begins to mature in the new year. The plot of the 30 day CP is drawn

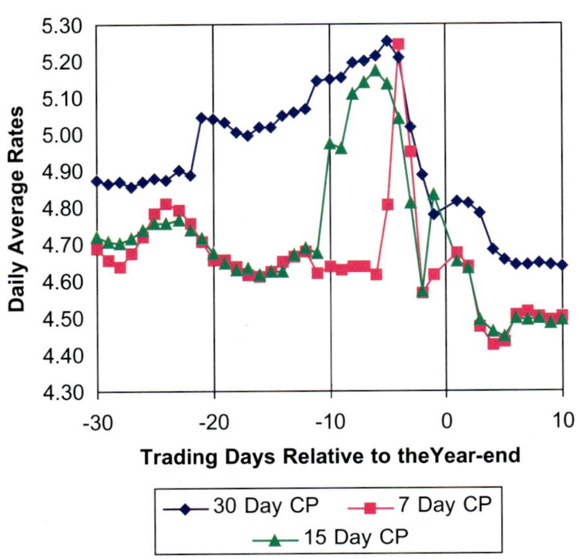

Figure 1 AA rated CP.

so that trading day −21 is the first day the new 30 day CP matures in the new year. To get the switch days to align across years, some minor adjustments were made to the 30 day CP data, while the switch day for all the 7 day CP data is day −4 and all the 15 day CP is day −10.[8]

In Figure 1 we see the same pattern in 30 day AA non-financial CP as identified in Griffiths and Winters (2003) and this regularity is consistent with a preferred habitat for liquidity at the year-end. The 30 day AA non-financial CP rates increase on trading day −21 when the maturity of new 30 day CP begins to span the year-end and rates decrease to normal levels across the last few trading days of the year. A similar pattern of the rates increasing when maturity begins to span the year-end followed by rate decreases over the last few trading days of the year also occurs in the 15 and 7 day AA-rated CP, which suggests a year-end preference for liquidity across maturities in the 30 day and under CP market. Recall that rates would have to remain elevated to support the risk-shifting window dressing hypothesis. We note that there is an unusual increase in average daily rates for 15 day CP on trading day −1. The largest daily rate increase in our 15 day AA non-financial CP occurs on the last trading day of 1999, which may be associated with Y2K liquidity provided by the Federal Reserve.[9] We chose to leave the outlier observation in our analysis.

Figure 2 is similar to Figure 1 using the rates for A2/P2 non-financial CP. Figure 2 shows that the plots for each maturity resembles the plots in Figure 1. That is, for each maturity the A2/P2 rates increase when the maturity begins to span the year-end and rates decrease across the last few trading days of the year. This suggests that the evidence to support a preferred habitat for liquidity at the year-end generalizes across risk classes of CP.

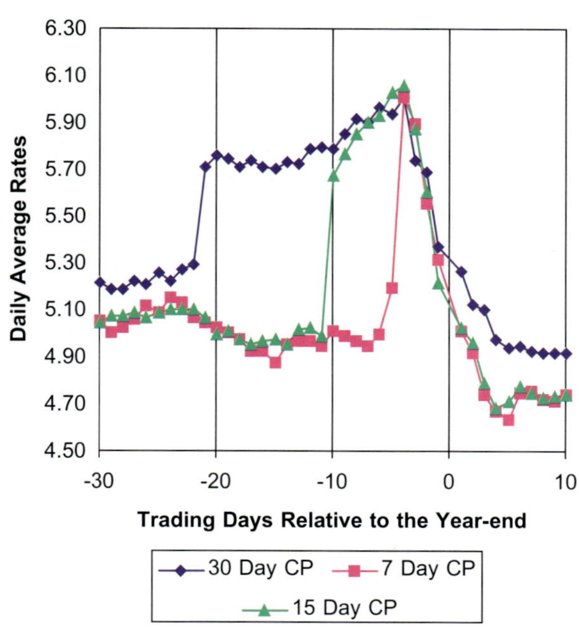

Figure 2 A2/P2 rated CP.

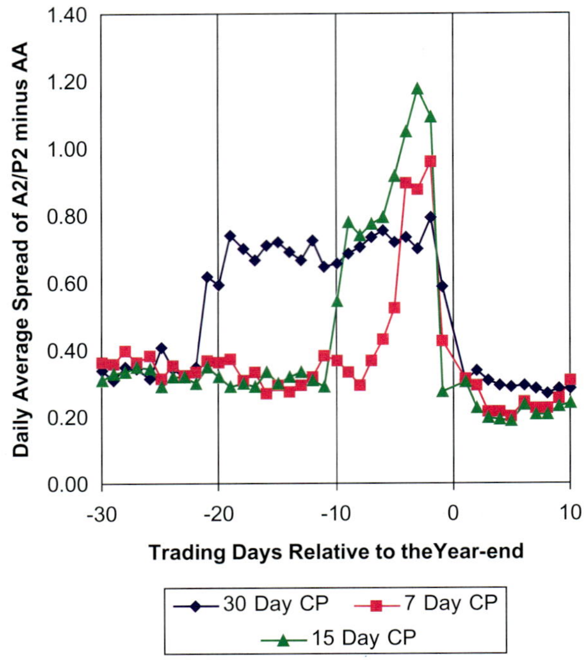

Figure 3 Spread of AA to A2/P2 rated CP.

Figure 3 plots the AA to A2/P2 spread at the year-end and provides our first look at the price of risk at the year-end. If the price of risk does not increase at the year-end then the spread should remain constant. Figure 3 shows that the spread for each maturity increases dramatically at the year-end arguing in favor of a price of risk increase at the year-end. However, the timing of the spread changes is consistent with the timing hypothesized for a preferred habitat for liquidity. That is, each spread increase aligns with the maturity of the instruments beginning to span the year-end and each spread decrease occurs across the last few trading days of the year. Spreads would have to remain abnormally high through the year-end to be consistent with the risk-shifting window dressing hypothesis. The observed pattern suggests that in this market, when liquidity gets squeezed at the end-of-the-year the price of risk increases, but that this effect is not associated with portfolio disclosure dates. That is, the instrument gets expensive for the borrower as expected but, then, cheapens prior to the last trading day of the year.

Even without the benefit of tests for statistical significance, we note that the spread increases are economically significant. Stigum (1990) states money market traders view 10–20 basis points (bps) as a significant arbitrage opportunity, while Figure 3 shows that the CP spreads increase at least 30–60 bps at the year-end. To provide the numbers for the daily average spreads in Figure 3, we provide Figure 4 with three panels. Each panel plots a different maturity from Figure 3 with the *X*-axis modified to focus on the period of increased spread for each maturity and each daily plot point is accompanied by the numerical value (in percentage points) of the average daily spread.

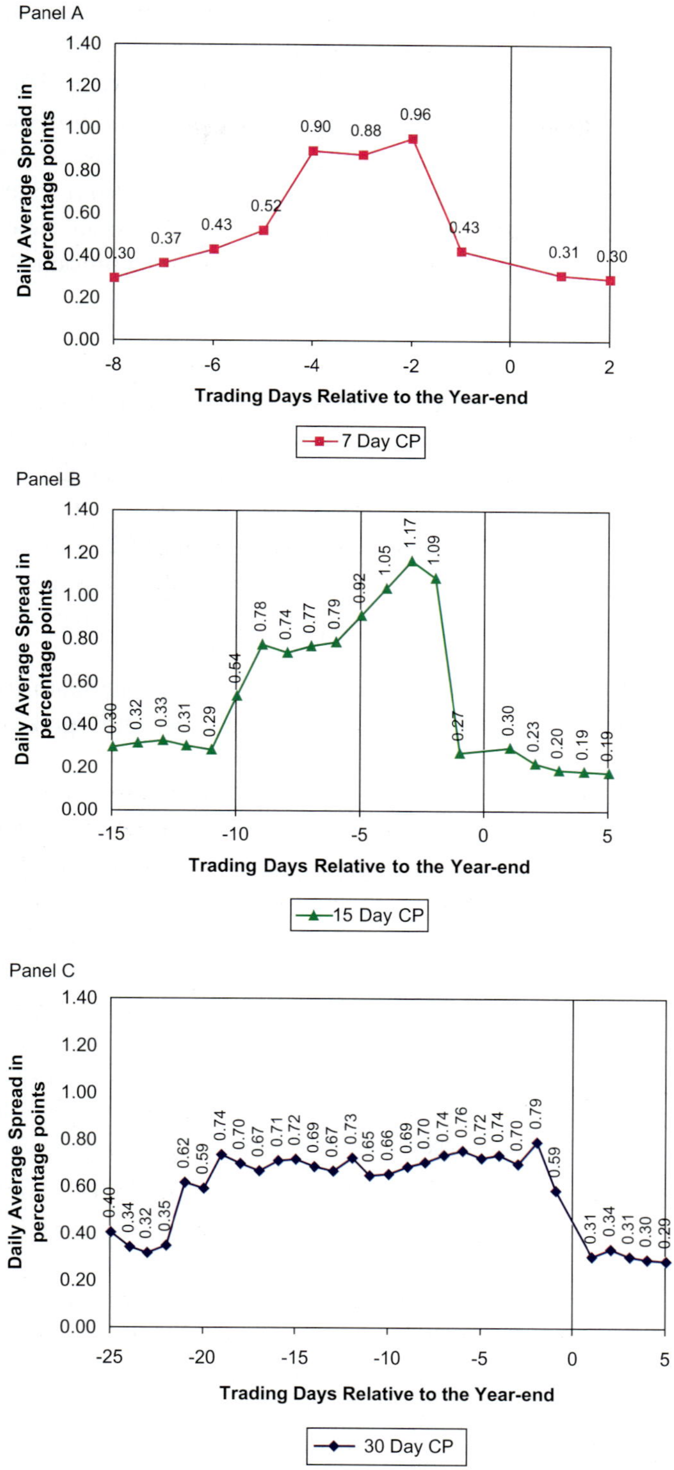

Figure 4 Spread of AA to A2/P2 rated CP. (A) 7-day spreads; (B) 15-day spreads; (C) 30 day spreads.

Figure 4, Panel A shows that 7 day average spreads increase on trading day −4 from 52 to 90 bps with spread remaining around 90 bps for 3 days: a year-end spread increase of at least 40 bps. Figure 4, Panel B shows that 15 day average spreads increase from 29 bps on trading day −11 to 78 bps on trading day −9 and over the next 7 days range between 74 bps and 117 bps: an increase of at least 50 bps. Figure 4, Panel C shows that 30 day average spreads increase on trading day −21, from 35 to 62 bps and, over the next 20 trading days, remain between 59 and 79 bps: an increase of about 35 bps. Again, all of these spread increases are economically significant.[10]

3.2 Regression Analysis

In this section, we take a closer look at the year-end break points in each time series of data in a regression analysis. The regression analysis controls for changes in the general level of short-term interest rates so that the dummy variables for the break points can isolate calendar-time specific effects. We estimate Eq. (1) for the daily rate changes in AA non-financial CP for each maturity and in A2/P2 non-financial CP for each maturity. In addition, we estimate Eq. (1) for the daily changes in the spread between AA CP and A2/P2 CP for each maturity. The results from estimating Eq. (1) are reported in Tables 1–3.

Table 1 provides the results from estimating Eq. (1) for each maturity of the AA-rated non-financial CP. All three maturities show a positive and significant (at better

Table 1 Regression for daily rate changes in AA-rated non-financial CP (Eq. (1)).

	7 Day	15 Day	30 Day
Intercept	−0.0036 (0.2685)	−0.0039 (0.1548)	−0.0019 (0.1679)
ΔX_{t-1}	0.0337 (0.2907)	−0.1276 (<0.0001)	0.1265 (<0.0001)
BCross	0.0062 (0.8643)	0.0089 (0.7675)	0.0431 (<0.0001)
ACross	0.2955 (<0.0001)	0.1833 (<0.0001)	−0.0096 (0.5197)
BYearend	−0.1585 (<0.0001)	−0.0209 (0.4992)	−0.1004 (<0.0001)
AYearend	0.0186 (0.6051)	−0.0853 (0.0045)	0.0231 (0.1183)
ΔTB	0.4053 (<0.0001)	0.3275 (<0.0001)	0.2541 (<0.0001)
F-statistic	26.00 (<0.0001)	16.53 (<0.0001)	37.00 (<0.0001)
Adjusted R-square	0.1308	0.0855	0.1475

Note: p-Values appear in parentheses under each parameter estimate.

Table 2 Regression for daily rate changes in A2/P2-rated non-financial CP (Eq. (1)).

	7 Day	15 Day	30 Day
Intercept	−0.0040	−0.0029	−0.0028
	(0.2413)	(0.3177)	(0.1680)
ΔX_{t-1}	−0.1285	−0.1667	−0.1547
	(<0.0001)	(<0.0001)	(<0.0001)
BCross	0.0664	−0.0073	0.2223
	(0.0819)	(0.8175)	(<0.0001)
ACross	0.5974	0.4336	0.0945
	(<0.0001)	(<0.0001)	(<0.0001)
BYearend	−0.3212	−0.3653	−0.1974
	(<0.0001)	(<0.0001)	(<0.0001)
AYearend	−0.2266	−0.1727	−0.1481
	(<0.0001)	(<0.0001)	(<0.0001)
ΔTB	0.3169	0.1845	0.1599
	(<0.0001)	(0.0003)	(<0.0001)
F-statistic	58.65	52.58	38.55
	(<0.0001)	(<0.0001)	(<0.0001)
Adjusted R-square	0.2576	0.2369	0.1529

Note: p-Values appear in parentheses under each parameter estimate.

Table 3 Regression for daily spread changes in non-financial CP for the spread between A2/P2 and AA Rated CP (Eq. (1)).

	7 Day	15 Day	30 Day
Intercept	0.0002	0.0015	−0.0002
	(0.9242)	(0.5671)	(0.8790)
ΔX_{t-1}	−0.2411	−0.4189	−0.4129
	(<0.0001)	(<0.0001)	(<0.0001)
BCross	0.0619	−0.0168	0.1477
	(0.0187)	(0.5683)	(<0.0001)
ACross	0.2688	0.2759	0.1122
	(<0.0001)	(<0.0001)	(<0.0001)
BYearend	−0.0952	−0.3342	−0.0438
	(0.0003)	(<0.0001)	(0.0141)
AYearend	−0.2916	−0.1725	−0.2260
	(<0.0001)	(<0.0001)	(<0.0001)
ΔTB	−0.1088	−0.1462	−0.1232
	(0.0102)	(0.0019)	(<0.0001)
F-statistic	40.69	71.49	65.87
	(<0.0001)	(<0.0001)	(<0.0001)
Adjusted R-square	0.1928	0.2978	0.2377

Note: p-Values appear in parentheses under each parameter estimate.

than the 1% level) parameter estimate on the daily change in 3 month T-bill yields, indicating that the AA-rated CP rates tend to move with changes in the general level of short-term interest rates. For the 7 day rate changes, we find that the parameter estimate for ACross (measuring the date the instrument begins to span the year-end) is positive and significant at better than the 1% level and BYearend (measuring the last two trading days of the year) is negative and significant at better than the 1% level. These results suggest that the 7 day AA-rated non-financial CP rates increase significantly when the instrument begins to mature in the new year and that the rates decline significantly over the last two trading days of the year. This is consistent with a preferred habitat for liquidity but does not support the risk-shifting window dressing hypothesis. For the 15 day rate changes we find that the parameter estimate for ACross is positive and significant at better than the 1% level and AYearend (measuring the first two trading days of the new year) is negative and significant at better than the 1% level. These results appear to support the risk-shifting window dressing hypothesis. However, a review of Figure 1 shows that rates decrease dramatically before the year-end, but that the majority of the rate decrease occurs earlier than the last two trading days of the year so that the rate decrease is not captured in our regression dummy variables (BYearend equals 1 only on the last two trading days of the year). For the 30 day rate changes, we find that the parameter estimate for BCross (measuring the last two trading days before the instrument spans the year-end) is positive and significant (at better than the 1% level) and BYearend is negative and significant (at better than the 1% level). These results suggest that the 30 day AA-rated non-financial CP rates increase significantly when the instrument still matures in the current year and that the rates decline significantly over the last two trading days of the year.

Table 2 provides the results from estimating Eq. (1) for each maturity of the A2/P2-rated non-financial CP. All three maturities show a positive and significant (at better than the 1% level) parameter estimate on the daily change in 3 month T-bill yields, which indicates that the riskier A2/P2-rated CP rates also tend to move with changes in the general level of short-term interest rates. For the 7 day A2/P2-rated rate changes, we find that the parameter estimate: for ACross is positive and significant at better than the 1% level, for BYearend is negative and significant at better than the 1% level, and for AYearend is negative and significant at better than the 1% level. The rate changes for 15 day A2/P2 rated non-financial CP follow the same pattern as the 7 day A2/P2 paper. For the 30 day A2/P2-rated rate changes, we find that the parameter estimate: for BCross is positive and significant at better than the 1% level, for ACross is positive and significant at better than the 1% level, for BYearend is negative and significant at better than the 1% level, and for AYearend is negative and significant at better than the 1% level. These results suggest that, in all cases, the rate increase begins by the time maturity spans the year-end and that the rate decrease occurs across the turn-of-the-year with the decrease beginning before the switch to the new year.

Table 3 provides the results from estimating Eq. (1) for each maturity on the spread between AA-rated and A2/P2-rated non-financial CP. All three maturities show negative and significant (at better than the 5% level) parameter estimates on the daily change in 3 month T-bill yields. This result is somewhat surprising and suggests that spread changes decrease when T-bill yields increase. However, this result is consistent with the results on the change in 3 month T-bill yields from Tables 1 and 2, which show that AA-rated CP is more responsive to changes in the general level of short-term interest rates than A2/P2 CP. For the 7 day spread changes, we find that the parameter estimate: for BCross is positive and significant at better than the 5% level, for ACross the estimate is positive and significant at better than the 1% level, for BYearend the estimate is negative and significant at better than the 1% level, and for AYearend the estimate is negative and significant at better than the 1% level. For the 15 day spread changes, we find that the parameter estimate: for ACross is positive and significant at better than the 1% level, for BYearend is negative and significant at better than the 1% level, and for AYearend is negative and significant at better than the 1% level. For the 30 day spread changes, we find that the parameter estimate: for BCross is positive and significant at better than the 1% level, for ACross the estimate is positive and significant at better than the 1% level, for BYearend the estimate is negative and significant at better than the 5% level, and for AYearend the estimate is negative and significant at better than the 1% level. These results suggest that, in all cases, spreads also begin to increase when maturity begins to span the year-end and that spreads decrease across the turn-of-the-year with the decrease beginning before the switch to the new year. These spread change results are consistent with the timing of the year-end preference for liquidity and are inconsistent with expectations based on risk-shifting window dressing arguments.[11]

3.3 Discussion About Market Participants

Burghardt and Kirshner (1994) discuss the effect of the turn-of-the-year interest rate increases on LIBOR and euro-dollar futures contract prices. They note that the turn effect in interest rates has gained notoriety among bankers because of the pressures applied to year-end financing rates. They note further that the source of the effect is said to be demand for cash. To address this year-end rate pressure the Chicago Mercantile Exchange (CME) has developed the Turn (interest rate) Futures contract, which the CME describes as "the first transparent, objective, and simple vehicle for taking advantage of opportunities presented by this closely scrutinized annual phenomenon."

In CP, the year-end rate increase could occur because the borrowers do not have any viable options for their year-end financing. However, CP is generally viewed as a less costly alternative to bank debt for high quality borrowers, so these borrowers can access bank debt if they get squeezed in the CP market. Saindenberg and Strahan (1999) examine this possibility by examining the decrease in non-financial CP across the fourth quarter of 1998. They find that over the same period covered by the reduction in CP outstanding, borrowing under bank commercial lines of credit increased by the same amount. Hence, when lenders squeeze borrowers in the CP market, borrowers have a readily available alternative source of funds. To further this point, Downing and Oliner (2004) show that tier-2 CP outstanding balances decline at the year-end and rebound in January.

When borrowers exit the CP market, the supply of available CP declines, resulting in prices rising and rates falling, *ceteris paribus*. However, our results suggest that rates increase at the year-end, suggesting a more than offsetting decline in amount loaned. That is, investors are withholding their cash from the markets in larger dollar amounts than the borrowers are switching to alternative funding sources. Shen (2003) states that the primary investors in CP are: money market mutual funds, trust funds, insurance companies, pension funds, and large firms with extra cash. Why would these firms hold back their available cash at year-end when rates in CP are high? We contend that it is precisely these investors who, at the margin, need the cash to meet their year-end cash obligations.

4 Conclusion

Musto (1997) identifies a year-end effect in CP rates and suggests that either the price of risk, or the quantity of risk, increases at the year-end. Griffiths and Winters (2003) show that the timing of the year-end rate changes in CP is not consistent with risk-shifting window dressing, but with a year-end preferred habitat for liquidity. Griffiths and Winters were unable to determine if the price of risk increases at the year-end in the CP market.

We examine whether the price of risk increases at the year-end in CP by using CP rates from two different risk classes. We determine that the spread between the risk classes increases at the year-end and that the spread increase occurs across CP with initial maturities of 30 days or less. Further, we show that the timing of the year-end spread changes is consistent with the year-end timing suggested by a year-end preferred habitat for liquidity, but does not support risk-shifting window dressing. We conclude that in a market for liquidity, when liquidity becomes paramount to the investors (at the year-end) the price of risk increases dramatically.

Acknowledgments

The authors thank an anonymous referee, John Krainer, Robin Grieves, and participants at the 2003 FMA Conference for helpful comments. The opinions in the paper are those of the authors and do not reflect any position by the Federal Reserve Bank of St. Louis nor the Board of Governors of the Federal Reserve System. A portion of this paper was completed while Griffiths was a faculty member at Thunderbird, The Garvin School of International Management.

Notes

1 The risk-shifting window dressing hypothesis is a variant on the traditional year-end window dressing hypothesis suggested by Haugen and Lakonishok (1987) and Ritter (1988).

2 The preferred habitat hypothesis was developed by Modigliani and Sutch (1966). Ogden (1987) adapts the preferred habitat hypothesis to the money markets to explain the month-end and year-end effect in the T-bill market identified by Park and Reinganum (1986).

3 The rates reported each day are for new instruments with initial maturities of 7, 15, 30, 60, and 90 days, instead of, for pre-existing instruments with these numbers of days remaining until maturity.

4 We limit our analysis to CP with initial maturities of 30 days or less because previously Griffiths and Winters (1997) find a year-end preferred habitat for liquidity in repos with initial maturities of 1, 2, and 3 weeks, and 1 month but not with maturities of 2 or 3 months.

5 The numerical ratings correspond to the numerical ratings from the credit rating agencies. Moody's short-term debt ratings and rating definitions can be found at www.moody's.com/moodys/cust/ and provide an excellent example of a rating agency's short-term debt ratings and definitions.

6 We recognize that 3 month T-bills is a maturity mismatch relative to all of the rates and spreads that we use as dependent variables. However, we believe that it is the best available proxy for the general level of short-term interest rates. Musto (1997) and Griffiths and Winters (2003) find no evidence of a significant year-end effect in 3 month T-bill yields, while Longstaff (2000) describes 1 month T-bills as special and Griffiths and Winters (2003) find significant year-end yield changes in 1 month T-bills.

7 We note that money market instruments trade in immediately available funds, which means we do not need to adjust the alignment of trading days relative to the year-end from any delay in settlement.

8 The adjustment to the data does not materially alter the plot. A few spaces were inserted in the middle of the year-end period in a couple of years, so that all the switch days would align in 30 day CP.

9 Our sample period includes the year-end switch from 1999 to 2000 and its associated concerns about technology problems. One of the responses to the Y2K concerns was the increase in market liquidity by the Federal Reserve. This action by the Federal Reserve could affect our results. We re-drew our plots and re-estimated our regressions controlling December 1999 and the switch to the year 2000 and the results are similar to the results reported in our figures and tables. That is, the increase in general market liquidity for the switch to the year 2000 does not drive our results and the patterns in December 1999 and January 2000 are similar to those in the other years of our sample (with the notable exception of the outlier in 15 day AA CP on trading day −1).

10 As a final reference point for the size of the year-end spread effect, we note that the 90 bps spread in 7 day CP is about four standard deviations above the mean, the year-end spreads in 15 day CP are between three and six standard deviations above the mean, and the year-end spreads in 30 day CP are two to three standard deviations above the mean.

11 Liquidity changes in the overnight markets could affect our results. We examined this possibility by estimating the unexpected daily rate changes in the effective Federal funds rate and then using the unexpected change as an explanatory variable in our Eq. (1). See Spindt and Hoffmeister (1988), Griffiths and Winters (1995) and Hamilton (1996) for models of daily changes in Federal funds rates and volatility. The unexpected rate change in the overnight market does not provide information about the year-end effect in CP during our sample period. Accordingly, we chose not to include the unexpected rate change in Eq. (1).

References

Burghardt, G. and Kirshner, S. (1994). "One Good Turn." *Risk Magazine* November.

Downing, C. and Oliner, S. (2004). "The Term Structure of Commercial Paper Rates." Working Paper, Federal Reserve Board.

Garbade, K.D. (1999). *Fixed Income Analytics.* Cambridge Massachusetts: The MIT Press.

Griffiths, M.D. and Winters, D.B. (1995). "Day-of-the-Week Effects in Federal Funds Rates: Further Empirical Findings." *Journal of Banking and Finance* **19**, 1265–1284.

Griffiths, M.D. and Winters, D.B. (1997). "On a Preferred Habitat for Liquidity at the Turn-of-the-Year: Evidence from the Term-Repo Market." *Journal of Financial Services Research* **12**, 21–38.

Griffiths, M.D. and Winters, D.B. (forthcoming). "The Turn-of-the-Year in Money Markets: Tests of the Risk-Shifting Window Dressing and Preferred Habitat Hypotheses." *Journal of Business.*

Hamilton, J. (1996). "The Daily Market for Federal Funds." *Journal of Political Economy* **104**, 26–56.

Haugen, R. and Lakonishok, J. (1987). *The Incredible January Effect.* Homewood, IL: Dow Jones-Irwin.

Kidwell, D.S., Peterson, R.L. and Blackwell, D.W. (1997). *Financial Institutions, Markets and Money*, 6th edn. Forth Worth, Texas: Dryden Press.

Longstaff, F. (2000). "The Term Structure of Very Short-Term Rates: New Evidence for the Expectations Hypothesis." *Journal of Financial Economics* **58**, 397–415.

Modigliani, F. and Sutch, R. (1966). "Innovations in Interest Rate Policy." *American Economic Review* **56**, 178–197.

Musto, D. (1997). "Portfolio Disclosures and Year-end Price Shifts." *Journal of Finance* **52**(4), 1861–1882.

Ogden, J.P. (1987). "The End of the Month as a Preferred Habitat: A Test of Operational Efficiency in the Money Market." *Journal of Financial and Quantitative Analysis* **22**(3), 329–344.

Park, S.Y. and Reinganum, M.R. (1986). "The Puzzling Price Behavior of Treasury Bills that Mature at the Turn of Calendar Months." *Journal of Financial Economics* **16**, 267–283.

Ritter, J. (1988). "The Buying and Selling Behavior of Individuals at the Turn-of-the-Year." *Journal of Finance* **43**(3), 701–717.

Saidenberg, M. and Strahan, P. (1999). "Are Banks Still Important for Financing Large Businesses?" *Federal Reserve Bank of New York Current Issues in Economics and Finance* **5**, 1–6.

Shen, P. (2003). "Why has the Nonfinancial Commercial Paper Market Shrunk Recently?" *Federal Reserve Bank of Kansas City Economic Review* 55–76.

Spindt, P. and Hoffmeister, R. (1988). "The Micromechanics of the Federal Funds Market: Implications for Day-of-the-Week effects in Funds Rate Variability." *Journal of Financial and Quantitative Analysis* **23**, 401–416.

Stigum, M. (1990). *The Money Market*, 3rd edn. Dow Jones-Irwin.

White, H. (1980). "Heteroscedasticity-Consistent Covariance Matrix Estimator and a Direct Test for Heteroscedasticity." *Econometrica* **48**, 817–838.

Keywords: Risk; year-end effect

Journal Of Investment Management
Vol. 1, No. 4 (2003), pp. 9–25

RESAMPLED FRONTIERS VERSUS DIFFUSE BAYES: AN EXPERIMENT

Harry M. Markowitz[a] *and Nilufer Usmen*[b]

1 Introduction

This paper reports on an experiment which compares two methods of handling the fact that empirically observed means, variances, and covariances, for a mean–variance analysis, are themselves noisy. One method is Bayes inference using diffuse priors which the present authors, among many others, have recommended. (Markowitz and Usmen, 1996a,b). The other is the method of Resampled Efficient Frontiers™ recommended by Richard O. Michaud (Michaud, 1998).[1]

The experiment is a computer simulation "game" with two players and a referee. In the game the referee generates 10 "truths" about eight asset classes. For each truth the referee draws 100 different possible "histories" of 216 monthly observations. (We chose eight asset classes and 216 months to keep the experiment as close as possible to that of Michaud.)

Each history is presented to each player. The players know that the truth is a joint normal distribution with unchanging means, variances, and covariances but do not know the parameter values. The Michaud player uses the observed history to generate a resampled frontier. That is, for a given history the player randomly generates many mean–variance efficient frontiers and averages these. The Bayes player uses the observed history to update beliefs, from prior to posterior, then uses these beliefs to compute one efficient frontier. Because of the high dimensionality of the "hypothesis-space," Monte Carlo sampling must be used to approximate the Bayes player's *ex post* means, variances, and covariances. Given their respective frontiers each player picks three portfolios, namely, the portfolios which each player believes maximizes

$$EU = E - \lambda V \tag{1}$$

for $\lambda = 0.5, 1.0, 2.0$, where E and V are the portfolio mean and variance. The referee notes the player's actual expected utility using the true means, variances, and covariances—known only to the referee. The referee also notes each player's estimate of its expected utility. This is repeated for the 100 randomly drawn histories for a given truth and the 10 truths of the game.

[a]Harry Markowitz Company, 1010 Turquoise Street Suite 245, San Diego, CA 92109, USA. Tel.: (858) 488-7212 (corresponding author).

[b]School of Business, Montclair State University, Upper Montclair, New Jersey, USA.

The assumption of normality and unchanging distributions may be unrealistic, but both players are apprised of the rules of the game. It is not obvious that the assumptions favor one methodology over the other. The authors expected the Bayesian approach with diffuse priors to do better than the resampled frontier approach. In fact, the opposite turned out to be the case. Section 2 of this paper describes how the referee generates truths and, from these, the histories "observed" by the players; Section 3 describes the actions of the Michaud player; Section 4 describes the actions of the diffuse Bayesian player; Section 5 presents the results of the experiment; Section 6 points out some questions raised by these results; Section 7 summarizes.

2 The Referee and The Game

The experiment ("game") is outlined in Exhibit A. The referee generates 100 histories from 10 "truths," each history consisting of returns on eight asset classes during 216 consecutive months. Each truth is itself randomly generated by the referee by

Exhibit A The Experiment.

Referee chooses First/Next "Truth"

> "Truth" is a joint normal return distribution with fixed mean vector μ and covariance matrix C not known to the players.

Referee draws First/Next historical sample randomly from Truth

For Player = {Bayesian, Resampler}

> Referee gives historical sample to Player.

Player applies its procedure to sample. (See write-ups of respective procedures.)

For the given sample and for each utility function (specifically, for $EU = E - \lambda V$ for $\lambda = \frac{1}{2}$, 1, and 2) the Player returns:

> Selected Portfolio
> Estimate of its Expected Utility
>
> For each (Player, Utility function):
>
> Referee computes True expected utility.
>
> Repeat for Next Historical Sample

After all historical samples have been generated and processed, and with Truth still fixed:

> For each utility function, see which player had higher EU on average.
> Compare EU achieved versus EU anticipated on average.

Repeat for Next Truth

Did one of the players do better for most Truths or on average?

Table 1 Asset classes used in experiment.[a]

Asset class	Data source
Canadian Equities	Morgan Stanley Capital International[b]
French Equities	Morgan Stanley Capital International[b]
German Equities	Morgan Stanley Capital International[b]
Japanese Equities	Morgan Stanley Capital International[b]
United Kingdom Equities	Morgan Stanley Capital International[b]
United States Equities	S & P 500 Index total return
United States Bonds	Lehman Brothers[c]
Euro Bonds	Lehman Brothers[d]

[a] Source: Michaud (1998) p. 13, footnote 16.
[b] Dollar return indexes net of withholding taxes.
[c] Government/Corporate US bond index.
[d] Eurobond global index.

computing the means, variances and covariances of 216 draws of eight returns each from a "seed" distribution. This seed distribution is normally distributed with means, variances, and covariances equal to the historic excess return over the US 30-day T-bill rate of the eight asset classes listed in Table 1 for the 216 months from January 1978 through December 1995, as in Michaud (1998).

Having thus established a truth, the referee generates a 216 month "history" from this truth by sampling joint normally from the truth's mean vector and covariance matrix. Each history is presented to each of the two players. Each player tells the referee, for each history, the portfolio which the player believes maximizes EU in (1) for $\lambda = 0.5, 1.0, 2.0$, respectively. The player also provides the referee with the player's own estimate of EU. The referee computes the actual value of EU from the truth, known only to the referee. The referee tabulates the actual value and the players' estimates of this value for the two players. This is repeated for 100 histories per truth and 10 truths for the experiment.

3 The Michaud Player

Michaud proposes the following procedure to handle the fact that observed means, variances, and covariances are not the true parameters but contain noise. In private conversations with the present authors, Michaud points out that more sophisticated procedures could be incorporated into the resampling philosophy. We grant this, but note that it would be difficult to formulate an experiment that encompasses all the possible nuances of both the resampling and Bayesian approaches. The experiment we report here, admittedly, compares "vanilla" resampled frontiers with diffuse Bayes implemented by a particular Monte Carlo analysis.

Following Michaud (1998), the "Michaud player" in our experiment proceeds as follows: given a specific history O ("O" for "Observation") generated by the referee with its means, variances, and covariances, the Michaud player draws 500 new samples of returns on the eight asset classes for 216 months, drawing these from a joint normally distributed i.i.d. random process with the same means, variances, and covariances as O. For each of these 500 samples the Michaud player generates an efficient frontier and then averages these 500 efficient frontiers. Specifically, it notes the first, second, third.... 101st points on the frontier spaced by equal increments of standard deviation. The first point is the one with the highest expected return on the frontier; the 101st point is the one with the lowest standard deviation. The "resampled frontier" has as its first portfolio the average holdings of the first portfolios of the 500 particular frontiers, its second portfolio is the average holdings of 500 second portfolios, etc.

The portfolio mean and variance ascribed to each of the 101 portfolios of the resampled frontier are computed using the original means, variances, and covariances of the observation O. (The present authors thank Richard and Robert Michaud for clarification on this point.) The task that each of the players is assigned is to provide portfolios which maximize the expected value of (1). Therefore, for a given history the Michaud player picks from his resampled frontier the points which maximize the expected value of its estimated EU for $\lambda = 0.5$, 1.0, and 2.0. This process is repeated for each of the 100 randomly drawn histories for each of the 10 truths presented to the player by the referee.

4 The Diffuse Bayes Player

4.1 *Basics*

At any moment in time (say $t = 0$) the Bayesian rational decision maker (RDM) acts as if it ascribes a probability distribution $P_0(h)$ to hypotheses h in some space H of possible hypotheses. In the present discussion, a hypothesis is a vector of eight means and 36 distinct variances and covariances:

$$h' = \left(\mu_1^h, \ldots, \mu_8^h, \sigma_{11}^h, \sigma_{12}^h, \ldots, \sigma_{88}^h\right) \tag{2}$$

plus the assertion that the variables

$$r' = (r_1, \ldots, r_8) \tag{3}$$

are joint normally distributed with these parameters. The hypothesis space H may be taken as all possible values of h:

$$H = R^{44} \tag{4}$$

It is inconsequential whether we restrict H to the set H^* of 44-tuples that can possibly be parameters of a joint normal distribution, or define it as in (4) and understand that

$$P_0(R^{44} - H^*) = 0 \tag{5}$$

The probability distribution $P_t(H)$ changes over time, as we review below. We assume that, as of any time t, the RDM chooses an action α so as to maximize a single-period utility function

$$EU = \underset{h}{E}[E(U(r;\alpha)|h)] \tag{6}$$

In other words, the action α is chosen so as to maximize EU where U depends on returns r and action α, and the expected return in (6) is computed as if Nature randomly drew a hypothesis h using probability distribution P_t, then drew r given h. In the present experiment the action α is the choice of a portfolio.[2]

To pick a portfolio which maximizes EU in (6) using the utility function in (1), the RDM uses only its estimated portfolio mean (E) and portfolio variance (V) which depend only on its estimated means μ_i of securities and the covariances σ_{ij} (including variances $V_i = \sigma_{ii}$) between pairs of securities. These are given by

$$\mu_i = E(r_i) = \underset{h}{E}\,(E(r_i)|h) = \underset{h}{E}\,\mu_i^h = \text{Avg}\,\mu_i^h \tag{7}$$

$$\begin{aligned}\sigma_{ij} &= E(r_i - \mu_i)(r_j - \mu_j) = E\big(r_i - \mu_i^h + \mu_i^h - \mu_i\big) \times \big(r_j - \mu_j^h + \mu_j^h - \mu_j\big)\\ &= E\big(\sigma_{ij}^h\big) - E\big(\mu_i^h - \mu_i\big)\big(\mu_j^h - \mu_j\big)\\ &= \text{Avg}\,\sigma_{ij}^h - \text{cov}\big(\mu_i^h, \mu_j^h\big)\end{aligned} \tag{8}$$

since, e.g.

$$\underset{h}{E}\big[\big(r_i - \mu_i^h\big)\big(\mu_j^h - \mu_j\big)|h\big] = 0$$

In particular, for $i = j$ (Eq. 8) says

$$V_i = \text{Avg}\,V_i^h - \text{Var}\big(\mu_i^h\big) \tag{9}$$

The last line of (7) and (8) are mnemonics for the immediately preceding lines. These formulas tell us that, for the Bayesian RDM, the expected value of r_i at time t is the average, using $P_t(h)$ over $h \in H$, of μ_i^h; whereas covariance between r_i and r_j is the average σ_{ij}^h plus the covariance between μ_i^h and μ_j^h. In particular, the variance of r_i is the average V_i^h *plus* the variance of μ_i^h.

As evidence accumulates, $P_t(h)$ changes over time, according to the Bayes rule. If $P_t(H)$ has a probability density function $P_t(h)$, and O is an observation taken between t and $t+1$ (e.g., O is the set of monthly returns r_{it} for $i = 1, \ldots, 8$, $t = 1$ to 216 as described before), with $L(O|h)$ the probability density of O given hypothesis h, then,

$$p_{t+1}(h) = \frac{p_t(h)L(O|h)}{\int_H p_t(h)L(O|h)\,\mathrm{d}h} \tag{10}$$

The human decision maker (HDM) who wishes to emulate an RDM sometimes avoids the burden of specifying $p_t(h)$ by assuming that

$$p_t(h) = 1/\text{vol}(\Omega^*) \quad \text{for all } h \in \Omega^* \tag{11}$$

where "vol" stands for volume and $\Omega^* \subset H$ is assumed to be sufficiently large that

$$\int_{H-\Omega^*} p_t(h)L(O|h)\,\mathrm{d}h \tag{12}$$

is negligible. With (11) assumed, the updated beliefs of (10) become

$$p_{t+1}(h) = L(O|h)/D \tag{13}$$

where

$$D = \int_{\Omega^*} L(O|h)\,\mathrm{d}h \tag{14}$$

and the expected value [with respect to $P_{t+1}(h)$] of any integrable function $v(h)$ is

$$\mathop{E}_{H} v(h) = N/D \tag{15}$$

where

$$N = \int_{\Omega^*} v(h)L(O|h)\,\mathrm{d}h$$

In principle, (15) can be used to compute $\mathop{E}_{H} \mu_i^h$, $\mathop{E}_{H} \sigma_{ij}^h$, and $\mathop{E}_{H} \mu_i^h \mu_j^h$ which are necessary to compute Avg μ_i^h, Avg σ_{ij}^h and cov $\left(\mu_i^h, \mu_j^h\right)$ in (7) and (8). The practical problem is that N and D are integrals over 44-dimensional spaces. As is often done, we will use Monte Carlo analysis to approximate a high-dimensional integral. The specifics of how we do this are described in a following subsection. First, we discuss the fact that a hypothesis space can often be parameterized in different ways, and present a parameterization of the present situation that will be very convenient for the Monte Carlo analysis that follows.

4.2 *Diffuse Priors*

Suppose, for the moment, that there was only one unknown parameter, an expected value μ of one random variable r. Then, the standard diffuse prior spreads probability belief concerning μ uniformly over some large interval:

$$p(\mu) = \begin{cases} \dfrac{1}{2\Delta} & \text{for } \mu \in [-\Delta, \Delta] \\ 0 & \text{otherwise} \end{cases} \tag{16}$$

The choice of Δ is not important as long as Δ is sufficiently large, since the contribution to $E(r)$ becomes negligible beyond a sufficiently large Δ. Admittedly, this is often not a very plausible prior. For example, if r is the return on an asset class it is not plausible for the asset class to have a large constant-through-time negative expected return. Such an asset class would disappear. However, the use of (16) is justified as convenient because it saves making a decision as to the exact form to be used for prior beliefs. In effect, it assumes that posterior beliefs are proportional to the likelihood function $L(O|h)$. One justification for assuming posterior beliefs are proportional to $L(O|h)$ is the Edwards *et al.* (1963) principle of stable estimation. "To ignore the departures from uniformity, it suffices that your actual prior density change gently in the region favored by the data and not itself too strongly favor some other region" (p. 202). In particular, it suffices if the likelihood function is much more concentrated than the prior beliefs are, and prior beliefs do not strongly favor any region.

Next, suppose that there are two parameters to be estimated, namely an expected return μ and a standard deviation σ. Now, there are competing choices for a diffuse prior such as

$$p(\mu, \sigma) = \begin{cases} \dfrac{1}{2\Delta_1\Delta_2} & \text{for } \mu \in [-\Delta_1, \Delta_1] \\ & \quad \sigma \in [0, \Delta_2] \\ 0 & \text{otherwise} \end{cases} \tag{17}$$

$$p(\mu, V) = \begin{cases} \dfrac{1}{2\Delta_1\Delta_2} & \text{for } \mu \in [-\Delta_1, \Delta_1] \\ & \quad V \in [0, \Delta_2] \\ 0 & \text{otherwise} \end{cases} \tag{18}$$

$$p(\mu, \log\sigma) = \begin{cases} \dfrac{1}{4\Delta_1\Delta_2} & \text{for } \mu \in [-\Delta_1, \Delta_1] \\ & \log\sigma \in [-\Delta_2, \Delta_2] \\ 0 & \text{otherwise} \end{cases} \tag{19}$$

Since $\log \sigma = \frac{1}{2} \log V$, a similar expression for $p(\mu, \log V)$ would not be a new alternative. Since the use of (16) is justified by convenience and the principle of stable estimation, even when not plausible, one should be permitted the choice between (17), (18), and (19) on the basis of convenience, since the principle of stable estimation would seem to apply about equally to any of them.

With two normally distributed random variables, $r = (r_1, r_2)$, the hypothesis space would most naturally include the choice of

$$h' = (\mu_1, \mu_2, \sigma_1, \sigma_2, \sigma_{12}, \text{ or } \rho_{12}).$$

One way of forming diffuse priors for the above is to assume that μ_1, σ_1 and μ_2, σ_2 each have as priors (17), (18), or (19) and that ρ_{12} is independently drawn with a prior density of

$$p(\rho) = \begin{cases} \frac{1}{2} & \text{for } -1 \le \rho \le 1 \\ 0 & \text{otherwise} \end{cases} \tag{20}$$

It might seem that one could repeat the process for $n = 8$ with μ_i, σ_i, $i = 1, \ldots, 8$ having priors (17), (18), or (19) and with each ρ_{ij} independently having (20) as a prior for $i = 1, \ldots, 7, j = i + 1, \ldots, 8$. One problem with this is that it assigns positive probabilities to correlation matrixes which are logically impossible. For example, it is impossible to have $\rho_{ij} < -\frac{1}{7}$ for every $i \neq j$ for eight returns.

We use a different "diffuse approach" which avoids the above difficulty and is computationally quite convenient for the Monte Carlo analysis described below. This approach uses priors equivalent to nature drawing r_{it} according to

$$p(r_{it}) = \begin{cases} \dfrac{1}{2\Delta} & \text{for } r_{it} \in [-\Delta, \Delta] \\ 0 & \text{otherwise} \end{cases} \tag{21}$$

independently for $i = 1, \ldots, 8$, $t = 1, \ldots, 216$, then computing μ_i, σ_i, and ρ_{ij} as the means, standard deviations, and the correlations of the randomly drawn r_i. The distribution of $(\mu_1, \mu_2, \ldots, \sigma_{88})$ is implicit. In other words, we will find it most convenient to assume that prior probability distribution of $(\mu_1, \ldots, \sigma_{88})$ is the same as that of the sample statistics of random variables $r_1, \ldots, r_8$ drawn uniformly and independently, for sample size $T = 216$. For example, for a very large Δ in (21) the distribution of μ_1 is approximately normally distributed with a large standard deviation.

4.3 *Importance Sampling*

Let

$$K = R^8 \times R^{216} \tag{22}$$

be the space of 8×216 real matrices. Examples of members of K include O, the historical observation handed to each player, and $k_1, \ldots, k_{500}$, the 500 histories which the Michaud player generates. Recall, H is defined in (4) as R^{44}. Members of H include h in (2), the parameters of a joint normal distribution of $(r_1, \ldots, r_8)$.

Let f_{KH} be a function $f_{KH} : K \to H$ which associates with each point $k \in K$ the $(\mu_1, \ldots, \sigma_{88})$ vector $h \in H$ obtained by computing these parameters from the returns matrix k. For two points k_1, and k_2 in K we define

$$L(k_1|k_2) = L[k_1|f_{KH}(k_2)] = \prod_{t=1}^{216} N[r^t; f_{KH}(k_2)] \tag{23}$$

where $N(r; h)$ is the normal density of the random vector r given the parameters h. In other words, (23) defines the likelihood of k_1 given k_2 to mean the likelihood of getting the sample k_1 from a normal distribution with parameters $f_{KH}(k_2)$.

Let

$$K^* = \{r \in K| \quad |r_{it}| \leq \Delta \forall\, i, t\} \tag{24}$$

for some large Δ. We assume that the prior density is uniformly distributed over this set, K^*. To evaluate an expected value as in (15) by integration would require integration over a large rectangle in an 8×216-dimensional space. This is not feasible. On the other hand, an estimate of $E(v)$ by Monte Carlo, for randomly drawn v, depends on sample size and the moments of v rather than on the dimensionality of K.

Given any function $v(k)$ of the sample point k, in principle, one could estimate the Bayes player's $E(v)$ given O, by sampling k from K^* with probability

$$p(k) = L(O|k)/D \tag{25a}$$

where

$$D = \int_{K^*} L(O|k)\, \mathrm{d}k \tag{25b}$$

Instead, we will have the Bayes player use the same 500 samples from K which the Michaud player uses to compute its resampled frontier. We must keep in mind that these 500 samples were drawn with probability density

$$q(k) = L(k|O) \tag{26}$$

That is, the 8×216 matrices (r_{it}) in Michaud's samples are drawn joint normally assuming the parameters of the "historical" observation O. Observe that $L(k|O)$ in (26) is not the same as $L(O|k)/D$ in (25a).

There is a standard correction applicable when we wish to estimate an expected value

$$E(v) = \int_{K^*} p(k)v(k)\,\mathrm{d}k \tag{27}$$

and we draw a sample, e.g. $v_1, \ldots, v_{500}$, with probability $q(k)$ rather than $p(k)$. The sample average

$$v^* = \frac{1}{500}\sum_{i=1}^{500} v_i \tag{28}$$

has expected value

$$E(v^*) = \int_{K^*} q(k)v(k)\,\mathrm{d}k \tag{29}$$

which may differ from $E(v)$ in (27). Instead, we may use a weighted average

$$\bar{v} = \frac{1}{500}\sum \left[p(k)/q(k)\right] v(k_i) \tag{30}$$

This has expected value

$$E(\bar{v}) = \int q(k)\left[p(k)/q(k)\right] v(k)\,\mathrm{d}k = E(v) \tag{31}$$

as desired.

The weights in (30) correct for sample probabilities $q(k)$ provided $q(k) > 0$ when $p(k) > 0$. This does not mean that all sampling distributions $q(k)$ are equally good. Since all are adjusted to have the correct $E(v)$, the variance of v depends only on

$$E(v^2) = \int q(k)\left(\frac{p(k)\cdot v(k)}{q(k)}\right)^2 \mathrm{d}k = \int \frac{\left[p(k)v(k)\right]^2}{q(k)}\mathrm{d}k \tag{32}$$

The minimum of this subject to

$$\int q(k)\,\mathrm{d}k = 1.0 \tag{33}$$

is

$$q(k) = p(k)|v(k)| \tag{34}$$

Since our sample will serve to estimate the expected value of many different $v(k)$, perhaps all we can conclude from (34) is that it is best to avoid large $q(k)$ where $p(k)$ is relatively small. $q(k) = p(k)$ seems at least good and perhaps ideal.

To compute $p(k)$ we need D from (25b). We now discuss how we approximate this. Let "Vol" be the volume of K^* in (24). Assuming $L(O|k)$ may be ignored in $K - K^*$, Eq. (25b) may be written as

$$D = \text{Vol} \int_{K^*} \frac{L(O|k)\,\mathrm{d}k}{\text{Vol}} \tag{35}$$

This is the volume of K^* times the expected value of $L(O|k)$ in K^* when k is drawn uniformly from it; i.e., with probability density

$$p(k) = 1/\text{Vol} \tag{36}$$

We can approximate this expected value using the sample of 500 k_i drawn with probability density $L(k_i|O)$ by weighing the observed $L(O|k_i)$ by the ratio of desired density (1/Vol) to the density used $L(k_i|O)$. That is, we can approximate the integral (expected value) in (35) by

$$\bar{L} = \frac{1}{500} \sum \frac{L(O|k_i)}{L(k_i|O) \cdot \text{Vol}} \tag{37}$$

But D in (35) is "Vol" times the integral, so the approximation to D is

$$\bar{D} = \frac{1}{500} \sum \frac{L(O|k_i)}{L(k_i|O)} \tag{38}$$

i.e., the observed average ratio of $L(O|k_i)$ to $L(k_i|O)$. It may be objected that if $\bar{D}$ is substituted for D in (25a), $p(k)$ is a ratio of unbiased estimators, which is not necessarily unbiased. On the other hand, with $\bar{D}$ thus used for D in (25a), the weights in (30) sum to one. In this case $\bar{v}$ is a weighted average of $v(k)$, which seems attractive.

Our procedure then is as follows. To approximate the RDMs posterior mean vector μ and covariance matrix C we approximate the expected values of variables v, such as Er_i and Er_ir_j for all i, j, then use the relationships in (7) and (8). To estimate $E(v)$, we evaluate v for each of the Michaud samples from O, namely $k_1, \ldots, k_{500}$, then form the weighted average $\bar{v}$ of the $v(ki)$ where the weights are shown in (30) with $q(k)$ denned in (26) and $p(k)$ defined in (25a) and (38).

For the one case we checked, most weights $q(k)/p(k)$ are close to unity. Table 2 shows the deciles of the 500 weights computed for Truth 1 History 1. All weights were greater than 0.80 and not greater than 1.025. Ninety percent of the weights were between 0.96 and 1.025. This says that the Michaud sample is a good one for the present purpose, according to (34) and the discussion that follows it.

5 Results

The results of the experiment are presented in Tables 3 and 4. The first panel of Table 3 shows averages of estimated and actual expected utility achieved by the two players. Specifically, for $\lambda = 0.5$, 1.0, and 2.0, as indicated by the row labeled "Lambda," and for each player, as indicated by the row labeled "Player," the table presents two columns

Table 2 Distribution of weights $p(k)/q(k)$ for Truth 1 History 1.

Deciles	From	To
1st	0.809	0.961
2nd	0.961	0.984
3rd	0.984	0.999
4th	0.999	1.005
5th	1.005	1.012
6th	1.012	1.015
7th	1.015	1.019
8th	1.019	1.021
9th	1.021	1.023
10th	1.023	1.025

of information. The first column is the average (over the 100 histories generated for a truth) of the players' estimate of expected utility. The second column is the average of actual utility as evaluated by the referee. For example, on the line labeled Truth 1 we see that, on average over the 100 histories generated for Truth 1, the Bayesian player believed it had achieved an expected utility of 0.01181 whereas the average of its actual *EU* was 0.00712. The comparable numbers for the Michaud player are 0.01032 and 0.00753. Thus, both players overestimated how well they did, but the Michaud player overestimated less and achieved more. On the next nine lines similar numbers are reported for Truth 2 through Truth 10. The final three lines of the panel summarize results for the 10 truths. In particular, the average over the 10 truths of the Bayesian player's estimate was 0.01383 but it actually achieved 0.00861. In the average over all 10 truths, again, the Michaud player overestimated less and achieved more. In fact, comparing the average *EU* each player achieved in each of the 10 truths, the average over the 100 histories was greater for the Michaud player than the Bayes player in the case of each of the 10 truths, as noted in the last line of Panel A.

A similar story holds for $\lambda = 1.0$ and 2.0. Looking at the last row of Panel A for the actual *EU* achieved by the two players for these cases we see that the Michaud player achieved a higher average (over the 100 histories for a given Truth) in 10 out of 10 truths for $\lambda = 1.0$ and 2.0.

For some individual histories of the 100 histories of a given truth, the Bayes player had a higher *EU* than the Michaud player. In fact, in Panel B of Table 1 the entry for $\lambda = 0.5$, Bayes player, Truth 1 reports that the Bayes player achieved a higher *EU* than the Michaud player in 54 out of the 100 histories, despite having a lower average over the 100. Sticking with Truth 1, the Bayes player also "won" 54 out of 100 times for $\lambda = 1.0$, and 50 out of 100 for $\lambda = 2.0$. The Bayes player's "win count" was even more favorable in the case of Truth 6. In this case, the Bayes player "beat" the Michaud player 62 times out of 100 for $\lambda = 0.5$, 60 for $\lambda = 1.0$ and 66 for $\lambda = 2.0$. Nevertheless, the average *EU* achieved, averaged over the 100 histories, was higher for the Michaud player in each of these Truths.

Table 3 Player's choice of portfolio.

λ Player: Eval. by:	0.5 Bayes Player	0.5 Bayes Referee	0.5 Michaud Player	0.5 Michaud Referee	1.0 Bayes Player	1.0 Bayes Referee	1.0 Michaud Player	1.0 Michaud Referee	2.0 Bayes Player	2.0 Bayes Referee	2.0 Michaud Player	2.0 Michaud Referee
Panel A: EU averaged over 100 histories, for each of 10 truths												
Truth 1	0.01181	0.00712	0.01032	0.00753	0.01004	0.00564	0.00886	0.00594	0.00754	0.00394	0.00678	0.00426
Truth 2	0.01528	0.00885	0.01194	0.00901	0.01389	0.00783	0.01085	0.00801	0.01160	0.00616	0.00902	0.00664
Truth 3	0.01011	0.00614	0.01009	0.00737	0.00887	0.00534	0.00904	0.00636	0.00692	0.00410	0.00721	0.00481
Truth 4	0.01457	0.00850	0.01147	0.00862	0.01324	0.00746	0.01041	0.00763	0.01094	0.00573	0.00849	0.00600
Truth 5	0.01170	0.00641	0.00984	0.00694	0.00988	0.00480	0.00846	0.00549	0.00706	0.00282	0.00612	0.00322
Truth 6	0.01646	0.01056	0.01304	0.01078	0.01462	0.00890	0.01149	0.00914	0.01173	0.00670	0.00911	0.00700
Truth 7	0.01590	0.01147	0.01408	0.01152	0.01412	0.00989	0.01271	0.01015	0.01124	0.00758	0.01036	0.00793
Truth 8	0.01502	0.00956	0.01261	0.01005	0.01329	0.00811	0.01119	0.00861	0.01053	0.00578	0.00866	0.00610
Truth 9	0.01402	0.00906	0.01241	0.00961	0.01204	0.00719	0.01087	0.00798	0.00892	0.00462	0.00812	0.00521
Truth 10	0.01343	0.00846	0.01130	0.00900	0.01176	0.00676	0.00975	0.00735	0.00909	0.00402	0.00712	0.00453
Grand mean	0.01383	0.00861	0.01171	0.00904	0.01217	0.00719	0.01036	0.00767	0.00956	0.00514	0.00810	0.00557
Std Dev	0.00205	0.00171	0.00138	0.00150	0.00200	0.00161	0.00133	0.00145	0.00190	0.00148	0.00129	0.00142
No. times better		0		10		0		10		0		10
Panel B: Number of "wins" out of 100 histories, for each of 10 truths												
Truth 1		54		46		54		46		50		50
Truth 2		52		48		54		46		65		35
Truth 3		46		54		43		57		41		59
Truth 4		57		43		61		39		64		36
Truth 5		43		57		27		73		30		70
Truth 6		62		38		60		40		66		34
Truth 7		57		43		53		47		42		58
Truth 8		54		46		48		52		41		59
Truth 9		32		68		28		72		27		59
Truth 10		61		39		49		51		52		48
Avg No. wins		51.80		48.20		47.70		52.30		47.80		52.20
No. times better		7		3		5		5		5		5

Table 3 (*Continued*)

λ	0.5	0.5	0.5	0.5	1.0	1.0	1.0	1.0	2.0	2.0	2.0	2.0
Player:	Bayes	Bayes	Michaud	Michaud	Bayes	Bayes	Michaud	Michaud	Bayes	Bayes	Michaud	Michaud
Eval. by:	Player	Referee	Player	Referee	Player	Referee	Player	Referee	Player	Referee	Player	Referee
	Panel C: Standard deviation of EU over 100 histories, for each of 10 truths											
Truth 1	0.00516	0.00210	0.00401	0.00132	0.00470	0.00160	0.00359	0.00102	0.00356	0.00116	0.00265	0.00077
Truth 2	0.00445	0.00149	0.00395	0.00084	0.00416	0.00185	0.00372	0.00113	0.00364	0.00258	0.00331	0.00121
Truth 3	0.00354	0.00244	0.00339	0.00109	0.00331	0.00231	0.00321	0.00092	0.00286	0.00178	0.00284	0.00080
Truth 4	0.00413	0.00203	0.00369	0.00101	0.00398	0.00221	0.00356	0.00118	0.00377	0.00235	0.00331	0.00117
Truth 5	0.00514	0.00161	0.00347	0.00077	0.00475	0.00126	0.00329	0.00064	0.00396	0.00077	0.00275	0.00058
Truth 6	0.00469	0.00223	0.00476	0.00114	0.04427	0.00227	0.00438	0.00101	0.00379	0.00242	0.00373	0.00117
Truth 7	0.00544	0.00178	0.00347	0.00088	0.00515	0.00155	0.00331	0.00086	0.00447	0.00111	0.00296	0.00073
Truth 8	0.00399	0.00217	0.00413	0.00119	0.00391	0.00169	0.00398	0.00112	0.00376	0.00117	0.00360	0.00073
Truth 9	0.00584	0.00144	0.00371	0.00056	0.00551	0.00130	0.00359	0.00070	0.00467	0.00089	0.00319	0.00065
Truth 10	0.00399	0.00283	0.00445	0.00155	0.00391	0.00212	0.00422	0.00130	0.00360	0.00166	0.00353	0.00077
Avg Std Dev		0.00201		0.00104		0.00182		0.00099		0.00159		0.00086
No times better		0		10		0		10		0		10

Table 4 Referee's choice of portfolio.

λ Player: Eval. by:	0.5 Bayes Referee	0.5 Michaud Referee	1 Bayes Referee	1 Michaud Referee	2 Bayes Referee	2 Michaud Referee
	Panel A: EU *averaged over 100 histories, for 10 truths*					
Truth 1	0.007811	0.007709	0.006303	0.006253	0.004852	0.004899
Truth 2	0.009625	0.009407	0.008641	0.008594	0.006967	0.007104
Truth 3	0.007111	0.007552	0.006198	0.006647	0.004741	0.005139
Truth 4	0.009157	0.008915	0.008109	0.008049	0.006220	0.006395
Truth 5	0.006721	0.007008	0.005200	0.005662	0.003504	0.003661
Truth 6	0.011378	0.011183	0.009781	0.009608	0.007486	0.007481
Truth 7	0.011935	0.011571	0.010425	0.010303	0.008178	0.008260
Truth 8	0.009674	0.010071	0.008225	0.008714	0.005799	0.006309
Truth 9	0.009423	0.009641	0.007712	0.008169	0.005112	0.005576
Truth 10	0.008193	0.008854	0.006665	0.007339	0.004151	0.004718
Grand mean	0.009103	0.009191	0.007726	0.007934	0.005701	0.005954
Std dev	0.001701	0.001509	0.001654	0.001473	0.001506	0.001414
No. times better	5	5	5	5	1	9
	Panel B: Number of wins out of 100 histories, for 10 truths					
Truth 1	65		60		53	
Truth 2	66		64		58	
Truth 3	56		52		47	
Truth 4	69		67		59	
Truth 5	52		32		40	
Truth 6	67		60		60	
Truth 7	74		64		54	
Truth 8	44		45		37	
Truth 9	55		43		27	
Truth 10	58		58		41	
Avg wins	60.6		54.5		47.6	
No. times greater	9		7		5	
	Panel C. Std Dev of EU *over 100 histories, for 10 truths*					
Truth 1	0.00169	0.00112	0.00113	0.00082	0.00063	0.00043
Truth 2	0.00110	0.00058	0.00128	0.00060	0.00127	0.00061
Truth 3	0.00186	0.00083	0.00163	0.00071	0.00117	0.00060
Truth 4	0.00143	0.00062	0.00153	0.00060	0.00139	0.00056
Truth 5	0.00145	0.00053	0.00106	0.00042	0.00054	0.00027
Truth 6	0.00106	0.00086	0.00074	0.00058	0.00099	0.00059
Truth 7	0.00131	0.00084	0.00102	0.00070	0.00090	0.00054
Truth 8	0.00137	0.00089	0.00121	0.00076	0.00093	0.00051
Truth 9	0.00137	0.00053	0.00125	0.00049	0.00082	0.00039
Truth 10	0.00274	0.00145	0.00223	0.00114	0.00120	0.00067
Avg Std Dev	0.00154	0.00082	0.00131	0.00068	0.00098	0.00052
No. times lower	0	10	0	10	0	10

Panel C of Table 1 shows that, for a given Truth, the standard deviation of the achieved *EU* was higher for the Bayesian than the Michaud player. For example, for Truth 1, $\lambda = 0.5$, the standard deviation of *EU* for the Bayesian player was 0.00210 as compared to 0.00132 for the Michaud player. In fact, for all three values of λ and all 10 truths, the variance of the actual *EU* was lower for the Michaud player than the Bayes player.

Most significant for our purpose is the fact that the Michaud strategy delivered higher average *EU* in 10 out of 10 truths for three out of three values of λ. Thus, the Michaud player did a better job of achieving the objective, namely high *EU*.

Table 4 displays the results of a slightly different game. In this second game, for each history and each truth each player computes an efficient frontier as in the first game. But instead of picking a point from the frontier for each λ, the player passes its entire frontier to the referee. For each λ the referee picks the point on the player's frontier that has the highest true *EU*. Game 2 thus addresses the question of whether the superiority of the Michaud player over the diffuse Bayesian player in the first game is due to a better frontier or to a better pick from an equally good frontier.

The Bayes player does much better in Game 2 than it did in Game 1. In particular, for $\lambda = 0.5$ and 1.0 Panel A of Table 4 shows that with five out of 10 truths the Bayesian player achieves higher average *EU* than the Michaud player as compared to 0 out of 10 in Game 1. Also, Panel B shows that for $\lambda = 0.5$ and 1.0 the Bayesian player has a higher *EU* in many more histories for a given Truth than the Michaud player. On the other hand, the Michaud player comes out ahead overall. In particular, for every λ the "Grand Mean" of achieved *EU* averaged over all truths is greater for the Michaud player than the Bayesian player. However, the out-performance of the Michaud player over the Bayes player is smaller in the second game than in the first. In particular, for $\lambda = 0.5$ the difference in performance between the two players is only about 20% as great in the second game as it is in the first ($0.000088 = 0.009191 - 0.009103$ versus $0.00043 = 0.00904 - 0.00861$), about 44% as great when $\lambda = 1.0$ and 59% as great when $\lambda = 2.0$.

As explained in the next section, for $\lambda = 0.5$, *EU* in (1) is approximately[3] $E(\ln(1+r))$. This, in turn, is $\ln(1+g)$ where g is the geometric mean or growth rate. We can, therefore, give the results in Tables 3 and 4 a more concrete interpretation for the case of $\lambda = \frac{1}{2}$ Annualizing, the Bayes player believes it can achieve an "average"[4] annual growth rate of 18.05% ($0.180548 = \exp(12 \cdot (0.01383)) - 1$), whereas the portfolios it chose had an average actual growth rate of 10.89% and the best from its frontier averaged a growth rate of 11.54%. The Michaud player thought it could achieve an average annual growth of 15.09%; the portfolios it chose had an average growth rate of 11.46%; the actual average highest growth portfolio on its frontier was 11.66%. Thus, in game 1, the Michaud methodology adds 0.57 to the average growth rate. In game 2 it adds 0.12.

The relatively better performance of the Bayesian player in Game 2 (as compared to its performance in Game 1) suggests that the Game 1 superiority of the Michaud player is more due to a wise pick from its frontier than due to a superior frontier, though the latter reason is also applicable.

6 Questions

The preceding results raise questions for portfolio theory and practice. In particular, the results represent something of a crisis for the theoretical foundations of portfolio theory as presented in Part IV of Markowitz (1959), Chapters 10–13. Chapters 10 through 12 present introductory accounts of utility analysis as justified by Von Neumann and Morgenstern (1944), personal probability as justified by Savage (1954), and dynamic programming as presented by Bellman (1957). Chapter 13 applies these principles to the problem of selecting a portfolio. Specifically, mean–variance analysis is justified as an approximation to the single-period "derived" utility function always associated with many-period utility maximization. It is argued that the mean–variance approximation should be good as long as the probability distribution of return is not spread out too much. Calculations—by Markowitz (1959), Young and Trent (1969), Levy and Markowitz (1979), Dexter *et al.* (1980), Pulley (1981, 1983), Kroll *et al.* (1984), Simaan (1987) and Hlawitschka (1994)—show that, for most utility functions proposed for practice, the mean–variance approximation to expected utility is quite robust. As Levy and Markowitz conclude

> If Mr. X can carefully pick the E,V efficient portfolio which is best for him then Mr. X, who still does not know his current utility function, has nevertheless selected a portfolio with maximum or almost maximum expected utility.

In addition, Markowitz and van Dijk (2003) illustrate the ability of a suitably constructed "single-period" mean–variance analysis to give near-optimum results in the case of transaction costs and changing probability distributions. One caveat however: as Grauer (1986) illustrates, the return distributions from highly levered portfolios are too spread out for mean–variance approximations to do well. However, for unlevered return distributions as considered in the present paper, computations have generally shown mean–variance to be quite good.

Thus, until now, calculations seem to support the theoretical foundations for mean–variance analysis presented in Part IV of Markowitz (1959). An integral part of these foundations is that a RDM will use probability beliefs where objective probabilities are not known, and will update these beliefs according to the Bayes rule as evidence accumulates. Usually, when Bayesian inference is tried in practice it is assumed that, prior to the sample in hand, beliefs are "diffuse"—i.e., "neutral" in some sense with respect to which hypothesis is true—as recommended by Jefferies (1948) or Edwards *et al.* (1963).

Given this background, the results presented in this paper are badly in need of an explanation. Such explanation could be in terms of why Bayesian updating did not do better, or why the Michaud estimation did so well.

Concerning why Bayesian updating did not do better: it may have to do with the difference between the computation which we performed and which a RDM would perform. The latter is an integration over a high-dimensional space, well beyond foreseeable human computational abilities. We approximated this integral by Monte Carlo sampling. (Note the distinction between the sample which the referee handed both players, and the sample we used to approximately compute the integral which the RDM computes exactly.) If this—exact versus approximate calculation of updated beliefs—is the source of difficulty with the Bayesian approach taken here, then, maybe the conclusion will be that Bayesian inference is ideal for the RDM but not for the human, at least at the level of computational effort spent by the Bayesian and Michaud players in the reported experiment.

Alternatively, perhaps the problem with the approach taken here is the priors used. Perhaps "diffuse prior" should be defined differently. Or, perhaps, an informed prior should be used like those of Black and Litterman (1990)—but updating the priors using history rather than user estimates as in Black and Litterman.[5]

Expected utility and Bayesian inference were originally proposed, by Daniel Bernoulli and Thomas Bayes in the Eighteenth Century, as plausible rules for action when the future is unknown (see Bernoulli, 1954; Bayes, 1958). Von Neumann and Morgenstern (1944) and Savage (1954) derive these rules from more basic principles of rational behavior. The resampled frontier as presented by Michaud (1998) is a plausible procedure which, we find, works quite well. But how does it relate to the theory of rational behavior? Does it contradict one or more of Savage's axioms? If so, is this a black mark against the method or against the axioms? Or does Michaud's procedure somehow satisfy the Savage axioms? We would very much like to know the answers to some or all of these questions.

Practical questions, raised by the success of the Michaud method in the experiments reported here, include those of costs and benefits. In particular, how much expected return do these procedures add for a given level of risk—in practice. This may involve transaction costs, changing probability distributions, non-normal distributions—all assumed away in the current experiments. Historical backrests might shed some light on these matters.

Concerning costs, computation costs may or may not be a problem. It does not take long or cost much these days to generate a set of 500 frontiers and average these. But it might still be computationally burdensome to compute many such resampled frontiers in a backtest with many monthly re-optimizations, with the backtest frequently repeated to see the effects of alternate parameter settings. However, a Bayesian update of beliefs would also be computationally burdensome in such a case.

Finally, the cost of using a resampled efficient frontier depends on what the patent holder charges for the use of this patented procedure (see note 1).

7 Conclusions

This paper reports the results of an experiment comparing two procedures for dealing with sampling error in the inputs to a mean–variance analysis. One procedure is the Bayesian updating of diffuse priors. The other is Michaud's resampled efficient frontier. In the experiment a referee generates 10 "truths" at random from a "seed" distribution.

From each "truth" the referee randomly generates 100 histories. Each history is presented to a Bayesian player and a Michaud player. Each player follows its prescribed procedure to determine which portfolio would provide highest $E - \lambda V$ for $\lambda = 0.5$, 1.0, and 2.0. Sometimes one player, sometimes the other picks a portfolio with higher $E - \lambda V$. But in the case of each truth and each value of λ, the average of the 100 values of $E - \lambda V$ is higher for the Michaud player than the Bayes player. However, the Bayes player does almost as well as the Michaud player when each player presents its entire efficient frontier to the referee, and the referee picks the player's best portfolio from the frontier. This suggests that the chief problem with the Bayesian player's choice of portfolio is that the latter is more over-optimistic than is the Michaud player in estimating achievable portfolio mean and variance.

This result has practical implications for the estimation of inputs to a mean–variance analysis, even for methods other than the two considered explicitly here. For example, in practice, mean–variance analysis is often performed at an asset class level with estimates of means based partly on judgment, but using historical variances and covariances. The results of this paper imply that these variance estimates are too low. First, if you accept the theory of rational behavior under uncertainty developed by Savage (1954), as explained by Markowitz (1959) Chapter 12, then you should not use historical variance, nor even an average variance—averaged over possible explanations of history. Rather, you should use the latter *plus* a term reflecting your uncertainty in your estimate of the mean. Furthermore, the results of the present paper imply that, for reasons unknown to us, when this theoretical correction is made, the investor is still too optimistic for his or her own best interest.

Acknowledgment

The authors thank Anthony Tessitore for extremely valuable suggestions.

Notes

1 Resampled efficiency, as described in Michaud (1998, Chapters 6 and 7), was co-invented by Richard Michaud and Robert Michaud and is a US patented procedure, #6,003,018, December 1999, patent pending worldwide. New Frontier Advisors, LLC, has exclusive licensing rights worldwide.

2 The assumption of a single-period utility function is not less general than the assumption of many-period or continuous-time utility maximization, since many-period or continuous-time utility maximization may be reduced to a series of one-period or instantaneous utility maximizations using a "derived" utility function, as described by Bellman (1957). In general, the time-varying derived utility function U_t may be a complicated function that includes state variables as well as returns, and depends on what has gone before. Our specific assumption, that U_t is given by (1), is a vast simplification which we justify on the grounds that our objective is not to solve the dynamic programming problem for some many-period or continuous-time investment model, but to take a reading on the ability of two alternate methods to handle uncertainty.

3 For other values of λ, EU in (1) approximates the expected value of other utility functions. The choices made by a Bernoulli/Von Neumann and Morgenstern utility function are not

affected by adding a constant or multiplying by a positive constant. That is, the same decisions maximize $E[a + bU(r)]$, $b > 0$, as those that maximize $EU(r)$. It is, therefore, essential to the validity of the comparisons made in the text—e.g., that the difference in performance is only 20% as great in game 2 as game 1 when $\lambda = 0.5$—that this comparison is in fact unaffected by the arbitrary choice of a and $b > 0$.

[4] The "average" referred to here is the antilog of an average logarithm, therefore, a geometric mean.

[5] Harvey *et al.* (2003) reports the results of an experiment in which Bayes outperforms Michaud when conjugate priors are used.

References

Bayes, T. (1958). "Essay Toward Solving a Problem in the Doctrine of Chances: with a biographical note by G. A. Barnard." *Biometrika* **45**, 293–315. (Also published separately by the Biometrika Office, University College, London.) *Philosophical Transactions of the Royal Society* 370–418, 1763.

Bellman, R.E. (1957). *Dynamic Programming.* Princeton, New Jersey: Princeton University Press.

Bernoulli, D. (1954). "Specimen theoriae novae de mensura sortis. Exposition of a New Theory on the Measurement of Risk" (English translation by Louise Sommer). *Econometrica* **22**, 23–26. (Originally published in 1738. *Comm. Acad. Sci. Imp. Petropolitanae* **5**, 175–192.)

Black, F. and Litterman, R. (1990). "Asset Allocation: Combining Investor Views with Market Equilibrium." *Journal of Fixed Income* Goldman Sachs, September.

Dexter, A.S., Yu, J.N.W. and Ziemba, W.T. (1980). "Portfolio Selection in a Lognormal Market When the Investor Has a Power Utility Function: Computational Results." In: Dempster, M.A.H. (ed.) *Stochastic Programming.* New York: Academic Press, pp. 507–523.

Edwards, W., Lindman, H. and Savage, L.J. (1963). "Bayesian Statistical Inference for Psychological Research." *Psychological Review* **70**(3), 193–242.

Grauer, R.R. (1986). "Normality, Solvency, and Portfolio Choice." *Journal of Financial and Quantitative Analysis* **21**(3), 265–278.

Harvey, C.R., Liechty, J.C, Leichty, M.W. and Muller, P. (2003). "Portfolio Selection with Higher Moments." Working Paper, Duke University, Durham, NC.

Hlawitschka, W. (1994). "The Empirical Nature of Taylor-Series Approximations to Expected Utility." *The American Economic Review* **84**(3), 713–719.

Jeffreys, H. (1948). *Theory of Probability.* Oxford: Clarendon Press.

Kroll, Y., Levy, H. and Markowitz, H.M. (1984). "Mean Variance Versus Direct Utility Maximization." *Journal of Finance* **39**(1) 47–61.

Levy, H. and Markowitz, H.M. (1979). "Approximating Expected Utility by a Function of Mean and Variance." *American Economic Review* **69**(3), 308–317.

Markowitz, H.M. (1959). *Portfolio Selection: Efficient Diversification of Investments.* New York: John Wiley & Sons. 2nd edn. published by Cambridge, MA: Basil Blackwell.

Markowitz, H.M. and Usmen, N. (1996a). "The Likelihood of Various Stock Market Return Distributions, Part 1: Principles of Inference." *Journal of Risk and Uncertainty* **13**, 207–219.

Markowitz, H.M. and Usmen, N. (1996b). "The Likelihood of Various Stock Market Return Distributions, Part 2: Empirical Results." *Journal of Risk and Uncertainty* **13**, 221–247.

Markowitz, H.M. and van Dijk, E.L. (2003). "Single-Period Mean–Variance Analysis in a Changing World." *Financial Analysts Journal* **59**(2), 30–44.

Michaud, R.O. (1998). *Efficient Asset Management: A Practical Guide to Stock Portfolio Optimization and Asset Allocation.* Boston, MA: Harvard Business School Press.

Pulley, L.M. (1981). "A General Mean–Variance Approximation to Expected Utility for Short Holding Periods." *Journal of Financial and Quantitative Analysis* **16**, 361–373.

Pulley, L.M. (1983). "Mean–Variance Approximations to Expected Logarithmic Utility." *Operations Research* **31**(4), 685–696.

Savage, L.J. (1954). *The Foundations of Statistic*, 2nd edn. Dover Publications, Inc., New York: John Wiley & Sons.

Simaan, Y. (1987). "Portfolio Selection and Capital Asset Pricing for a Class of Non-Spherical Distributions of Assets Returns." PhD Thesis, Baruch College, The City University of New York.

Von Neumann, J. and Morgenstern, O. (1944). *Theory of Games and Economic Behavior*. Princeton University Press, 3rd ed., Wiley, 1967.

Young, W.E. and Trent, R.H. (1969). "Geometric Mean Approximation of Individual Security and Portfolio Performance." *Journal of Financial and Quantitative Analysis* **4**, 179–199.

Keywords: Resampled frontier; Bayesian analysis; diffuse Bayes; mean–variance analysis; sampling errors; Michaud

Journal Of Investment Management
Vol. 1, No. 3 (2003), pp. 64–76

FUND MANAGERS MAY CAUSE THEIR BENCHMARKS TO BE PRICED "RISKS"

Michael Stutzer[a]

The presence of a positive intercept ("alpha") in a regression of an investment fund's excess returns on a broad market portfolio's excess return (as in the CAPM), and other "factor" portfolios' excess returns (e.g., the Fama and French factors) is frequently interpreted as evidence of superior fund performance. This paper theoretically and empirically supports the notion that the additional factors may proxy for benchmark portfolios that fund managers try to beat, rather than proxying for state variables of future risks that investors (in conventional theory) are supposed to care about.

1 Introduction

The CAPM is a linear, single excess return factor model, derivable by assuming that all investors are "rational," in the sense of choosing the tangency portfolio of risky assets on the mean–variance efficiency frontier. This portfolio is the single factor. But authors, too numerous to mention, have argued that additional factors are also present. For example, Fama and French (1992) documented the ability of the following linear, 3-factor model (their Eq. (1)) to predict anomalous expected excess returns earned by some well-known stock portfolio strategies:

$$E(R_i) - R_f = b_i[E(R_M) - R_f] + s_i E(\text{SMB}) + h_i E(\text{HML}) \tag{1}$$

where M denotes the broad market portfolio, SMB denotes the return on a portfolio that sells relatively big cap stocks and buys relatively small cap stocks, and HML denotes the return on a portfolio that sells relatively low book-to-market stocks and buys relatively high book-to-market stocks. Because (1) arises by taking expectations of both sides of multiple linear regression specification without an intercept, it subsequently became quite common to regress the returns of managed investment funds on the factors in (1) with an intercept α, and then to interpret a statistically significantly positive α as indicative of superior fund performance (e.g., see Davis, 2002).

Fama and French (1992) could not find empirical support for the standard *theoretical* frameworks that permit derivation of factor models like this, concluding with the following summary:

> Finally, there is an important hole in our work. Our tests to date do not cleanly identify the two consumption–investment state variables of special hedging concern

[a] Professor of Finance and Director, Burridge Center for Securities Analysis and Valuation, University of Colorado, 419 UCB, Boulder, CO 80309-0419, USA. Tel.: 303 492 4348; e-mail: michael.stutzer@colorado.edu

to investors that would provide a neat interpretation of the results in terms of Merton's (1973) ICAPM or Ross' (1976) APT.

Researchers subsequently struggled to do this, focusing on the possibility that the additional factors proxy for state variables of financial distress. Yet, a recent paper by Vassalou and Xing (2002) concludes that:

> Fama and French [Fama and French (1996)] argue that the SMB and HML factors of the Fama and French (FF) model proxy for financial distress. Our asset pricing model results show that, although SMB and HML contain default-related information, this is not the reason that the FF model can explain the cross section. SMB and HML appear to contain important price information, unrelated to the default risk.

Of course, this failure has not and will not stop others from compiling statistics favorable to claims that the factors proxy for predictors of other future risks that investors (in conventional theory) should care about, although this should be done with some care (as noted by Cochrane, 2001, p. 171). Given the easily observed relative scarcity of alternative quantitative theories presented in finance journals (relative to statistical studies loosely guided by old theories or no theory at all), perhaps it is time to propose plausible alternative *theoretical* explanations for the success of multifactor models. In a refreshing attempt to do so, Shefrin and Statman (1995) provide evidence that investors (likely wrongfully) presume that the stock of healthy, thriving companies will be unusually good investments, and conjecture that this might be the cause of the additional Fama and French factors. But they did not produce a quantitative financial theory that derives an equation like (1), nor more importantly, derives additional quantitative equations that could be tested.

In contrast, this paper does provide an alternative quantitative financial theory for the presence of non-market factor portfolios' expected excess returns in the following linear, excess return factor generalization of the CAPM:

$$E(R_i) - R_f = \beta_{im}[E(R_m) - R_f] + \sum_{b \in B} \beta_{ib}[E(R_b) - R_f]; \quad i = 1, \ldots, N \qquad (2)$$

where B is a set of n benchmark portfolios that different classes of portfolio managers (and/or other investors) try to "beat." While Fama and French did not write the linear model (1) in the excess return form (2), many other studies do use the excess return form, e.g., Gruber (1996) or Elton *et al.* (1996). It is a very widely accepted assumption that portfolio managers are motivated to try to outperform specific benchmark portfolios, e.g., see Bailey (1992) and Bailey and Tierney (1993, 1995). A typical example of benchmarking, which is of more than just professional interest to academic readers of this paper, is contained in the following statement by the TIAA-CREF Trust Company:

> Different accounts have different benchmarks based on the client's overall objectives ... Accounts for clients who have growth objectives with an emphasis on equities will be benchmarked heavily toward the appropriate equity index—typically the S&P 500 index—whereas an account for a client whose main objective is income and safety of

principal will be measured against a more balanced weighting of the S&P 500 and the Lehman Corporate/Government Bond Index. [TIAA-CREF (2000, p. 3)]

Roll (1992, p. 13) argued that "This is a sensible approach because the sponsor's most direct alternative to an active manager is an index fund matching the benchmark." The ability of funds like TIAACREF to attract individual investors by the use of relative performance objectives implies the possibility that this may be the voluntary choice of (possibly bounded rational, or possibly differently motivated) investors, who think the funds are better able to beat their desired benchmarks and hence attain their desired objectives. In fact, it is certainly possible that *individual* investors also try to beat benchmarks.

Perhaps the best known quantitative model of benchmark beating behavior is the Tracking Error Variance (TEV) model of Roll (1992). TEV investors try to earn a higher expected return than a specific benchmark portfolio's expected return, while minimizing the variance of the difference of the two returns. This paper will show that the presence of benchmark portfolios as factors in (2) does not necessarily have to arise as a result of hedging of state variable risks by conventional investors, but instead could be due to the concurrent portfolio choice behavior of TEV investors attempting to beat the benchmark portfolios. That is, the very attempt to beat these benchmarks results in them occurring as priced factors in (2).

To eventually establish this, Section 2 starts by briefly contrasting conventional mean–variance investor behavior in the presence of a riskless asset with Roll's TEV behavior. Proposition 1 shows that in the presence of a riskless asset, the Information Ratio (Goodwin, 1998; Gupta *et al.*, 1999; Clarke *et al.*, 2002) produced by substituting a benchmark portfolio return for the riskless return in the conventional Sharpe Ratio (1994), plays a role analogous to that played by the Sharpe Ratio in conventional mean–variance theory. Despite the widespread use of both the TEV criterion and the Information Ratio, it does not appear that this result has been previously published. Proposition 2 provides the following plausible frequentist rationale for maximizing the Information Ratio: it is consistent with maximizing the probability of outperforming the benchmark on-average. Section 2.1 makes a brief descriptive and prescriptive case for this behavioral criterion.

Proposition 4 in Section 3 shows that the linear excess return factor model (2) is a capital market equilibrium relation resulting from the aggregate asset demands of both conventional investors (if any) and TEV investors. This proves that the theory is capable of delivering any linear multifactor model, after substituting a set of factor mimicking benchmark portfolios for the proposed factors. Because of this, empirical tests different from the mere goodness-of-fit of a particular specification of (2) must be used to differentiate this theory from others that imply (2). Fortunately, Proposition 3 shows that this theory implies an unusual sign restriction on the intercepts in regressions of each (i.e., the market and the benchmarks) portfolio's excess returns on the others' excess returns. This sign restriction—an inherently sharper test than the mere search for statistical connections between the factors and financial distress and/or other conjectured risk variables—is tested in Section 4, where we show that some of the explanatory power of multiple factors appearing in stock returns may be explained by the presence of separate classes of TEV investors who respectively try to beat growth and value benchmarks. Section 5 concludes, and suggests some topics for future research.

2 Conventional Mean–Variance versus TEV Investing

The concise derivation of conventional mean–variance investing in Huang and Litzenberger (1988, pp. 76–78) is presented and then contrasted with its TEV generalization. Conventional investors choose an unrestricted weight vector q_p of the N risky assets, investing the rest of their investable funds in the riskless asset. They do so by minimizing the return variance, subject to a portfolio expected return constraint:

$$\min_q \frac{1}{2} q' V_q \quad \text{s.t. } q'[E(R) - \mathbf{1}R_f] = E(R_p) - R_f = E(R_p - R_f) \tag{3}$$

where V denotes the covariance matrix of the return vector R with expectation vector $E(R)$, and $\mathbf{1}$ denotes a vector of ones. Note that $E(R_p)$ denotes the expected return on a portfolio that could contain the riskless asset. The risky asset vector q_p satisfies the following Lagrangian first-order condition:

$$Vq_p = \lambda[E(R) - \mathbf{1}R_f] \tag{4}$$

Premultiplying both sides of (4) by V^{-1}, and then dividing each side of the resulting equation by the sum of its respective components (assuming that the sum of the risky asset weights is not equal to zero), we obtain the tangency portfolio w_T of the risky assets:

$$\frac{q_p}{\mathbf{1}'q_p} = \frac{V^{-1}[E(R) - \mathbf{1}R_f]}{\mathbf{1}'V^{-1}[E(R) - \mathbf{1}R_f]} \equiv w_T \tag{5}$$

Expression (5) is the familiar result that all conventional investors purchase risky assets in the same proportions as the tangency portfolio w_T. Letting $q^i_{pf} \equiv 1 - \mathbf{1}'q_p$ denote conventional investor i's weight on the riskless asset, (5) shows that the risky asset weight vector of the ith conventional investor is:

$$q^i_p = (1 - q^i_{pf})w_T \tag{6}$$

A few more routine calculations (see Huang and Litzenberger, 1988, pp. 76–77) show that the conventional Sharpe Ratio of the chosen portfolio is:

$$\frac{E(R_p - R_f)}{\sqrt{\text{Var}(R_p - R_f)}} = \frac{E(R_p) - R_f}{\sqrt{\text{Var}(R_p)}} = \sqrt{[E(R) - \mathbf{1}R_f]'V^{-1}[E(R) - \mathbf{1}R_f]} \equiv \sqrt{H} \tag{7}$$

where $\sqrt{H}$ is the *maximum* conventional Sharpe Ratio among mean–variance efficient risky asset portfolios, attained by the tangency portfolio (5).

Now, consider another class of investors, comprised of individuals and/or fund managers who use a portfolio q_b with return R_b as a benchmark against which performance is measured. According to the TEV hypothesis of Roll (1992), they would choose a risky asset weight vector q_p by solving

$$\min_q \frac{1}{2}[q - q_b]'V[q - q_b] \quad \text{s.t.} \, [q - q_b]'[E(R) - \mathbf{1}R_f] = E(R_p - R_b) \geq 0 \tag{8}$$

That is, a TEV-efficient investor minimizes the TEV $\text{Var}(R_p - R_b)$ required to exceed the expected return of the benchmark by some chosen amount. The tradeoff between that chosen amount, and the minimum TEV required to achieve it, is dubbed the TEV frontier. Just as the conventional mean–variance frontier is simplified by the introduction of a riskless asset, I will now show that the TEV frontier is similarly simplified. Define $x \equiv q - q_b$ to be the unrestricted risky asset vector in excess of the benchmark's. Substituting x into (8), we have the equivalent problem:

$$\min_x \frac{1}{2}x'Vx \quad \text{s.t.} \, x'[E(R) - \mathbf{1}R_f] = E(R_p) - R_f - (E(R_b) - R_f) = E(R_p - R_b) \tag{9}$$

which is formally equivalent to (3). Assuming the solution $x_p \equiv q_p - q_b$ does not sum to zero, i.e., the weight placed on the riskless asset in the managed portfolio does not equal the weight placed on the riskless asset in the benchmark, the solution is found by substitution into (5), yielding

$$\frac{x_p}{\mathbf{1}'x_p} = \frac{V^{-1}[E(R) - \mathbf{1}R_f]}{\mathbf{1}'V^{-1}[E(R) - \mathbf{1}R_f]} \equiv w_T \tag{10}$$

and substituting $\mathbf{1}'x_p = 1'[q_p - q_b] = (1 - q_{pf}) - (1 - q_{bf}) = q_{bf} - q_{pf} \neq 0$ into (10) results in the following risky asset weight vector for the jth TEV investor, now denoted by q^j_{pb}:

$$q^j_{pb} = q_b + (q_{bf} - q^j_{pbf})w_T \tag{11}$$

Because (11) shows that $q^j_{pb} - q_b$ is proportional to the tangency portfolio whose Sharpe Ratio is the right-hand side of (7), the analogous finding for TEV investors is

$$\frac{E(R_p - R_b)}{\sqrt{\text{Var}(R_p - R_b)}} = \frac{E(R_p) - E(R_b)}{\sqrt{\text{Var}(R_p - R_b)}} = \sqrt{[E(R) - \mathbf{1}R_f]'V^{-1}[E(R) - \mathbf{1}R_f]} \equiv \sqrt{H} \tag{12}$$

The left-hand side of (12) is the *Information Ratio* (Goodwin, 1998; Gupta *et al.*, 1999; Clarke *et al.*, 2002). A survey of the TEV literature failed to uncover the following proposition characterizing the symmetry between the conventional mean–variance and TEV optimal portfolios in the presence of a riskless asset:

Proposition 1: *When a riskless asset exists, conventional mean–variance investors choose risky asset weight vectors by maximizing the conventional Sharpe Ratio. Normalization of the vectors produces the Tangency Portfolio. Analogously, TEV investors choose risky* *asset weight vectors by maximizing the Information Ratio. Normalization of the difference between a risky asset weight vector and the benchmark's risky asset weight vector produces the same Tangency Portfolio.*[1]

Proposition 1 uses traditional theorizing to establish that in the presence of a riskless asset, the TEV hypothesis is a natural extension of the mean–variance hypothesis relative to a benchmark. But there is also a quite plausible frequentist foundation for TEV behavior. Anyone desiring to beat the benchmark return R_b will, at the very least, endeavor to beat it *on-average* over some span of time T that possibly differs across them. That is, anyone desiring to beat the benchmark would like $\sum_{t=1}^{T} R_{pt}/T > \sum_{t=1}^{T} R_{bt}/T$ for some T. If $T = \infty$, the law of large numbers dictates that he/she needs only choose a portfolio p with $E[R_p] > E[R_b]$ in order to ensure this. But over the finite time horizons T faced by real-world managers and/or investors, there is a nonzero probability that this might not happen, i.e., $\text{Prob}\left[\sum_{t=1}^{T} (R_{pt} - R_{bt})/T \leq 0\right]$. Assuming that $R_{pt} - R_{bt}$ is an IID normally distributed process, as commonly (albeit sometimes implicitly) assumed in textbook presentations of applied mean–variance analysis, $\sum_{t=1}^{T} (R_{pt} - R_{bt})/T \sim \mathcal{N}\left(E[R_p] - E[R_b], \sqrt{(\text{Var}[R_p - R_b])/T}\right)$. So, by transforming this normally distributed variate to the standard normal variate Z, the underperformance probability is

$$\begin{aligned} \text{Prob}\left[\sum_{t=1}^{T} (R_{pt} - R_{bt})/T \leq 0\right] &= \text{Prob}\left[Z \leq \frac{-(E[R_p] - E[R_b])}{\sqrt{(\text{Var}[R_p - R_b])/T}}\right] \\ &= \text{Prob}\left[Z > \sqrt{T}\frac{E[R_p] - E[R_b]}{\sqrt{\text{Var}[R_p - R_b]}}\right] \end{aligned} \quad (13)$$

Someone who wants to minimize the left-hand side of (13), i.e., the probability of failing to beat the benchmark on-average over a finite time horizon T, will choose the risky asset portfolio p that minimizes the right-hand side of (13). We immediately see that this is the same portfolio that maximizes the Information Ratio, *independent of the time horizon T*. Because the probability of *out* performing the benchmark on-average is one minus the left-hand side of (13), it is equally valid to state that this portfolio maximizes the probability of outperforming the benchmark on-average.

This frequentist interpretation of the Information Ratio is exactly true only when returns in excess of the benchmark are IID normal, no matter how many periods T are used to form the average return. But Central Limit Theorems (e.g., see Lehmann, 1999, Chap. 2) prove that this interpretation is still *approximately* true for suitably large T, in many cases when returns in excess of the benchmark are independently, non-normally distributed. That is, the average of T returns will be approximately normally distributed once T is large enough, making the above probability calculations accurate once T is suitably large.[2] These results are summarized in the following proposition.

Proposition 2: *Assuming the presence of independent, normally distributed returns measured in excess of a TEV investor's benchmark, maximization of the Information Ratio is* *equivalent to maximization (minimization) of the probability of outperforming (underperforming) the benchmark portfolio on-average over any number of evaluation periods T. Without the normality assumption, this interpretation is approximately valid for suitably large T.*[3]

In conjunction with Proposition 1, Proposition 2 shows that the criterion of maximizing (minimizing) the probability of outperforming (underperforming) the benchmark on-average is a natural generalization of the TEV hypothesis and its associated Information Ratio criterion function [see Browne (1999a,b) for analyses of portfolio choice based on more complex outperformance probability based criteria]. It provides a new, frequentist interpretation of existing studies that used the Information Ratio, e.g., Gupta *et al.* (1999) and Clarke *et al.* (2002).[4]

Finally, comparing (11) to (6), we see that a TEV investor's risky asset weight vector is no longer proportional to the tangency portfolio w_T, but instead is an affine transformation of it, displaced by the benchmark portfolio's risky asset weight vector q_b. Hence, TEV investors' portfolios will not be mean–variance efficient, i.e., a linear combination of two mean–variance efficient portfolios, unless the benchmark itself is.

2.1 *Description Versus Prescription*

The TEV hypothesis, and especially its aforementioned interpretation as maximizing (minimizing) the probability of outperforming (underperforming) a benchmark, is at least as plausible a *description* of fund manager behavior as the conventional mean–variance hypothesis is. Chan *et al.* (1999, p. 938) note that "Since managers are evaluated relative to some benchmark, it has become standard practice for them to optimize with respect to tracking error volatility." They provide further corroboration of the outperformance probability interpretation given in Proposition 2 above, by stating that (Chan *et al.*, 1999, p. 956) "Since professional managers are paid to outperform a benchmark, they are in general not concerned with the absolute variance of their portfolios, but are concerned with how their portfolio deviates from the benchmark. Underperforming the benchmark for several years typically results in the termination of a manager's appointment." Some direct evidence for this was provided by Olsen (1997), who conducted a series of surveys of portfolio managers and strategists, randomly selected from US-based Chartered Financial Analysts (CFAs). He asked these professionals to "list those things that first come into your mind when you think about *investment risk*," and found that 47% of them placed either "a large loss" or "return below target" first on their lists, which was more than twice as high as any other response. Finally, Goodwin (1998, p. 34) notes that "Most money managers routinely report their products' information ratios to investors, and some investors rely on information ratios to hire and fire money managers." The close connection between Information Ratio maximization and outperformance probability maximization, detailed in Proposition 2, shows that those money managers and their clients are at least implicitly concerned with the probability of outperforming their benchmark. Is it not reasonable to presume that the massive amount of professionally managed capital, invested in attempts to beat benchmarks, has had *some* influence on the returns of assets favored or disfavored by this criterion? Those proposing alternative explanations for multiple priced factors implicitly presume that fund management is irrelevant.

While it may be a better *description* of portfolio managers' behavior than the conventional mean–variance hypothesis, Roll (1992) worried that it may not be a good *prescription* for funds' investors. *If* a manager's benchmark portfolio is not on the mean–variance efficiency frontier, Roll (1992) foresaw a role for portfolio constraints that would induce fund managers to choose more mean–variance efficient portfolios. But, it is quite difficult for investors, fund managers, and/or regulators to ascertain whether or not a particular benchmark portfolio is on the mean–variance frontier. As Roll (1992, p. 19) notes:

> Estimation error is severe in portfolio analysis. No one knows where the global total return efficient frontier is really located. Its position depends, *inter alia*, on individual asset expected returns, which can be estimated only with substantial error because of the large component of noise in observed returns.

Furthermore, it is possible that measuring performance relative to a benchmark is a second-best, principal-agent mechanism desirably employed by investors (i.e., the principals), coping with an asymmetry in which portfolio managers (the agents) have better information about the efficiency frontier than they do. Measuring performance relative to a benchmark subtracts out a common shock faced by investors, which in the words of Brown *et al.* (1996, p. 87) would "allow the principal to separate some of the variation in outcome due to the state of nature from the agent's contribution." Moreover, Roll (1992, p. 20 and footnote 10) notes that doing so helps cope with estimation error, because when the correlation coefficient of the benchmark portfolio's return with a managed portfolio's return is in excess of half the ratio of their volatilities, "estimated *differences* between portfolio returns can be estimated more precisely."

Finally, the prescriptive case against measuring performance relative to a benchmark presumes that all investors *should* be worried about possible portfolio mean–variance inefficiency. *A priori*, it is equally plausible that *some* investors *should* be worried that their investments will not outperform a particular benchmark that provides a floor for their satisfaction, and accordingly either seek to employ a manager that will choose a portfolio with the highest probability of beating that benchmark on-average, or attempt to do it themselves.

3 Capital Market Equilibrium

Following Brennan (1993), capital market equilibrium is derived analogously to the standard CAPM: one imposes the equilibrium condition that the aggregate risky asset demand vector must equal the vector of market supplies. The demand arises from both conventional investors and the different classes of benchmark investors. The equilibrium condition is:

$$\sum_{i} W^i q_p^i + \sum_{b \in B} \sum_{j} W_b^j q_{pb}^j = W^m w_m \tag{14}$$

where the W^i in the first term denotes the total wealth invested by the conventional mean–variance investor i, q^i_p denotes the risky asset weight vector chosen by that investor, W^j_b is the total wealth invested by the TEV investor j utilizing the benchmark b, and q^i_{pb} denotes the risky asset weight vector chosen by that TEV investor. The right-hand side of (14) multiplies the vector of market portfolio weights w_m by the total value of the market W^m to obtain the vector of risky assets' market supplies.

Now substitute (6) into the first term on the left-hand side of (14), and (11) into the rest of it, to produce the aggregate demand vector. The sums can be simplified by noting that the factor portfolios identified in the literature, e.g., the aforementioned papers of Fama and French, are comprised solely of risky assets, in which case we can let $q_{bf} = 0$ in (11). Letting W^c_r denote the aggregate value of wealth invested by conventional mean–variance investors in *risky* assets, W^b_f denote the aggregate wealth invested in the *riskless* asset by TEV investors with benchmark b, and W^b denote the aggregate wealth invested by TEV investors with benchmark b, we derive

$$w_T * \left(W^c_r - \sum_{b \in B} W^b_f \right) = W^m w_m - \sum_{b \in B} W^b q_b \tag{15}$$

Now, substitute (5) for w_T in (15), multiply both sides by the covariance matrix V of the risky assets' returns, and rearrange to obtain:

$$\begin{aligned}
E(R) - 1R_f &= \frac{1'V^{-1}[E(R) - 1R_f]}{W^c_r - \sum_{b\in B} W^b_f}\left[W^m V w_m - \sum_{b \in B} W^b V q_b\right] \\
&= \frac{A}{W}\left[W^m V w_m - \sum_{b \in B} w^b V q_b\right] \\
&= \frac{A}{W}\left[W^m \operatorname{Cov}(R1, R_m) - \sum_{b \in B} W^b \operatorname{Cov}(R_1, R_b)\right] \\
&\quad \vdots \\
&\quad \frac{A}{W}\left[W^m \operatorname{Cov}(R_N, R_m) - \sum_{b \in B} W^b \operatorname{Cov}(R_N, R_b)\right] \\
&\equiv \operatorname{COV}\frac{A}{W}[W^m, -W^{b_1}, \ldots, -W^{b_n}]'
\end{aligned} \tag{16}$$

where COV denotes the matrix of the N risky assets' covariances with the market and the n benchmark portfolios' returns, $A = \mathbf{1}'V^{-1}[E(R) - 1R_f]$ is one of the four numbers that Huang and Litzenberger (1988, p. 64) used to characterize the mean–variance efficient set, and $W = W^c_r - \sum_{b\in B} W^b_f$. The covariance terms arise because the product of V and any portfolio weight vector is the vector of the risky assets' return covariances with that portfolio's return. This will soon be transformed into the exact linear factor model (2). But first, let us examine an important implication of it.

Premultiplying both sides of (16) by any portfolio's risky asset weight vector produces a linear relationship between that portfolio's expected excess return and its covariances with the market and benchmarks' returns. Successively doing so for market and the n benchmark portfolios yields the following system of linear equations:

$$\begin{aligned} E(R_m) - R_f &= \frac{A}{W}\left[W^m \operatorname{Cov}(R_m, R_m) - \sum_{b\in B} W^b \operatorname{Cov}(R_m, R_b)\right] \\ E(R_{b_1}) - R_f &= \frac{A}{W}\left[W^m \operatorname{Cov}(R_{b_1}, R_m) - \sum_{b\in B} W^b \operatorname{Cov}(R_{b_1}, R_b)\right] \\ \vdots &= \vdots \\ E(R_{b_n}) - R_f &= \frac{A}{W}\left[W^m \operatorname{Cov}(R_{b_n}, R_m) - \sum_{b\in B} W^b \operatorname{Cov}(R_{b_n}, R_b)\right] \end{aligned} \tag{17}$$

It is convenient to write (17) in matrix form as:

$$E(\mathcal{R}) - \mathbf{1}R_f = \Sigma \frac{A}{W}[W^m, -W^{b_1}, \ldots, -W^{b_n}]' \tag{18}$$

where $E(\mathcal{R})$ denotes the vector of market and benchmark portfolios' expected returns on the lefthand side of (17) and Σ is the square covariance matrix of the market and benchmark portfolios' returns. Premultiply both sides of (18) by Σ^{-1} to produce $\Sigma^{-1}[E(\mathcal{R}) - \mathbf{1}R_f]$, and then use the seminal result in Stevens (1998, Eq. (9), p. 1826) to rewrite it as follows:

$$\begin{aligned} \frac{A}{W}[W^m, -W^{b_1}, \ldots, -W^{b_n}]' &= \Sigma^{-1}[E(\mathcal{R}) - \mathbf{1}R_f] \\ &= \left[\frac{\alpha_m}{\operatorname{Var}(\varepsilon_m)}, \frac{\alpha_{b_1}}{\operatorname{Var}(\varepsilon_{b_1})}, \ldots, \frac{\alpha_{b_n}}{\operatorname{Var}(\varepsilon_{b_n})}\right]' \end{aligned} \tag{19}$$

where α_m is the intercept and $\operatorname{Var}(\varepsilon_m)$ is the variance of the error term in the following linear excess return factor model for the market portfolio:

$$R_m - R_f = \alpha_m + \sum_{j=1}^{n} \beta_{mb_j}(R_{b_j} - R_f) + \varepsilon_m \tag{20}$$

and αb_i and $\operatorname{Var}[\varepsilon_{b_i}]$ are the counterparts in the following linear excess return factor model for the ith benchmark portfolio:

$$R_{b_i} - R_f = \alpha_{b_i} + \beta_{b_i m}(R_m - R_f) + \sum_{j\neq i} \beta_{b_i b_j}(R_{b_j} - R_f) + \varepsilon_{b_i} \tag{21}$$

Because the theory does not imply a particular sign for A/W,[5] (19) only implies that α_m in the factor model (20) for the market portfolio has a sign opposite to the predicted common sign of each α_{b_i} in the factor model (21) for the benchmark portfolio i. This implication is summarized as the following proposition:

Proposition 3: *The intercept (i.e., alpha) in a linear factor regression model of the market portfolio's excess return on the benchmark portfolios' excess returns should be opposite in sign to the intercept in a linear factor regression model of any benchmark portfolio's excess return on the excess returns of the market portfolio and the other benchmark portfolios.*

While a test of the sign restriction in Proposition 3 is conducted in Section 4, there is another implication of the theory that has already received vast testing and commentary. This is (2), the general linear, multi-excess return factor generalization of the CAPM. Let us derive (2) as an equilibrium relationship; (19) permits the substitution of $\Sigma^{-1}[E(\mathcal{R}) - \mathbf{1}R_f]$ for $(A/W)[W^m, -W^{b_1}, \ldots, -W^{b_n}]'$ in (16), resulting in the vector of equations

$$E(R) - \mathbf{1}R_f = \text{COV}\ \Sigma^{-1}[E(\mathcal{R}) - \mathbf{1}R_f] \tag{22}$$

whose ith component is the factor model (2), i.e., COV Σ^{-1} is the $N \times n+1$ matrix of the N risky asset returns' betas on the market, and the n benchmark portfolios that separate classes that TEV investors want to beat. This is summarized in the following proposition:

Proposition 4: *The linear, excess return factor model (2) of expected asset returns arises as a market equilibrium in the presence of a riskless asset, with both mean–variance investors and classes of TEV investors, who respectively attempt to beat one of the benchmarks in (2).*

4 Some Empirical Evidence

Let us test the theory's implied sign restriction given in Proposition 3, using the portfolios that were essential in the Fama and French equity factor model tests. Fama and French (1996, Table IX, pp. 70–71) documented that "equivalent descriptions of returns" are provided when omitting an explicit size factor from their three factor model (1), using just $R_M - R_f$, $R_L - R_f$, and $R_H - R_f$ as excess return factors in a three factor model, where R_M is the return on the CRSP Value Weighted portfolio, R_L is the return on their portfolio of low book-to-market ratio (i.e., growth) stocks, and R_H is the return on their portfolio of high book-tomarket ratio (i.e., value) stocks. In fact, even their earlier study (Fama and French, 1992, pp. 447–448) concluded that "Unlike the size effect, the relation between book-to-market equity and average return is so strong that it shows up reliably in both the 1963–1976 and the 1977–1990 subperiods ... The subperiod results thus support the conclusion that, among the variables considered here, book-to-market equity is consistently the most powerful for explaining the cross-section of average stock returns." Corroborating this emphasis on book-to-market equity, Knez and Ready (1997) employed an outlier-robust regression technique to re-examine the Fama and French evidence, concluding that (Knez and Ready, 1997, p. 1380) "the negative relation between firm size and average returns is driven by a few extreme positive returns in each month," that (Knez and Ready, 1997,

p. 1356) "most small firms actually do worse than larger firms," but (Knez and Ready, 1997, p. 1357) "that the risk premium on book-to-market is not affected by extreme observations once you control for size."

In light of this evidence for the efficacy of a linear model (2) of stock returns with three excess return factors $R_m - R_f$, $R_L - R_f$, and $R_H - R_f$, let us follow Fama and French in using the CRSP Value Weighted equity portfolio as the "market" portfolio, and test Proposition 3 assuming that there are two classes of TEV investors: one class tries to beat a growth stock benchmark, proxied by the Fama and French growth stock portfolio L, while the other class tries to beat a value stock benchmark that is proxied by the Fama and French value stock portfolio H. Using the same July 1963 to December 1993 data period adopted by Fama and French, the OLS-estimated (with t-statistic in parentheses) $\alpha_m = -0.059\%$ per month (-2.42) in (20). The L benchmark portfolio's $\alpha_L = 0.059\%$ per month (1.64) in (21). The H benchmark portfolio's $\alpha_H = 0.277\%$ per month (4.21). The significantly negative sign of the market alpha is opposite to the significantly positive signs of the L and H alphas, consistent with Proposition 3. Given the aforementioned Fama and French evidence on the efficacy of the L and H benchmark factors in explaining stock returns, it is not surprising that the market regression (20) and the two benchmark factor regressions (21) all had values for their adjusted R^2 in excess of 90%.[7]

Additional corroborating evidence for this theory was found in the two factor model of Gomez and Zapatero (in press). They used the MSCI US equity index as the proxy for the market portfolio, and the S&P 500 as a benchmark portfolio that all TEV investors try to beat. They estimated an orthogonalized version of the resulting linear two-factor model (2) on a large number of stocks, and concluded that the addition of the S&P 500 factor did indeed help explain the expected returns of those stocks. Because of Fama and French's (1992, p. 446) finding that "large stocks are more likely to be firms with . . . lower book-to-market equity," the findings of Gomez and Zapatero overlap with Fama and French's findings about the explanatory ability of their low book-to-market "L" portfolio. Gomez and Zapatero (in press) did not derive an analog of the sign restriction in Proposition 3, and hence did not subject their proposed factor model to the additional test conducted above.

5 Conclusion

A linear excess return factor model was derived as a consequence of equilibrium asset demands from a class of conventional mean–variance investors and different classes of other investors, each of whom tries to beat a different benchmark portfolio in accord with the TEV hypothesis of Roll (1992). That is, each TEV investor chooses a portfolio to minimize the variance of its return about a benchmark portfolio's return, while trying to exceed the benchmark's expected return by some amount. In the presence of a riskless asset, this is equivalent to choosing a risky asset weight vector portfolio that maximizes the well-known Information Ratio, calculated by using the benchmark portfolio's return in place of the riskless asset return in the conventional Sharpe Ratio. It was shown that maximization of the Information Ratio is also consistent with maximization (minimization) of the probability of outperforming (or underperforming) the benchmark used to compute it, particularly so over longer time horizons. This frequentist criterion seems plausible, and there does not appear to be any direct evidence that either institutional investors (e.g., managed mutual funds, banks, insurers, and other financial intermediaries) or individual investors behave more in accord with conventional mean–variance theory than TEV theory.

The theory implies that an asset's expected excess return is linearly related to the excess return of the market portfolio's excess return, as in the CAPM. But the excess returns of each of the benchmark portfolios in wide use will also be factors priced in this way, whether or not they are mean–variance efficient portfolios. The theory also implies that if one builds a separate excess return factor model for the market portfolio with the benchmarks as factors, and builds separate excess return factor models for each benchmark portfolio with the market and the *other* benchmark portfolios as factors, the market model's alpha must have a sign opposite to that of the usual one for all the benchmark portfolios' alphas. An empirical test of this implication indicated that the seemingly anomalous empirical multifactor findings of Fama and French (1992, 1996) may be explained by the presence of two classes of TEV investors, trying to beat growth stock and value stock benchmarks, respectively.

An ambitious future theoretical topic is to use the generalized theory of benchmark investing developed in Stutzer (2003) and Foster and Stutzer (2002) to extend the theoretical predictions beyond the normally distributed TEV paradigm. This should yield analogous nonlinear multifactor models. A good empirical topic would be to incorporate a widely adopted bond benchmark and a value weighted blended market portfolio, in order to jointly test the theory on both stocks and bonds.

Acknowledgment

I am indebted to Richard Roll, whose encouraging correspondence helped produce this version of the paper.

Notes

1 Here is the proof. A risky asset vector that maximizes the Information Ratio also maximizes the squared ratio. Again, using the notation $q - q_b \equiv x$ as in (9), the squared Information Ratio is $\left(\sum_i x_i[E(R_i) - R_f]\right)^2 / \sum_i \sum_j V_{ij}x_ix_j$. Because q_b is fixed, maximizing over q can be achieved by maximizing over x. Because neither risky asset vectors q nor q_b need sum to one, the x_k are unrestricted variables, so the first derivatives of the Information Ratio with respect to each must be zero at a maximum. The kth first derivative condition can be written as $\sum_j V_{kj}\lambda x_j = E(R_k) - R_f$, where $\lambda = \left(\sum_i x_i[E(R_i) - R_f]\right)/2\sum_i \sum_j v_{ij}x_ix_j$. Substituting variables defined by $y_j \equiv \lambda x_j$ transforms these into an exactly determined system of linear equations, with solution vector $y = V^{-1}[E(R) - 1'R_f \equiv \lambda x$. Dividing both sides of this expression by $\sum_i y_i = 1'y = \lambda 1'x$ we obtain $y/1'y = x/1'x = w_T$. This is the same as Eq. (10), which is used to characterize the TEV portfolio.

2 Restrictions on the process $R_{pt} - R_{bt}$ that are required for a CLT approximation of the average return's distribution are given in many texts, e.g., Lehmann (1999). Such process restrictions are often implicit in commonly applied time series analyses of financial returns.

3 The Gärtner–Ellis Large Deviations Theorem (Bucklew, 1990, Chap. 2) provides an alternative to the CLT approximation when T is large. In the special case of IID, but not necessarily normally distributed $R_p - R_b$, Stutzer (2000) used it to show that the Information Ratio should be replaced by the alternative performance criterion $\max_\theta E[-e^{-\theta(R_p - R_b)}]$, i.e., the expected CARA utility of $R_p - R_b$, when evaluated at the coefficient of absolute risk aversion θ that maximizes the expected CARA utility of $R_p - R_b$. A straightforward calculation shows that this is half the squared Information Ratio when $R_p - R_b$ is normally distributed, and is thus equivalent to using that ratio, consistent with Proposition 2.

4 It is also possible to formulate the probability of cumulatively outperforming the benchmark by a specific *calendar* time T, rather than on-average over T periods, by substituting $\log R_p - \log R_b$ for $R_p - R_b$ before forming the average. Stutzer (2003) and Foster and Stutzer (2002) studied and applied this formulation of the outperformance probability hypothesis. But the on-average criterion is needed here to derive the exact linear factor model (2) of non-log returns that is commonly used in practice.

5 Remember that $A/W \equiv (\mathbf{1}'V^{-1}[E(R) - \mathbf{1}R_f])/\left(W_r^c - \sum_{b\in B} W_f^b\right)$. The case analysis and figures in Huang and Litzenberger (1988, pp. 77–78) assume that $A/\mathbf{1}'\Sigma^{-1}\mathbf{1} > 0$. Because Σ^{-1} is positive definite, this is tantamount to assuming that $A > 0$. But the sign of W depends on whether or not the aggregate wealth invested by conventional mean–variance investors in risky assets exceeds the aggregate wealth invested by all TEV investors in the riskless asset. Because there appears to be no direct evidence that conventional mean–variance investing in risky assets is any more common than TEV investing (among individuals as well as institutional investors) in riskless assets, the theory does not imply that $W > 0$. Hence, the sign of A/W is indeterminate.

6 The derivation simplifies the development in Brennan (1993). Brennan only allowed conventional investors the right to invest in the riskless asset. In his model, the TEV investors are not allowed to use the riskless asset. As a result, Brennan derives a more complicated relationship than (2), which necessitates replacing R_f in (2) by a complicated function of it, the return on the minimum variance portfolio, and investors' wealths and absolute coefficients of risk aversion (see Brennan (1993) for details). By symmetrically allowing the TEV investors the same right to invest a fraction of the funds in the riskless asset that conventional investors have, the simpler relationship (2) results, which has a form commonly used in empirical studies (e.g., in Fama and French, 1996, Table IX, pp. 70–71; Gruber, 1996; Elton *et al.*, 1996).

7 A referee wrote that a small cap benchmark should be included in these regressions, because small cap benchmarks "are in common usage among investors." Adding the excess returns from a benchmark portfolio of small cap stocks (specifically, a portfolio representing the smallest 20% of CRSP stocks' market capitalization, as reported on Kenneth French's website) resulted in a sign pattern analogous to that reported above. That is, the estimated α_m in (20) is statistically significantly negative, while the intercepts in two of the three possible regressions (21) of a benchmark portfolio excess return on the market's and the other two benchmarks' excess returns were statistically significantly positive. While the estimated intercept in the other regression (the excess return of the small cap benchmark on the excess return of the market and the excess returns of the L and H benchmarks) was negative, it was statistically insignificant (its t-statistic was only 1.10). Hence, the addition of a small cap benchmark does not change the empirical support for the theory's Proposition 3.

References

Bailey, J. (1992). "Are Manager Universes Acceptable Performance Benchmarks?" *Journal of Portfolio Management* **18**(3), 9–13.

Bailey, J. and Tierney, D. (1993). "Gaming Manager Benchmarks?" *Journal of Portfolio Management* **19**(4), 37–40.

Bailey, J. and Tierney, D. (1995). "Benchmark Orthogonality Properties." *Journal of Portfolio Management* **21**(3), 27–31.

Brennan, M. (1993). "Agency and Asset Pricing." Finance Working Paper no. 6-93, Anderson Graduate School of Management, University of California, Los Angeles.

Brown, K.C., Harlow, W.V. and Starks, L.T. (1996). "Of Tournaments and Temptations: An Analysis of Managerial Incentives in the Mutual Fund Industry." *Journal of Finance* **51**(1), 85–110.

Browne, S. (1999a). "The Risk and Rewards of Minimizing Shortfall Probability." *Journal of Portfolio Management* **25**, 76–85.

Browne, S. (1999b). "Beating a Moving Target: Optimal Portfolio Strategies for Outperforming a Stochastic Benchmark." *Finance and Stochastics* **3**, 275–294.

Bucklew, J.A. (1990). *Large Deviation Techniques in Decision, Simulation, and Estimation*. Wiley.

Chan, L.K.C., Karceski, J. and Lakonishok, J. (1999). "On Portfolio Optimization: Forecasting Covariances and Choosing the Risk Model." *Review of Financial Studies* **12**(5), 937–974.

Clarke, R., de Silva, H. and Thorley, S. (2002). "Portfolio Constraints and the Fundamental Law of Active Management." *Financial Analysts Journal* **58**(5), 48–66.

Cochrane, J.H. (2001). *Asset Pricing*. Princeton: Princeton University Press.

Davis, J.L. (2002). "Mutual Fund Performance and Management Style." *Financial Analysts Journal* **57**(1), 19–27.

Elton, E.J., Gruber, M.J. and Blake, C.R. (1996). "Survivorship Bias and Mutual Fund Performance." *Review of Financial Studies* **9**(4), 1097–1120.

Fama, E.F. and French, K.R. (1992). "The Cross-Section of Expected Stock Returns." *Journal of Finance* **47**(2), 427–465.

Fama, E.F. and French, K.R. (1996). "Multifactor Explanations of Asset Pricing Anomalies." *Journal of Finance* **51**(1), 55–84.

Foster, F.D. and Stutzer, M. (2002). "Performance and Risk Aversion of Funds with Benchmarks: A Large Deviations Approach." Working Paper, University of Colorado Finance Department.

Gómez, J.P. and Zapatero, F. (forthcoming). "Asset Pricing Implications of Benchmarking: A Two-Factor CAPM." *European Journal of Finance*.

Goodwin, T.H. (1998). "The Information Ratio." *Financial Analysts Journal* **54**(4), 34–43.

Gruber, M.J. (1996). "Another Puzzle: The Growth in Actively Managed Mutual Funds." *Journal of Finance* **51**(3), 783–810.

Gupta, F., Prajogi, R. and Stubbs, E. (1999). "The Information Ratio and Performance." *Journal of Portfolio Management* **25**(1), 33–39.

Huang, C.-F. and Litzenberger, R.H. (1988). *Foundations for Financial Economics*. North-Holland.

Knez, P.J. and Ready, M.J. (1997). "On the Robustness of Size and Book-to-Market in Cross-sectional Regressions." *Journal of Finance* **52**(4), 1355–1382.

Lehmann, E.L. (1999). *Elements of Large Sample Theory*. Springer-Verlag.

Olsen, R.A. (1997). "Investment Risk: The Experts' Perspective." *Financial Analysts Journal* **53**(2), 62–66.

Roll, R. (1992). "A Mean/Variance Analysis of Tracking Error." *Journal of Portfolio Management* **18**(4), 13–22.

Sharpe, W. (1994). "The Sharpe Ratio." *Journal of Portfolio Management* **21**(1), 49–58.

Shefrin, H. and Statman, M. (1995). "Making Sense of Beta, Size, and Book-to-Market." *Journal of Portfolio Management* **21**(3), 26–34.

Stevens, G.V.G. (1998). "On the Inverse of the Covariance Matrix in Portfolio Analysis." *Journal of Finance* **53**(5), 1821–1827.

Stutzer, M. (2000). "A Portfolio Performance Index." *Financial Analysts Journal* **56**(3), 52–61.
Stutzer, M. (2003). "Portfolio Choice with Endogenous Utility: A Large Deviations Approach." *Journal of Econometrics* **116**, 365–386.
TIAA-CREF. (2000). TIAA-CREF Trust Company's personal touch. TIAA-CREF Investment Forum, September.
Vassalou, M. and Xing, Y. (2002). "Default Risk in Equity Returns." Working Paper, Columbia University Graduate School of Business.

Keywords: Benchmark investing; performance evaluation; asset pricing